Doing Statistical Mediation and Moderation

Methodology in the Social Sciences

David A. Kenny, Founding Editor
Todd D. Little, Series Editor
www.guilford.com/MSS

This series provides applied researchers and students with analysis and research design books that emphasize the use of methods to answer research questions. Rather than emphasizing statistical theory, each volume in the series illustrates when a technique should (and should not) be used and how the output from available software programs should (and should not) be interpreted. Common pitfalls as well as areas of further development are clearly articulated.

RECENT VOLUMES

DIAGNOSTIC MEASUREMENT: THEORY, METHODS, AND APPLICATIONS
André A. Rupp, Jonathan Templin, and Robert A. Henson

ADVANCES IN CONFIGURAL FREQUENCY ANALYSIS
Alexander von Eye, Patrick Mair, and Eun-Young Mun

APPLIED MISSING DATA ANALYSIS
Craig K. Enders

PRINCIPLES AND PRACTICE OF STRUCTURAL EQUATION MODELING, THIRD EDITION
Rex B. Kline

APPLIED META-ANALYSIS FOR SOCIAL SCIENCE RESEARCH
Noel A. Card

DATA ANALYSIS WITH Mplus
Christian Geiser

INTENSIVE LONGITUDINAL METHODS: AN INTRODUCTION TO DIARY AND EXPERIENCE SAMPLING RESEARCH
Niall Bolger and Jean-Philippe Laurenceau

DOING STATISTICAL MEDIATION AND MODERATION
Paul E. Jose

LONGITUDINAL STRUCTURAL EQUATION MODELING
Todd D. Little

INTRODUCTION TO MEDIATION, MODERATION, AND CONDITIONAL PROCESS ANALYSIS: A REGRESSION-BASED APPROACH
Andrew F. Hayes

Doing Statistical Mediation and Moderation

Paul E. Jose

Series Editor's Note by Todd D. Little

THE GUILFORD PRESS
New York   London

© 2013 The Guilford Press
A Division of Guilford Publications, Inc.
370 Seventh Avenue, Suite 1200, New York, NY 10001
www.guilford.com

Printed in the United States of America

This book is printed on acid-free paper.

Last digit is print number: 9   8   7   6   5   4   3   2

Library of Congress Cataloging-in-Publication Data

Jose, Paul E. (Paul Easton), 1952–
    Doing statistical mediation and moderation / Paul E. Jose.
        p. cm. — (Methodology in the social sciences)
    Includes bibliographical references and index.
    ISBN 978-1-4625-0815-0 (pbk.) — ISBN 978-1-4625-0821-1 (hardcover)
    1. Mediation (Statistics)   2. Social sciences—Statistical methods.   I. Title.
    QA278.2.J67 2013
    519.5'36—dc23

                                                            2012047804

*To my wife, Mary, and to my three sons, Ben, Easton,
and Isaac, who have had to tolerate many hours of
"I've got to work on my book now" instead of time with me
doing other, more enjoyable family things*

*My wife's enduring support, love, and belief in me
has sustained me through many hours of hard work,
and my sons remind me to enjoy and savor the journey
through life.*

Series Editor's Note

Mediation and moderation are two ubiquitous concepts in social and behavioral science research. These concepts pervade the hypotheses of researchers from the world of business to the realm of education. Given their common invocation in the theories and hypotheses of researchers, one would think that the meanings of mediation and moderation would be well understood and that their distinction would be clear and never conflated. Unfortunately, they are oft confused and researchers appear rather perplexed about how to define and test for evidence of their influence. Enter Paul Jose's book, *Doing Statistical Mediation and Moderation*.

I am delighted to introduce this book to you. I first met Paul at one of our very first Kansas University Stats Camps held every June (see *www.statscamp. org* for more details on this annual event). Paul was there to hone his skills on recent advances in structural equation modeling. The enthusiasm that he shared with us on his interest in writing a book on mediation and moderation was inspiring. A few years later, when I took the helm of The Guilford Press Methodology in the Social Sciences Series from David Kenny, I solicited Paul to bring his dream to the series. Paul has pitched this book precisely at the level that I hoped he would. It is a disarming treatment of the sometimes intimidating concepts of mediation and moderation. His writing style is a reflection of his kind personality, wry wit, and statistical scholarship. He brings you in for an enjoyable learning experience, employing a terrific balance of humor and active voice with just the right dosage of how-to procedure and postresults interpretation. The book does not require more than a basic understanding of statistics because Paul is careful to introduce and define concepts along the way.

Paul emphasizes that there are more than two ways to analyze data with three variables—for example, a third way is simple additive effects. As Paul outlines, moderator-oriented research is more interested in when certain effects will hold. In contrast, mediator-oriented research is more interested in the mechanisms of how and why effects occur. A moderator is often introduced when X and Y have a weak or inconsistent relationship. In contrast, a mediator is often introduced when X and Y have a strong relationship to start with. As I mentioned, researchers often confuse these ideas. They also conflate them with simple additive effects of multiple predictors! Here, the additive effect is the simple linear combination of unique effects that contribute to an outcome. In my consultations with others, I frequently have to help them understand that one's standing on an outcome can directly relate to one's standing on the multiple predictors, with nothing being mediated or moderated. That is, researchers often confuse how different people can have different profiles on the independent variables, which lead to the same or different outcome with none of the process being related to mediation or moderation. I like that Paul cautions readers and researchers that not all multivariate problems are mediated or moderated processes. The outcome can be multiply caused. Now, with this book, I have a definitive resource that I can share with researchers to help them understand these essential distinctions.

The bottom line is, kudos to Paul. After enjoying his book, you not only will finally get the distinction between a mediator and a moderator squared away and know how to properly test for the existence of a mediator or a moderator, you will also more deftly understand the complexities of such processes as mediated moderation and moderated mediation.

TODD D. LITTLE
Postconferencing in Edmonton, Alberta

Preface

My goal from the very inception of this project, as reflected in the book's title, has been to teach researchers how to conduct both mediation and moderation analyses, with an emphasis on the "how to." I have tried to emphasize hands-on procedures for performing these analyses so that someone reading this book can quickly and readily acquire the set of skills necessary for these analyses. I hope that students who are learning the essentials of statistical analyses will be able to learn from this book what mediation and moderation can do and to more quickly integrate these approaches into their theory, research, and writings.

As I say later in the book, I am convinced that the best learning in statistics occurs through the hands-on experience of setting up a dataset, doing computations, reading the statistical output, graphing the results, and interpreting the resulting patterns. We learn by doing. So I want you, dear reader, to learn these techniques by conducting analyses on sample datasets that I have provided while you are reading this book. In addition, I have provided extra exercises and problems at the end of the substantive chapters so that you can practice these techniques and expand your expertise. (Suggested answers to exercises appear at the end of the book.) Appendix A relates SPSS, Amos, and Mplus syntax for conducting the key types of analyses, and Appendix B contains URLs for useful online material and applets to run related analyses. I have a very pragmatic, practical streak in my personality; I learned from an early age, growing up on a dairy farm in the Midwestern United States, that theory is nice and all, but it is not worth much if it cannot be applied.

I have written this book to encompass both mediation and moderation, harking back to Baron and Kenny's (1986) seminal article that alerted many of us to the benefit of jointly considering these two statistical techniques.

It is true that both methods describe interesting relationships among three variables (in the simpler versions of both), so it is natural to discuss them together; but it is also true that they sit next to each other uneasily, like teenage boys and girls at a school-sponsored dance. It is not clear how they are similar and different, and although I have taken some pains to explicate this enduring issue in this book, I remain unconvinced that we have utterly resolved the tension between these two techniques. Still, I believe that understanding one assists in the understanding of the other, and this is particularly germane once we begin to learn about and use combinations such as moderated mediation and mediated moderation.

The last issue that I would like to raise concerns the level of this book. For whom is this book written? I believe that higher-level undergraduates and graduate students will benefit chiefly from Chapters 2 (Historical Background), 3 (Basic Mediation), and 5 (Basic Moderation). The other chapters—Chapters 4 (Special Topics in Mediation), 6 (Special Topics in Moderation), and 7 (Mediated Moderation and Moderated Mediation)—will prove more difficult for these readers because they are written with the assumption that the reader knows structural equation modeling and multilevel modeling. Established researchers who know the basics of mediation and moderation and want to be stimulated to learn cutting-edge variations in these techniques (e.g., latent variable moderation) may wish to skim or skip the basic chapters and focus on the three higher-level chapters. I believe that a single book can encompass both entry-level instruction in mediation and moderation and instruction in advanced techniques, and that book is now in your hands. However, I do not believe that *all* readers will read and benefit from *everything* in this book; some will read only the basic material and some will read only the advanced material. I want the book to be used in statistics classes, and I also want it to function as a reference book to be taken down and perused from time to time to refresh one's memory as to how to do a particular analysis. These are my hopes for this progeny of mine that I am launching into the world, and whether it fulfills all of these goals remains to be seen. I realize that certain errors may remain in the book (even after careful vetting from multiple readers), so I would appreciate feedback from readers concerning these issues. If this book serves a useful function, I will be keen to revise, improve, and polish the book for another edition in a few years (after I recover from the exhaustion caused by this one). Finally, I hope that you benefit from reading this book, and enjoy learning about these techniques.

Acknowledgments

I want to thank the key people who have encouraged me to embark on and finish this arduous journey. I'd like to say a special (posthumous) thank you to Bob Abelson, who early on in my career showed me that a teacher of statistics could have a great sense of humor, be human and real, and be a great statistics educator as well. Other important influences are Fred Bryant and Grayson Holmbeck at Loyola University Chicago, who taught me about mediation and moderation, structural equation modeling, and life. Grayson's interest in and passion for mediation and moderation started me in a serious way on this path, and Fred convinced me that I could do amazing things in statistics. In brief encounters that I've had with Dave Kenny, Dave MacKinnon, and Andrew Hayes, I have found them to be very supportive and encouraging, and I would like to thank them for their outstanding work in this area, which permits someone like me to come along and create a book such as this. I would like to specifically mention Dave MacKinnon's book *Introduction to Statistical Mediation Analysis* (2008), which came out while I was in the middle of my work on my own book; it has been very useful as an authoritative source on mediation. Dave has also graciously helped me understand some of the more mysterious aspects of mediation in multilevel modeling. Todd Little and Kris Preacher have been, in their own ways, very encouraging and supportive, and Todd, in particular, has been an extremely helpful guide in his role as the editor of the Guilford Methodology in the Social Sciences series. And thanks are extended to Kathy Modecki, who guided me into the world of Mplus syntax. My main editor, C. Deborah Laughton, has exuded confidence and belief in this book idea since the beginning, and her attitude that I could write a book on this topic *and actually finish it* has been motivating, helpful, and necessary. Reviewers of earlier versions of the manuscript who provided perspective, information, corrections, and suggestions have been extremely valuable in the process as well, and I would like to particularly mention Maria M. Wong, Department of Psychology at Idaho State University, and Alex M. Schoemann, Center for Research Methods at the University of Kansas. Although I have received much appreciated guidance and assistance while on the path of writing this book, any remaining errors are mine.

Contents

Data and syntax files for examples and exercises, plus links to the author's online graphing and calculation programs (MedGraph and ModGraph), are available at *www.guilford.com/jose-materials*.

1

A Basic Orientation

Do not undertake the study of structural equation
models . . . in the hope of acquiring a technique that can
be applied mechanically to a set of numerical data with the
expectation that the result will automatically be "research."

[Avoid] the instinct to suppose that any old set of data,
tortured according to the prescribed ritual, will yield up
interesting scientific discoveries.
—DUNCAN (1975, p. 150)

MY PERSONAL JOURNEY

My experiences with the statistical techniques of mediation and moderation
are not unique, and I feel that it might be useful to share them with you to
make a point about how researchers have typically gone about acquiring such
knowledge (before this book was written, that is). At the time that I obtained
my PhD in psychology, I took required courses in statistics and methodology.
I learned a great deal about analysis of variance (ANOVA) and correlation,
and since then I have relied greatly on ANOVA and multiple regression to
make sense of the data that I have collected. Through the years I've heard
increasing use of the terms *mediation* and *moderation* but looked in vain in
statistics textbooks for a clear delineation of these techniques. I learned most
of what I know about these methods from talking with colleagues and modeling my efforts on their suggestions. I have been surprised that there hasn't
been a place where a novice could go to obtain the basic "how-to" knowledge
to perform these statistical functions, and I've been surprised that no statistics package with which I've become acquainted provides a quick, easy,

1

and clear set of procedures to conduct mediation or moderation. At the same time, more and more researchers and writers in the social sciences, management sciences, business, biology, and other fields have included these techniques in their reports.

For these reasons, I decided to write a book to describe *how to perform these two statistical techniques*. My goal is to provide a resource book that will be particularly helpful to the beginning user but also useful to the person who is looking to upgrade to more sophisticated approaches (e.g., moderation in hierarchical linear modeling, moderated mediation, quadratic moderation). If I have been successful in writing this book, then the uninitiated user will be able to read through the first several chapters of this book, analyze his or her data with a basic statistics program such as SPSS, and create useful findings within short order. I have included a number of examples throughout my book so that a novice user can gain practice in these techniques before launching into analyses of his or her own data. At the same time I am confident that a thorough reading of the book will lead a person to become facile with cutting-edge approaches that are not commonly used or appreciated.

I should probably state at this juncture that I am not a statistician by training. I received my PhD in developmental psychology some time ago (let's not dwell on how long ago it was), and I've grown interested in mediation and moderation because I have increasingly used these techniques in my own research. In this way, I share the same background as many of the readers of this book: We want to understand the basic facts about these techniques so that we can use them correctly. To this end, I emphasize "how-to" procedures, plain explanations, and concrete examples over general mathematical formulae typical of a statistics book. However, I have included critical and necessary mathematical and statistical equations in places because they are helpful in showing how abstract equations are translated into actual statistical procedures performed by a program. In the long run those readers who do master the "foreign language" of statistical notation will be able to connect the procedures described here with other useful papers and books.

I have tried to write this book in simple language so that it will be accessible to the novice reader. There are many books and articles written for the statistics community on the present topics, but they are not generally accessible and comprehensible for the beginner researcher. To my knowledge, there is no book on the market that is specifically written to address the needs of the uninitiated in the two areas of statistical mediation and moderation. I have a fair amount of experience teaching undergraduate students in psychology the basics of research methodology and statistics, and over time I've hit upon the following approach:

1. State a basic definition in plain, everyday language.
2. Give an example.
3. Actually do the procedure or analysis.
4. Review the definition in light of what you did.

I adopt this approach in the present book. I first plainly state what mediation or moderation is. Then I give you an example. The next step is up to you: You can actually perform the analysis with a statistics program. And finally, I invite you to review what you've learned conceptually and pragmatically. In my view, statistics is one of those things that a person *learns by actually doing it.* Many books on statistics are like manuals that describe the structure and functions of bicycles. It is often far from obvious how one should actually perform the statistical procedure, just as it is not obvious how to ride a bicycle from seeing a diagram of its structure. These statistics books are fine as far as they go; they convey abstract knowledge about important and useful concepts and techniques. The present book is an attempt to do it somewhat differently. My vision is that you'll be able to read and do the analyses at virtually the same moment as you progress through the book. This is the way true learning is likely to occur, in my opinion, and I hope that you take advantage of this possibility. Study the manual and then get on that bike and ride it. When you fall off, read the manual again, and ride it better next time.

Although much of this book is intended for the novice (in particular see Chapters 1, 2, 3, and 5), I have also written several chapters that move beyond the basic ideas of mediation and moderation to topics of interest to the high-level researcher. In particular, if the reader is already familiar with basic mediation and moderation, then he or she may be interested in learning more about:

1. *Special topics in mediation* (see Chapter 4 for topics such as bootstrapping, multiple mediators, and logistic mediation).
2. *Application of mediation in longitudinal designs* (see Chapter 4).
3. *Special topics in moderation* (see Chapter 6 for topics such as quadratic moderation, moderation in multilevel modeling, and logistic moderation).
4. *Mediated moderation and moderated mediation* (see Chapter 7).

The scope of this book, then, is broad, and it is probably the case that no one individual will read this entire book from cover to cover. I envision that the beginning student/researcher will benefit from reading and seriously engaging with Chapters 1, 2, 3, and 5 and will, in contrast, skim the other chapters to get a general orientation to higher level analytic techniques. The more advanced student/researcher, in comparison, is likely to briefly review the basic material but put more time and investment in Chapters 4, 6, and 7. In the latter case, the reader will note that I assume that readers of these chapters are familiar with structural equation modeling and multilevel modeling, which would be a misplaced assumption for the beginning student/ researcher. I am confident that all readers will find edification somewhere in this book, but it may take some time and effort on the reader's part to find the most helpful sections of the book.

I would also like to warn the reader that the tone of this book in places will be different from that of the typical statistics textbook. Most statistics books are written with a sober and almost solemn attitude, and I've often been told in all seriousness by some students and colleagues that they read statistics to help them get to sleep at night. I take a somewhat different approach. As someone who is currently involved in conducting studies in positive psychology, I take seriously the notion that we shouldn't be serious all of the time. Perhaps a better way to put it is that, although I treat statistics as a serious subject, I also feel that it's desirable to have a bit of fun along the way. I make fun of myself and make the occasional jibe at no one in particular just to make sure that you're still paying attention. I mean no disrespect to statisticians or the general field of science, but I'd like to convey the notion that statistical analyses are performed by real flesh-and-blood people who have foibles, warts, and other human characteristics. If I could demystify a small piece of this field a bit, then I think that that would be a step forward.

The book is written in the first person. In other words, you will hear my voice continually throughout, and I do feature a lot of my own research in describing these statistical techniques. This is my effort to make the material accessible and human. However, it has occurred to me that some people may feel that I'm using this approach because I am egocentric and self-centered. Let me assure you that I'm not egotistical: I am very aware of the shortcomings in my research. It's just that I know this stuff backward and forward and I can shape it to show you, the reader, what I want to demonstrate better than I can with someone else's data and research. I also think that many people (albeit not everyone) will find the topics that I study interesting. And if my first-person narrative succeeds in keeping the reader going through some of the highly technical matter, then it will have served its function. Truly, this book is not about me; it's about empowering you to master some powerful tools, and this is my attempt to get it across to you in an engaging fashion.

So the next step is to launch into an introduction to the topics of mediation and moderation. It is interesting to me that there is a great deal of misinformation and confusion and many blind spots and incorrect assumptions about mediation and moderation—more so than any other statistical topic that I've ever encountered—so I think that one of my main jobs in this book is to clear these up as I stimulate the reader to learn how to do these techniques properly.

CONFUSIONS ABOUT MEDIATION AND MODERATION

Confusion seems to exist about precisely what each of these two techniques does and does not do. The present chapter is placed at the beginning of the book because I think it's an important entry point to understanding what mediation and moderation are. However, I would encourage you to revisit this section after you have read the entire book, because then your knowledge of the two techniques will allow you to better understand where the pitfalls and misunderstandings occur. In other words, it takes some knowledge to understand one's lack of knowledge. For the truly novice user (i.e., no or very little previous knowledge), this section may not be very helpful, but I think that it will be very helpful for those of you who have tried one or both methods or who have looked for authoritative information on one or both methods. In any case, I think that it has value in that it will prime you to think about my explanations in a deeper and more sophisticated way.

Common Language Usage of the Words *Mediation* and *Moderation*

The title of this book refers to "doing statistical mediation and moderation." I felt it necessary to distinguish this topic from books on labor mediation and treatises on how to moderate meetings. A Google search will quickly provide evidence that most of the world thinks of mediation and moderation in a different sense than do researchers. I would like to briefly touch on the lay-language definitional meanings of these two terms in order to make a point: These terms were chosen to describe statistical phenomena that are not all that different from what we experience in the wider world and particularly in human interactions.

The definition of *mediate* by the *Funk and Wagnalls Standard College Dictionary* (1978, p. 841) is:

(a) to settle or reconcile differences by intervening as a peacemaker; and

(b) to serve as the medium for effecting a result or conveying an object, information, etc.

The first meaning is the one that most people think of when they hear of mediation, and a large profession is made up of people who attempt to enact the desirable goal of creating a compromise between two differing positions. I draw attention, however, to the second meaning, which is remarkably close to what statistical mediation is about. In essence, a mediating variable conveys information from one place (the independent variable [IV]) to another place (the dependent variable [DV]). It is the medium or conduit of information between the IV and the DV, and therefore it passes information from one place to another. The word *mediation* has two definitional meanings, then, in line with the preceding definitions: reconciliation or interposition. Reconciliation occurs after a mediator has settled differences between two parties, and interposition accurately portrays the latter situation in which a person or mediating variable is placed in between two other objects.

Now let's turn to moderation. The definition of the verb *moderate* by the same dictionary is:

(a) to make less extreme; and

(b) to preside over. (p. 870)

We are familiar with the first meaning, as in "the wind is moderating the temperature today," and it is generally used to refer to affecting a phenomenon so that it is less extreme. This meaning is relevant to statistical moderation in the sense that it captures one aspect of statistical moderation. As you will see in Chapter 5, statistical moderation includes both *buffering* and *exacerbating* effects. The case of buffering is close to this first definitional meaning: namely, to make a relationship less strong. For example, stressed people generally feel depressed, and if we examine the impact of a moderator such as social support, we might find that individuals who talk to others about their problems show a weaker relationship between stress and depression. The relationship was therefore "buffered" by the moderator, social support, and this weakened or less extreme relationship is similar to the sense of making something less extreme. (Unfortunately, the analogy ends there, because the case of exacerbating is the case of making something worse or more extreme. More will be said about these two opposite characteristics of moderation later.)

The second meaning of moderation, that is, presiding over something, is appropriate to some extent, too. To preside over a meeting is to control the proceedings of a meeting; the word *control* is relevant here. In statistical moderation, the moderating variable affects (i.e., controls) the relationship between the IV and the DV. In that sense, a foreperson of a jury who moderates the discussion of 12 people deciding the fate of an accused person may be said to be similar to a moderating variable in a multiple regression.

I should note at this point that even the two terms *mediate* and *moderate* as used in common language have certain overlapping qualities. Note that the first definitions of these two terms, given previously, have a certain shared meaning: to settle differences and to make less extreme. When one mediates between two conflicting parties, one is quite likely to moderate the discussion. It is significant that the *Funk and Wagnalls* dictionary defines a moderator as "an arbitrator of a dispute; a mediator." So even in everyday language we have confusion between mediation and moderation. I am sometimes asked, "Can a moderator be a mediator?" My advice to people confused by this situation is to focus on the second meanings given here and to map them onto the statistical examples that I give you later in this book.

Five Areas of Confusion in Statistical Mediation and Moderation

First, because mediation and moderation have similar sounding names, most people assume that they are related and possibly derive from the same source. The reality is that they derive from different statistical sources: Moderation is a special type of ANOVA interaction, and mediation is a special type of path model. Their heritage, in other words, is quite different, although they can both be computed through multiple regression. The situation is a bit like koalas and bears: They look similar, but their genealogy and physiology are quite different.

Second, statistics textbooks typically do not do a very good job of explaining these two approaches. In my experience, I have found very few texts that discuss these two techniques *together*, drawing out their similarities and differences (for two exceptions, see Howell, 2007, and MacKinnon, 2008). Part of the reason for this omission is that the terms *mediation* and *moderation* are not common terms for statisticians to use for these phenomena. Mediation is often described by statisticians as "semipartial correlations within a multiple regression format," and moderation is described as "a statistical interaction within a multiple regression format." Statisticians don't see these two techniques as especially similar or related, and they don't tend to describe them in conjunction with each other. From my perspective, what has happened is that researchers have appropriated these labels to describe two techniques that share a characteristic—that is, they attempt to explicate relationships among three variables—and these two techniques have come over time to be associated in the minds of researchers by the fact that they can both be used to probe three-variable relationships.

Third, reports of moderation and mediation in the research literature are not always clear or accurately performed. What particular researchers did in performing their particular test or tests may be ambiguous. Holmbeck (1997) and Baron and Kenny (1986) have pointed out that some researchers have used the wrong label for what they actually did (or what they theorized was likely to happen). There is nothing quite as confusing as an author who has published in a reputable journal describing a phenomenon as "moderation" when, in fact, he or she has examined the data with a mediational paradigm (or vice versa).

Fourth, both are special cases of two separate broad statistical approaches, and therefore they do not receive as much attention and coverage as mainstream statistical approaches. Considerable coverage is given in statistics books on the topic of ANOVA, and there is a great deal of information concerning statistical interactions within an ANOVA context. There is also a great deal of information on correlations, part and partial correlations, and regression techniques. But I have found that there is little explication of how these two areas (mediation and moderation) touch each other. The uninitiated reader may not realize that they are related to each other, but more knowledgeable readers will know that the overarching model that incorporates both of them is called GLM (the general linear model; see Henderson, 1998). In fact, in the SPSS data analysis program, if you are interested in computing a univariate ANOVA, you click on an option called "GLM" to move to several variations of ANOVA. Note, however, that regression falls under a completely different option (REGRESSION), so it is not apparent that they are cousins, but I wish to make the point here that they are. Moderation and mediation fall into that gray area that exists between ANOVA and partial correlations that is not well understood by the novice researcher.

Fifth, it's not entirely clear what distinguishes a moderating variable from a mediating variable. For example, one researcher might use social support coping as a mediator in a study, and another researcher in a different study might use the same variable as a moderator. Is one wrong, and if so, which one? The definitions of mediating and moderating variables overlap to some extent, and this has led to a great deal of inconsistency in how certain variables are treated by researchers. On a related point, it is not common that researchers perform both moderation and mediation on the same dataset, so examples of this type of work are rare. In fact, many researchers believe that mediation and moderation are mutually exclusive, that is, that one can perform only one type of analysis on a given set of variables. The truth of this assertion is dependent on the nature of the mediating or moderating variable, and in some cases both techniques can be used on the same variables.

Several notable articles have appeared over the past decade or so that try to rectify the misperceptions and confusions surrounding these techniques. Baron and Kenny (1986) wrote an article about 20 years ago from the perspective of social psychological research, and it stands as the seminal article that behavioral researchers use to try to disambiguate these two techniques. Subsequently, excellent work by Holmbeck (1997, 2002) has extended these views to clinical psychology. I strongly recommend reading these works because they present considerable context for the use of these techniques and they point out common misunderstandings and pitfalls to which researchers may fall prey. (A recent book by MacKinnon [2008] focusing on mediation is also an excellent place to go for definitive information.) I intend for the book that you're reading now to stand as my effort to try to clear up misconceptions in this area. I would not pretend that this book will stand as the final set of answers to the many issues that vex mediation–moderation researchers, but hopefully it will clarify some basic issues and extend the search for consensus on a number of cutting-edge issues.

MEDIATION AND MODERATION: THE SYNERGISM OF THREE VARIABLES

When students begin to learn statistics, they usually begin with cases in which two variables are examined together:

1. A t-test, in which levels of one variable (e.g., social support) are compared across groups (e.g., males vs. females).
2. A chi-square test, in which frequencies of one variable (e.g., ethnicity) are compared with frequencies of another variable (e.g., religious affiliation).
3. A correlation, in which levels of one variable (e.g., depression) are associated with levels of another variable (e.g., altruism).

However, the situation becomes immensely more interesting and complicated when a third variable is introduced into the mix. I use multiple regression as the method for illustrating this extension, as it is the statistical technique of choice for computing basic mediation and moderation.

Let's take the example of a researcher who has performed a simple linear regression in which the variable of self-reported stress was used to predict self-reported levels of depression. (See Figure 1.1 for an example of a two-variable analysis such as I alluded to previously.) But then this imaginary researcher realizes that this relationship might be investigated by including a third variable, namely, perceived control. He or she knows that people who feel more in control of their situations are less likely to be affected by stressful events and are less likely to feel depressed. But how does one include this new variable?

Some researchers would merely add it to the regression (see Figure 1.2) as another predictor. This analysis would be somewhat interesting, and this involves using all three variables in the same analysis, but it's neither moderation nor mediation. This approach is an example of "additive effects" in that the effect of stress is added to the effect of perceived control in predicting scores of depression. Each of the two predictors contributes to some extent, and the regression "adds" them statistically. Much analytical work is of this type, and it can be illuminating in and of itself, but moderation and mediation are another step beyond additive effects.

FIGURE 1.1. Simple linear regression.

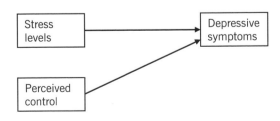

FIGURE 1.2. Adding a third variable to a simple linear regression.

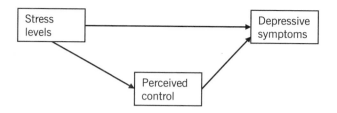

FIGURE 1.3. Depiction of simple mediation.

In mediation, the emphasis is on the *mechanism that operates between the two predictors and the outcome*, so one might want to examine the possibility that stress predicts perceived control, which in turn predicts depression. Note that the model in Figure 1.2 included nothing about the relationship between stress and perceived control. In that case, the two IVs are two coequal predictors, and their relationship to each other is considered to be merely a correlation, not directional or predictive. In mediation (see Figure 1.3), one explicitly examines the relationship between the IV (stress) and the mediating variable (MedV; perceived control), as well as the ability of both the IV and MedV to predict the DV (depression).

And then there is moderation, which explicitly *involves an interaction term* between the two independent variables. Moderation looks like the simple additive model described above, but the inclusion of the interaction term is a crucial addition (see Figure 1.4). This third term explains variability in the DV above and beyond the two additive effects and tells us important information about how the two independent variables *jointly* predict the DV.

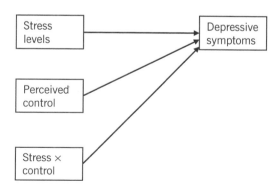

FIGURE 1.4. Depiction of simple moderation.

I assume that you, the reader, know how to do the simple additive model, and the rest of this book will convey material that goes beyond that simple first step in combining three variables in a single analysis. So how hard could it be to do these mediation and moderation analyses? Well, it turns out to be quite involved and complex, because there are many different ways in which three variables can be included in these analyses; in short, there are many different variations of mediation and moderation. To learn how to perform these analyses is to move to an entirely new level of complexity beyond simple correlations, *t*-tests, simple additive effects regressions, and ANOVAs, and it will take this entire book to sort through all of the various combinations and permutations of possibilities. The next chapter is my attempt to reconstruct a narrative of how these two statistical techniques developed over time in the hope that once a reader understands the historical and conceptual context for these approaches, then he or she will be better prepared to use these techniques wisely and well in the future.

2

Historical Background

In this chapter I first define statistics as a method of making "reasoned arguments." Then I review the schism within statistics between the investigation of mean group differences and a search for associations between variables. And finally I move on to recount the historical and contextual foundation for mediation and moderation that was built in the 20th century. Following this introduction, the largest portion of this chapter is devoted to an extended unpacking of the Baron and Kenny (1986) article that has served as the beacon for understanding statistical mediation and moderation for over 20 years. Most researchers have read, or at least skimmed, this article, yet areas of misunderstanding and confusion still exist despite this excellent orientation. I conclude the chapter by briefly touching on a couple of important developments in this area that occurred after the landmark Baron and Kenny paper was published.

THE HISTORY OF MEDIATION AND MODERATION

There is no coherent history of mediation and moderation. What I present here instead is a retrospective stitching together of descriptions of the work of various statisticians and researchers who have worked with these methods over time. I'm not sure that we can say that a particular person invented mediation, and probably the same is true for moderation, but we examine the earliest references to these methods.

Before we get started on mediation and moderation in particular, let me parenthetically note that there are some first-rate books written for the educated layperson that recount the general history of statistics: I recommend David Salsburg's (2001) *The Lady Tasting Tea: How Statistics Revolutionized Science in the Twentieth Century* and Peter Bernstein's (1996) *Against the Gods:*

13

The Remarkable Story of Risk. These are accessible accounts of the history of statistics and the estimation of probability, and they serve to remind the reader that statistics arose out of human needs to control and understand what seemed to be a chaotic and unpredictable world. Statistical techniques can be wonderful tools for exploring, explaining, and predicting the seemingly fickle happenstances of life, and I try to retain that spirit of adventure and excitement in my discourses on mediation and moderation. These are marvelous tools to unlock complicated interrelationships among variables, so we should learn where they come from and how to use them correctly.

At the same time, I think it's useful to bear in mind Robert Abelson's (1995) point that statistical findings are used to make arguments. There is nothing magical about statistical computations, and statistical results should be viewed with appropriate skepticism and caution. (See also Chinn & Brewer, 2001, for a similar view.) In this same vein, the section in Wikipedia ("Statistics," 2007) on the misuse of statistics notes: "Statistics is principally a form of rhetoric. This can be taken as a positive or a negative, but as with any means of settling a dispute, statistical methods can succeed only as long as both sides accept the approach and agree on the method to be used." The history of mediation and moderation that I briefly describe herein should be seen as an unfolding discussion about whether these two statistical techniques yield valid and useful information. I think that there is a growing consensus that these approaches can be helpful; however, there is also a growing unease about the indiscriminate and uncritical use of these approaches. Abelson (1995) would say that the user is on firmer ground in using a statistical technique if she or he knows more about the history, mathematical underpinnings, and limitations of an approach, and these things are what this book is about. Let's now review what little history exists about these techniques.

TWO STRANDS OF THOUGHT WITHIN STATISTICS

I think that it is illuminating to examine the early beginnings of statistics in the present context. We seem to have two major themes or strands of statistical thought represented in psychology: one from Ronald Fisher (1935, 1950) and one from Francis Galton (1869/1962).

Mean Group Differences

The first approach has led to techniques of examining mean group differences and features the use of *t*-tests, ANOVA, and the like. The goal is to determine whether the means of two or more groups are significantly different from each other given the amount of variability (standard deviation) associated with each mean. This tradition began with the use of the *t*-test that determines whether two groups' means are different. For example, a *t*-test can tell a researcher whether males and females differ in their reports of depression.

Subsequent developments gave rise to the technique of ANOVA as a statistical method, and an important characteristic of ANOVA design is relevant here. An important innovation of this approach is that one can "cross" IVs (or predictors). Thus one can simultaneously examine the effects of the IVs of gender and age (let's say younger and older male and female adolescents) on reports of depression. This analysis will tell the user whether a main effect exists for gender and whether a main effect exists for age. The entirely new and exciting aspect of ANOVA compared with the *t*-test, however, is determining whether a statistically significant interaction exists. The ANOVA analysis will produce output that will tell the user whether the interaction term of gender by age explains part of the variance in the depression variable. The user needs to examine the pattern of means obtained for this interaction and then interpret what it means. By definition, an interaction tells us that one predictor has a differential effect on the DV depending on different levels of the second predictor. Thus, in our preceding example, we may find that females report higher depression than males in general (i.e., a main effect). We may also find a significant interaction that tells us that this main effect depends on levels of the second predictor, age. Figure 2.1 shows that older female adolescents are significantly more depressed than older male adoles-

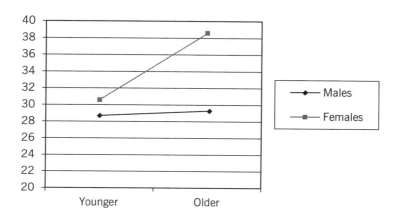

FIGURE 2.1. Interaction of gender and age on depression.

cents and that no significant difference exists between younger males and females. (This result is based on real data that I have collected, by the way, so I am not exactly making this up.)

This tradition gives us the concept of the interaction, and this is the tradition that gives rise to the statistical concept of moderation. In essence, moderation with regression could be said to be "a special case of ANOVA" insofar as one uses at least one continuous independent/predictor variable in the regression-based approach. As you probably know, when you attempt to perform an ANOVA, you are required to enter categorical IVs/predictors such as gender (0 = males; 1 = females) or dichotomized continuous variables such as our example of age here (0 = younger; 1 = older). Age is a natural continuous variable, but I had to create a categorical variable in order to make it work for an ANOVA. In moderation, I would leave age as a continuous variable because multiple regression can handle continuous variables.

Associations

The other tradition, termed the "associationist" perspective, has its roots in efforts to determine whether two variables are associated with each other. Francis Galton, in his quest to show that genetics largely determined the expression of intelligence, innovated the statistical method of correlation. He showed (Galton, 1869/1962) that a child's intelligence was positively correlated with his or her parents' intelligence, and he falsely concluded that genetic inheritance explained all of this relationship. Although he was overly enthusiastic about his hypothesis concerning the inheritance of intelligence, he was hugely influential in his creation of the correlation statistic, as well as the invention of the written survey. Ironically, he was probably the first person to fall prey to the admonition "correlation does not imply causality."

The statistical technique of correlation has spawned dozens of variations, and one of those variations concerns "partial" correlations. A "partial correlation" is one in which the effect of one variable is "taken out of" a second variable, which is correlated with a third. For example, a researcher collects data on academic professors' publications and salaries (see Cohen & Cohen, 1975, for a description of the data). He wishes to know whether number of publications is associated with salary level, so he computes a correlation between these two variables and finds that $r = .65$, $p < .01$. He is about to publish his result when a reviewer asks the question "Is this relationship changed by considering the number of years that the academic has been working since his/her PhD?" Consequently, he covaries out the number of years since PhD from the correlation between numbers of publications and salary, and he finds that the basic correlation drops significantly and is no longer statistically significant, $r = .12$, $p = .27$. This partial correlation may be a truer estimate of the relationship between the predictor (number of publications) and the outcome (salary) because, by covarying out the effect of the third variable, one determines the true strength of association between average number of publications per year and salary irrespective of number of years since graduation. This computation is similar to what one does when performing a mediation analysis.

Let me just make this point crystal clear, because it is an important one: Moderation derives from statistical work on ANOVA, whereas mediation derives from statistical work on correlation and regression. They do share some aspects in common—for example, both computations can be performed in regression—but I think it's fascinating that these two approaches emanated from different theoretical traditions.

THE HISTORICAL BASIS FOR THE METHODS OF MEDIATION AND MODERATION

The state of work and writing on mediation within the behavioral sciences (psychology, management sciences, sociology, nursing, etc.) is mushrooming. An outpouring of work in recent years amounts to a great deal of literature to read, understand, and use. I attempt to summarize the more seminal and more recent articles in an effort to alert the reader to the critical work in the field at this moment. The interested reader will find much to consider in this work.

From my reading, it seems that the social sciences' interest in mediation derived from work concerning path modeling invented by Sewell Wright. He, like Francis Galton, was fascinated by the topic of genetic inheritance. In 1921 he published a paper in the *Journal of Agricultural Research* titled "Correlation and Causation" that is widely credited with being the first paper describing path analysis. His subject matter, it is interesting to note, was tracing the multiple pathways of various causal genetic influences on guinea pig growth. He noted at the beginning of his paper that science is concerned with identifying causes for outcomes but that strict experimentation is not always desirable or possible. He goes on to state that we often have to deal with "a group of characteristics or conditions which are correlated because of a complex of interacting, uncontrollable, and often obscure causes" (p. 557). His paper was "an attempt to present a method of measuring the direct influence along each separate path in such a system and thus of finding the degree to which variation of a given effect is determined by each particular cause" (p. 557). He, you might notice, is describing direct and indirect effects among groups of variables, and although he originally described path models including four, five, or six variables, it can be seen that the general model applies equally well to the three-variable mediation context. Parenthetically, it can be mentioned in passing here that his reference to "interacting" variables refers to what we call moderation now. He didn't explain the role of interactions in path models, but he clearly envisioned from the beginning the potential role of interaction terms in path models. From a historical point of view, it is relevant to note that he did not use the words *mediation* or *moderation* in his article.

The first mentions of mediation and mediators in psychology occur in the work of psychologists at about the same time that Sewell Wright was creating path analysis. For example, Howard Warren in 1920 wrote a book titled *Human Psychology* in which he described the function of the organism's nervous system: "The neuro-terminal system is the mediator between the creature and his environment" (p. 92). He used the common-sense meaning of mediation to describe how the brain and nervous system were functional links between the organism's body and the environment, and this usage was eminently sensible to a researcher who described the interconnected linkages among neurons in the nervous system. Similarly, A. Rosenblueth, a physiological psychologist at Harvard College, published a series of articles in the 1930s concerning the function of a chemical mediator in nerve impulses (e.g., Rosenblueth & Rioch, 1933). In essence, it seems that the concept of mediation was appreciated in the disciplines of biology and chemistry early on and filtered out from these scientific fields into psychology and the rest of the social sciences during the first half of the 20th century.

Wright's path modeling approach was first used in biology, genetics, and agricultural research and was not widely appreciated in the social sciences until about mid-century. (I'm referring to the *20th* century, which I can still dimly remember.) Psychology at that time was very interested in process models, that is, models in which variables affected each other in sequence. A good example of this approach was the interest in the field of learning theory in the organism's role in stimulus–response (S-R) contingencies. Thorndike posed a stimulus–organism–response (S-O-R) model in which the organism was affected by the stimulus and then created a response. The "O" refers to cognition, drives, goals, and so forth, that the organism may use to respond to a particular stimulus. The organism becomes an "intervening variable," according to E. C. Tolman (1938, p. 344).

These ideas within learning theory formed a foundation for interest in process models, namely, how the effect of an IV on a DV can be mediated through an intervening variable. A classic paper in psychology by Mac-Corquodale and Meehl (1948) was pivotal in furthering this understanding. They referred to the work of Tolman (1938) and Hull (1943) as proposing the utility of considering intervening variables, and they contrasted this perspective with Skinner's (1938) position about S-R linkages, but they did not use the words *mediator* or *mediation* in their article. A bit later, Hyman (1955) wrote an influential methodology textbook that proposed a useful set of analytical approaches for intervening variables, but he did not use the *m*-word, either. According to Kenny (2008), he called this approach "elaboration." However, the very next year, in the journal *Psychological Review*, William Rozeboom (1956) wrote a paper with this word prominently included in his title (i.e., "Mediation Variables in Scientific Theory"), and his paper is replete with references to mediation and mediator variables. Somewhat surprisingly from today's perspective, he distinguished intervening variables from mediating variables, but his conception of mediation makes sense to us today: "We frequently have reason to believe, however, that given an empirical relation in which a variable *y* covaries with a variable *x*, there exist one or more 'real' variables *v* whose identities may be unknown to us but which causally mediate between *x* and *y*" (p. 259). Rozeboom's article is a dense tract written from a philosophy-of-science point of view and is infrequently read today, but it very well may be the pivotal article that introduced the common-sense word *mediation* into the social sciences.

When the cognitive revolution arose in psychology in the late 1950s and the early 1960s it was clear that cognitive models needed to be process models (Norman, 1977). Herbert Simon, at about the same time, approached the same issue from the perspective of philosophy (Simon, 1952). Shortly after this, within sociology and psychology, Blalock (1964), Duncan (1975), Heise (1975), and Kenny (1979) made significant advancements in formalizing the methodology of path analysis. In Kenny's 1979 book *Correlation and Causality*, he described mediation in the fashion used today, namely that a variable is interposed between two others in a path model. However, Duncan (1970, 1975) did not use the term *mediation*, although he clearly proposed models that involved what we call mediation now. Subsequently, more researchers in the social sciences began to use the term *mediation* to refer to indirect effects in path models (three variables or larger). An important but overlooked contribution was the article by James and Brett (1984) titled "Mediators, Moderators, and Tests for Mediation." (See also the book by James, Mulaik, and Brett [1982]).

At the same time, interest in "moderators" began to grow as well. The concept of moderation seemed to arise from an interest in combining the technique of multiple regression (path modeling techniques) with the concept of statistical interactions that enjoyed considerable enthusiasm in the ANOVA approach (Abrahams & Alf, 1972; Allison, 1977; Cohen, 1978; Cooley & Keesey, 1981; Sockloff, 1976; Southwood, 1978; Zedeck, 1971).

Initially, moderation was seen as separate and distinct from mediation, and one can appreciate that this occurred because they arose from two different sources. I think it's appropriate here to make a sociological observation: The terms *mediation* and *moderation* are not typically used by statisticians (in the past century or now), but they have come into common parlance because of the enthusiasm for these techniques evidenced by researchers and users. What has apparently happened is that a gulf has opened between mathematically based statisticians and users of statistical programs (i.e., researchers). Consequently, it is not uncommon for a researcher in a given field to approach a traditionally trained statistician to ask a question about these procedures and to be faced with puzzlement. I've been told by many students that when this occurs, they are asked to define, explain, and describe moderation and mediation to the statistician because she or he isn't familiar with these terms. I am relating this common story not to find fault with anyone, but to point out that as time passes, disciplines can draw away from each other with regard to terminology and procedures that they truly have in common. I hope that this book will enable researchers to approach statisticians concerning "part and partial correlations" and "interactions in multiple regression" and facilitate a fruitful interchange about these techniques.

BARON AND KENNY'S LANDMARK PUBLICATION

I choose now to discuss Baron and Kenny's seminal article "The Moderator–Mediator Variable Distinction in Social Psychological Research: Conceptual, Strategic, and Statistical Considerations," published in the *Journal of Personality and Social Psychology* in 1986. Although I realize that researchers outside of the field of psychology may find this somewhat tangential to their concerns, I do this for two reasons: (1) many researchers outside of psychology are aware of this far-reaching article; and (2) it contains many important definitions and observations about mediation and moderation that are germane to our concerns.

My approach to this article is a bit like that of a biblical scholar attempting to improve the knowledge of a congregation about what it is truly in the Bible. Many people believe that they know what is in the Bible, but few have actually read it thoroughly. Analogously, many people claim to follow Baron and Kenny's suggestions for mediation and moderation, but few have read this article closely and obtained definitive knowledge about it, so they may or may not actually be following the procedures the way they were laid down. I do not reiterate the entirety of the article, but I convey the basic points and try to clarify what they said about a number of controversial points.

Basic Overview

This article may be the most highly cited paper in the field of psychology. At my last check of PsychINFO (February 2013), it had been cited exactly 14,209 times. By 2014, their article might have been cited 15,000 times. Given that the average number of citations for the average article in psychology is probably less than 20, this is a phenomenally large number. Several points are worth noting here. First, it is apparently the only jointly published article by Baron and Kenny, proving that even a single fruitful collaboration can bear a great amount of fruit (in this case, truckloads of apples). Second, the article was published more than 20 years ago, and it is still going strong. Few papers continue to accrue citations after 2–3 years; the fact that this article is still current today indicates that it is undeniably a classic. The reason that it is still drawing attention is that the basic ideas laid out in the article are still accurate and germane today. The guidelines enunciated in this article are still widely accepted, and it has become an authoritative source to which people refer in order to resolve disagreements about mediation and moderation. I have been told countless times that "this is the Baron and Kenny method, so we should do it this way." Sometimes the person actually knows what Baron and Kenny said, and the method is sound, but I've found that a distressing number of times people will make the claim that Baron and Kenny said to do it "this way" when that way is at variance with what Baron and Kenny actually recommended. So let's get into their content and see where the controversies arise.

Unfortunately, the authors didn't contextualize their exposition against the backdrop of previous writings on mediation and moderation, but they alluded to "a relatively long tradition in the social sciences." I suspect that they were thinking of the work started by Sewell Wright and continued by other researchers in the area of path modeling. Unfortunately, Baron and Kenny did not elucidate this matter in their article, and one of my goals in the present book is to provide more of this history so that users can better appreciate how these terms came into being and how they are used. It's my belief that many of the early beginnings are still lying undiscovered in journals and books of the early 20th century.

The essential point of the article is that many people are confused about moderation and mediation and that a clear distinction between these two techniques is needed; the stated purpose of the article was to "distinguish between the properties of moderator and mediator variables in such a way as to clarify the different ways in which conceptual variables may account for differences in people's behavior" (p. 1173). I would say that despite the good work of this article (as well as others), we are still in pressing need of clear exposition on the distinction between these two procedures.

Moderation

The authors begin with an exposition of the moderation technique. They define a moderator as "a variable that affects the direction and/or strength of the relation between an independent, or predictor, variable and a dependent, or criterion, variable" (p. 1174), and they give as examples variables such as sex, race, and experimentally manipulated variables. Then they go on to give examples in both the ANOVA and correlational frameworks. Let's consider these two contexts.

KNOWLEDGE BOX. A Note about Terminology: IV/DV versus Predictor/Outcome

Notice that Baron and Kenny referred to both versions of these terms in the preceding quotation. The customary practice in the social sciences is to use "IV and DV" when one is describing an experimental study and "predictor and outcome" when one is describing a passive observational study. The essential point is that the IV refers to a manipulated variable, whereas the predictor variable is not manipulated.

In this book I strive for consistency in this matter, and you should as well. However, for many of the general models that I present here, it does not matter whether I say "IV" or "predictor." For both mediation and moderation, the IV, or predictor, variable is the origin of the basic relationship (x predicts y, where x is the IV, or predictor, and y is the DV, or outcome). Where it *does* matter is in your consideration of the causal pathways among the variables. If x is a manipulated variable in an experimental paradigm, then causality is assumed to flow from it toward the mediating and outcome variables, and one should use the *IV* and *DV* terms. If x is not manipulated and is measured concurrently with the mediating and outcome variables, then direction of causality is questionable, and one should use the terms *predictor* and *outcome variables.*

A close reading of Baron and Kenny's article, by the way, reveals that they were not all that consistent themselves in their use of these terms. For mediation, they posit that the "independent variable" predicts the "outcome variable." In any case, the take-home point is that terminology conveys important information about the nature of the relationships among the variables, so try to be accurate and consistent about these.

Baron and Kenny point out that an ANOVA analysis will yield an interaction term between two IVs/predictors and that this interaction should be conceptualized as moderation. The examples that they mentioned in this circumstance were social psychological variables, and if the reader is not familiar with the cognitive dissonance literature (which would be true of a lot of people), he or she would experience some difficulty understanding how the ANOVA framework is relevant. Let me give a brief example. I have a dataset on adolescent functioning, and I was curious as to whether reports of stress intensity would be predictive of reports of depressive symptoms among these youths. (I and other researchers typically find this result in a wide variety of cultural and national groups.) Further, I wanted to see whether this proposed relationship might vary by socioeconomic status (SES). The outcome variable was a measure of depressive symptoms assessed by the Minnesota Multiphasic Personality Inventory (MMPI) self-report questionnaire, and the two predictors were SES and stress intensity. Both of the predictors are continuous variables, so in order to make this analysis work in the ANOVA framework, I had to make these continuous variables categorical. I examined the distribution of scores and trichotomized these continuous variables into low, medium, and high groups, each composed of about 33% of the sample. Thus the recoded SES variable had three values—1 (low), 2 (medium), and 3 (high)—and the recoded stress intensity variable had the same three values. I then entered them as the "fixed factors" in the univariate analysis in SPSS with depressive symptoms as the DV. I found a significant main effect for stress intensity, $F(2, 1076) = 91.85$, $p < .001$, but the main effect for SES was nonsignificant, and, more important in the present context, the interaction was nonsignificant. The specific test of whether moderation occurred is whether the interaction term is statistically significant or not, so in the present case I found that SES did *not* moderate the relationship between stress intensity and depressive symptoms. In other words, the mean levels of depression for the high, medium, and low stress groups did *not* vary by level of SES. Individuals who experienced high levels of stress, for example, reported about the same levels of depression regardless of whether they came from high-, medium-, or low-SES households.

I described this ANOVA case in some detail because I want the reader to understand that moderation is not limited to multiple regression; it can be performed in ANOVA as well. (Technically, ANOVA is a special case of regression.) The difference is that ANOVA requires the researcher to use categorical variables for the predictors, whereas multiple regression does not. I reiterate this point later when I explicate moderation in gory detail in Chapter 5, but let me be clear about the similarities and differences between ANOVA and regression here. ANOVA requires the two predictors to be categorical (i.e., two or more discrete levels), whereas moderation in multiple regression requires that at least one predictor be continuous. Baron and Kenny laid out the four possibilities in their article: categorical IV and categorical moderating variable (ModV; ANOVA applies in this case); continuous IV and categorical ModV; categorical IV and continuous ModV; and continuous IV and continuous ModV (these three latter cases can be analyzed with multiple regression). In the preceding example, I converted two continuous predictors into categorical predictors in order to make an ANOVA analysis work. Let me say categorically (pun intended) that *this is nonoptimal* because one loses mathematical information when one cuts up a continuous distribution into various sized groups. (Some people—see Maxwell & Delaney, 1993— say that it is dangerous and risky to do this because this categorization may distort the distribution on which it was based and lead to biased results.) I did it here to demonstrate how a lot of researchers (particularly students) try to make their data fit a particular technique that they know how to use. What one should do here instead of an ANOVA is a multiple-regression-based moderation analysis because the moderator is a continuous variable. I explain this in further detail in Chapter 5.

The other context (correlational) should be touched on, too. Baron and Kenny point out that "a moderator is a third variable that affects the zero-order correlation between two other variables" (p. 1174). This general type of analysis can be performed easily in SPSS as a *partial correlation*. Choose "Partial" under "Analysis/Correlation," and the program will ask for two or more variables to be correlated, as well as "control variables." Thus one can ask whether the correlation between anxiety and depression is affected by a third variable, such as gender. In another dataset I found that the zero-order correlation between anxiety and depression (as expected) was moderately large in size, $r(653) = .605$, $p < .001$. I suspected that this correlation might differ between the two genders, so I conducted a partial correlation with some follow-up analyses. When I performed the partial correlation I obtained a lower correlation: $r(653) = .578$, $p < .001$. I then conducted a split file analysis—a correlation between anxiety and depression split by gender. I found that females reported a stronger relationship, $r(279) = .635$, $p < .001$, than males, $r(374) = .516$, $p < .001$. The partial correlation removes the effect of gender on the correlation between these other two variables, although the partial correlation analysis in itself does not allow the user to determine whether the change is statistically significant or not. In the present case one can see that the strength of the correlation for females is larger than for males, but I do not have a good way here (in partial correlation) to determine whether this difference is significant or not. A proper moderation analysis—performed in multiple regression—will tell me whether this difference is significant. (By the way, I have just gone away to properly test this hypothesis with the appropriate moderation analysis, and I found that it is significantly different.) What I think is interesting about this paragraph by Baron and Kenny (pp. 1175–1176) is that they do not mention "partial correlation," so it is hard for people who are familiar with correlation to make the connection between moderation and partial correlation.

Baron and Kenny presented a figure that depicts the basic moderation path model (see Figure 2.2). They appropriately drew the reader's attention to the third path (predictor × moderator) and said that whether this term is a significant predictor or not is the test of whether significant moderation occurred or not. A couple of comments are in order here. First, what they have drawn is a classic multiple regression path model in the sense that

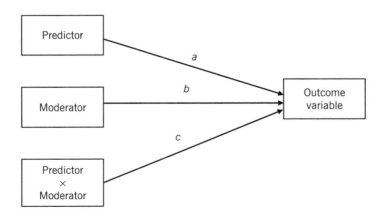

FIGURE 2.2. Baron and Kenny's depiction of basic moderation.

there is a single outcome and multiple predictors. Second, they appropriately focused on the third term, c, as the test of moderation, but this emphasis overshadows the fact that the other two terms, a and b, yield useful information as well. Some users skip over the main-effect findings and focus entirely on the interaction term. And third, it is not clear how one obtains this interaction term. Despite the fact that Baron and Kenny refer to it as "the interaction or product of these two [a and b]," the article does not make crystal clear that the user should generate this interaction term by literally multiplying these two variables together (although that is implied by the word *product*).

Another interesting tidbit that Baron and Kenny dropped into the article here concerns the relationship between the predictor and the ModV. They say that "it is desirable that the moderator variable be uncorrelated with both the predictor and the criterion (the dependent variable) to provide a clearly interpretable interaction term" (p. 1174). One reason that they say this, I believe, is that they were aware that a ModV highly correlated with the predictor would cause problems of multicollinearity. In essence, highly correlated predictors share considerable variance and adversely affect the ability of least squares computations involved in multiple regression to derive clear and unambiguous estimates of shared and unique variance. In lay language, it is not advisable to have highly correlated predictors. Aiken and West (1991) discuss this issue at some length. Does that mean that the predictor and ModV *must be or should be "uncorrelated,"* as Baron and Kenny recommend? This issue is controversial, in my experience. Baron and Kenny say that it is *desirable*, not necessary; but some users have raised this to the level of dogma, saying that the ModV *must* be uncorrelated with the predictor (and also the outcome). My position on this issue is that the ModV should not be highly correlated with either the predictor or the outcome but that strict nonsignificant correlation is not necessary.

Another issue that draws some attention but is generally ignored concerns the issue of quadratic moderation. I have received a few questions about linear versus quadratic moderation that have been stimulated by Baron and Kenny's description of a continuous moderator and categorical predictor (the so-called "Case 3"). They depict a straight line for the situation of linear moderation and an upwardly curving line to depict the quadratic moderation case, but many users do not clearly understand the distinction between linear and quadratic moderation. Baron and Kenny accurately say that the usual garden-variety moderation that most of us perform is of the linear type. In fact, rarely do researchers examine their data for quadratic moderation, and there are several reasons for this. First, researchers do not usually think in terms of quadratic predictions. Second, most researchers do not know how to perform quadratic analyses (despite the fact that Baron and Kenny explained how to do it in this article). And third, even if one accurately computes the analysis, most researchers do not have a graphing program that would allow them to quickly determine the shape of the resulting figure. A full explanation of quadratic moderation is given in Chapter 6.

And last, Baron and Kenny voiced concern throughout the moderation section about "measurement error." The average user skips over these references with a nagging sense of unease because, although it seems to be something important to consider, most readers do not begin to have a clue about how to account or adjust for it. Let me say that measurement error is a ubiquitous phenomenon in data of any sort. All variables are measured with some error, and statisticians spend a lot of time and effort to determine whether and how error obscures the ability of various statistical techniques to obtain accurate pictures of the data. Basically, two situations are to be avoided: (1) too much random error and (2) too much nonrandom error. In the first case we seek to use measures that measure constructs reliably, so we seek measures with high internal reliability and high test–retest reliability. In the second case, we use reliable measures and hope like heck that we are not picking up relatively more error in certain individuals or groups than in others. In essence, nonrandom error occurs when biases, response sets, and other extraneous influences lead to greater or lesser reliability of a measure between groups (e.g., Do males and females respond equally reliably to a given depression measure over time?). Users rarely examine for the presence of the latter problem, so for the most part it just remains lurking in datasets. Baron and Kenny raise this issue because nonrandom error can reduce one's confidence in claiming that a given moderation result is equally robust for all groups under all circumstances. They suggest that structural equation modeling (e.g., the statistical package LISREL) is helpful in correcting this problem. In my experience, researchers rarely check for systematic error, and it remains an issue that needs to be grappled with and resolved.

One way to cope with measurement error is to remove it statistically, and this is the goal of latent variable modeling performed in various structural equation modeling (SEM) programs such as LISREL, EQS, Amos, Mplus, and others. It is germane in this context to note that many statisticians have been working for a couple of decades to come up with a robust and valid way to perform latent variable moderation, that is, moderation in which error is removed from the measured predictors (Moulder & Algina, 2002). Among others, Ping (1996), Joreskog (cited in Algina & Moulder, 2001), Kenny and Judd (1984), Bollen (Bollen & Paxton, 1998), and Jaccard and Wan (1996) have proposed methods to test latent variable moderation. Achieving this goal has been somewhat like searching for the holy grail, because this goal has been perceived as highly desirable, yet no consensus has arisen in favor of one approach. I report in Chapter 6 a new method proposed by Todd Little (Little, Bovaird, & Widaman, 2006), which, in all due respect to those who have come before, I believe achieves this goal. I should also mention that the MPlus SEM program includes a feature called the "Xwith command," which permits latent variable moderation as well.

Mediation

Now we move on to the question of mediation. Baron and Kenny define a MedV as one that "accounts for the relation between the predictor and the criterion" (p. 1176). Then they make what I consider to be one of the best comparisons of mediation and moderation made by anyone: "whereas moderator variables specify when certain effects will hold, mediators speak to how or why such effects occur" (p. 1176). Let's expand on this a little. Moderation describes the case in which a third variable (i.e., the ModV) is used to describe under what conditions the predictor is correlated with the outcome in particular ways. The predictor and the ModV are assumed to be concurrent and not likely to affect each other, whereas, in contrast, in mediation the predictor and the MedV are assumed to be related to each other. In essence, what they are saying is that moderation does not have a causal aspect, whereas mediation does.

Then Baron and Kenny present a diagram of the mediational model (see Figure 2.3). It is noteworthy that they describe this as a "causal chain" involving two "causal paths" (*b* and *c*), because the issue of causality is one that bedevils the discussion of mediation models. We return to this issue later. (Also note that they use the term *IV* throughout this section, although this model can apply to nonmanipulated predictor variables.)

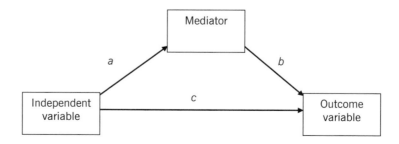

FIGURE 2.3. Baron and Kenny's depiction of basic mediation.

One of the most often cited aspects of Baron and Kenny's description of mediation is their list of "conditions" to test the mediation hypothesis. They say that a variable functions as a mediator when the following conditions are met:

1. The IV must be significantly correlated with the MedV (path a in Figure 2.3).
2. The MedV must be significantly correlated with the DV (path b in Figure 2.3).
3. "When paths a and b are controlled, a previously significant relation between the IV and DV is no longer significant, with the strongest demonstration of mediation occurring when path c is zero" (p. 1176).

Considerable information is packed into these three points, so I would like to deconstruct this section at some length. The first point to notice is that all three relations must be statistically significant (although the significance of the basic relationship, IV to DV, requires some further explication; see later discussion). Second, it is important to note (although not stated by Baron and Kenny) that these relations need not be positive in direction. The relationships can be positive or negative, but they must be significant. The third point is the one that causes the most confusion: Mediation is demonstrated when path c is reduced when the indirect path is introduced. I presented the verbatim quote that stipulates that mediation is demonstrated when a previously significant IV-to-DV relationship is "no longer significant." Many people (myself included at one point) concluded that this statement was definitive in saying that simply noting whether path c went from significance to nonsignificance was sufficient to support the view that mediation had occurred. However, if one reads a bit further in the article, Baron and Kenny note that, because psychology deals with multiple causation, it is probably unrealistic to ever expect to find path c reduced to zero (with the MedV included in the equation). Thus they argue that it is probably more realistic to try to find significant reductions in path c.

Then they proceed to lay out the technical procedures for testing mediation. They argue that three multiple regressions are necessary to test mediation:

1. MedV is regressed on the IV (which means that the IV is the predictor and the MedV is the outcome).
2. DV is regressed on the IV.
3. DV is regressed on the IV and the MedV.

On the basis of these three regression equations, Baron and Kenny argue, one can determine whether mediation occurred. Three conditions must hold in order for mediation to be supported:

1. The IV must predict the MedV in the first equation.
2. The IV must predict the DV in the second equation.
3. The MedV must predict the DV in the third equation.

The test of mediation, against the backdrop of these conditions, is:

4. Whether the effect of the IV on the DV is less in the third equation compared with the second equation.

Is this enough by itself to support mediation? Various authors (e.g., MacKinnon, Lockwood, Hoffman, West, & Sheets, 2002) have argued that it isn't. A simple "less than" decision rule seems to be too vague. To be fair, on this last point, Baron and Kenny then went on to cite Sobel (1982) and his significance test for the indirect effect. It will be helpful to repeat it here. They said that the following is the "standard error of the indirect effect or ab" of this test:

$$\text{SQRT}(b^2 s_a^2 + a^2 s_b^2 + s_a^2 s_b^2) \tag{2.1}$$

where a and b refer to the unstandardized regression coefficients (B's) of paths a and b, respectively, and s_a and s_b refer to the corresponding standard errors.

The involvement of the Sobel formula in computing the significance of the mediating effect was a great innovation in this area and still stands today as useful and relevant. The consensus now is that the "steps" approach is insufficient by itself, but Sobel's z-score or other statistical output (e.g., confidence intervals) is necessary to support or reject a mediation hypothesis.

Nine Continuing Areas of Confusion

The Baron and Kenny article has stood the test of time to become the definitive source for researchers wishing to conduct the two procedures of mediation and moderation, but it must be said that there are some continuing areas of confusion that users experience. In this section, I discuss the most common questions that I've received from researchers attempting to use these techniques.

1. It's not clear how one uses Baron and Kenny's restated Sobel formula. If the previous formula describes the standard error, what does one do with it? As it turns out, one divides the product of the coefficients of the two paths constituting the indirect path. A reading of Sobel's article or Kris Preacher's website (**http://www.quantpsy.org/sobel/sobel.htm**) reveals that the complete formula looks like this:

$$z\text{-value} = \frac{a*b}{\text{SQRT}(b^2 s_a^2 + a^2 s_b^2 + s_a^2 s_b^2)} \tag{2.2}$$

In other words, one should multiply the B's of paths a and b and divide by the square root of the sum of those three terms. This computation will yield a z-score that can be looked up in a z-score table, or a Web-based applet (e.g., **http://wise.cgu.edu/p_z/p_z.html**) can be used to obtain the significance level of the obtained z-score. According to Preacher, the formula cited by Baron and Kenny is the Aroian test formula, and it is slightly different from the original Sobel formula. However, the two formulas tend to yield the same result with sample sizes greater than 50.

2. How does one obtain the B's and standard errors? Baron and Kenny skim over this concern, but Preacher properly points out that these values must be obtained with care and precision. The a and s_a are obtained from the first regression equation stipulated by Baron and Kenny. The b and s_b are obtained from the third regression equation stipulated by Baron and Kenny, in other words, in the case in which both the IV and MedV are predictors of the DV.

3. Concerning the matter of "perfect mediation," Baron and Kenny say this: "Perfect mediation holds if the independent variable has no effect when the mediator is controlled" (p. 1177). Within the context of their argument on the previous page that "the strongest demonstration of mediation occur[s] when path c is zero" (p. 1177), the message that a lot of readers have picked up is that perfect mediation is desirable and obtainable. Baron and Kenny plainly state that in psychology (and this would apply to many other disciplines as well), we customarily deal with variables that have multiple causes. In a field such as chemistry, in which a particular chemical reaction may be caused by one and only one mixture of ingredients, we can obtain perfect mediation, but *not* in the social sciences or other disciplines that use probabilistic data. In my own research with self-report data provided by adolescents and young adults, I have obtained results in which path c approaches zero,

but these results are very rare, and they never achieve an absolute zero value. I have encountered a range of attitudes and beliefs in the field of psychology about this matter, and this leads me to think that there is still considerable ambiguity and confusion. In Chapter 3, I present a suggestion that I hope will help clarify this matter.

4. Baron and Kenny raise a concern with multicollinearity between the IV and the MedV. This issue arises in the third equation stipulated by Baron and Kenny, that is, when the IV and MedV jointly predict the DV. As you know, one of the preconditions of the mediation test is that the IV and MedV must be significantly correlated, and when a multiple regression with correlated predictors is computed, one of the results can be attenuated power in estimating the coefficients. The danger here, it would seem, is in the case in which the IV and MedV are too highly correlated. Just as with moderation, the researcher doesn't wish to have predictors that are too highly correlated. As I noted before, if correlations fall in the high range (i.e., above .70), then one may have a problem. If a correlation above .90 is obtained, then it is quite likely that the two variables are measuring essentially the same construct and may be parsimoniously combined.

5. Although Baron and Kenny state flatly that the MedV should be measured without error, they also recognize that in most datasets in the social sciences the MedV is measured with error. The presence of measurement error usually attenuates (reduces) the size of the coefficients in regression analyses and can lead to the error of concluding that significant mediation did not occur when in fact it did. The solution proposed by Baron and Kenny is to use latent variable path modeling to probe mediational relationships. This proposal is sound, and I give an example of this approach later in this book, but unfortunately even 20 years after this groundbreaking article came out, distressingly few researchers use this approach. One must use an SEM statistics package such as Amos, LISREL, or EQS to conduct these analyses, and not enough researchers have managed to acquire the skills to use such a program. As a consequence, many mediational analyses are still performed with observed variables in regression, and although this approach *may* yield a veridical answer, Baron and Kenny are correct in trying to steer researchers toward the more robust approach of latent variable analyses.

6. The question arises of causal direction among the variables. Baron and Kenny state that the DV should not cause the MedV, and they raise the issue of "feedback" from the DV back to the MedV. They do not devote much space to this thorny issue, but let me expand somewhat on this very impor-

tant and confusing problem. Throughout their article, Baron and Kenny are vague about the matter of the temporal order of mediation variables. In the absence of clear guidelines, many readers have concluded that they endorsed the use of mediation on concurrent data, that is, data collected at one point in time. That is not the case, but perhaps researchers believe that they have found a "loophole" that they can exploit for their own purposes. In various places Baron and Kenny alluded to *exogenous* and *endogenous* variables, terminology that is usually reserved for clear-cut *x* and *y* variables. In other words, the clearest example of an *x* (exogenous) variable would be an experimental manipulation because of the assumption that causality flows from that event or situation. For example, watching a video that portrays homeless people in a particular light (IV) may lead to a feeling of pity for the homeless (MedV), which in turn may lead an individual to donate more time or money to helping the homeless (DV). What Baron and Kenny are raising in this part of their article is the possibility that the DV may causally affect the MedV, and if this happens, then it will interfere with the researcher's efforts to identify a clear mediational pattern. Thus, if the individual knew that the video was designed to increase charitable contributions and if he or she resented this pressure, then the person might be less inclined to give money to the homeless and as a result may rate his or her empathy for the homeless lower. In essence, it is inherently difficult to obtain social science variables that behave in clear, step-like causal chains because people are incredibly complex organisms that think and behave in complicated ways that often involve feedback loops.

I discuss later in the book at great length the pros and cons of using concurrent or longitudinal data to explicate mediational patterns. I think that Baron and Kenny would have endorsed the longitudinal (or temporal sequenced) approach if they had explicitly considered this question, but there is little discussion in their article on this important issue. Suffice it to say at this juncture that Baron and Kenny were right in alerting researchers to the issue of the order of variables in their proposed mediational models and that they were correct in noting that some variables may exist in complicated bidirectional relationships.

7. The strength of the relationship between the IV and DV for moderation as compared with mediation analyses must be considered. Baron and Kenny note that this relationship is usually presumed to be moderate to strong for mediation, whereas it may be "unexpectedly weak or inconsistent" (p. 1178) for cases of moderation. The point of mediation is to examine whether a third variable (the proposed mediator) explains significant variance between

the IV and the DV, so apparently there should be a strong to moderate basic relationship to explain in this case. On the other hand, one might suspect that a moderation analysis would be useful in the case of surprisingly weak IV-to-DV relationships because the point of moderation is to find contexts in which this relationship varies in strength. As I noted earlier, Baron and Kenny remarked that the IV-to-MedV relationship should be significant for mediation, but it is desirable for it to be nonsignificant for moderation. These are helpful points for the researcher to remember when trying to determine whether to use one approach or the other in a particular situation.

8. Researchers need to consider how mediation and moderation may be combined. Baron and Kenny devote several paragraphs to the idea that a researcher may begin with a particular approach and then end up clarifying their phenomenon by switching to the other approach. In my experience, I've noted that this happens occasionally, so I agree that researchers should be aware of the different ways in which they can approach their data and eschew exclusive reliance on either moderation or mediation. Baron and Kenny's Figure 4 (p. 1179) depicted a path model that combined both moderation and mediation. In my experience talking with people who've read this article, this point by Baron and Kenny is rarely understood properly and even more rarely taken up in actual work. I devote some space to this issue because I think that it may be useful for researchers to understand this matter better so that they might better integrate it into their own work. Baron and Kenny's model looked like Figure 2.4.

What Baron and Kenny are attempting to show is that moderation, in particular the control × stressor interaction term (*cs*), is placed in the path

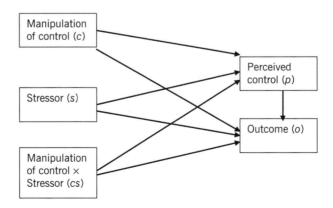

FIGURE 2.4. Baron and Kenny's depiction of mediated moderation.

model just like any other term, and in fact it is expected to predict the mediating variable (perceived control), as well as the outcome. The nature of these relationships was not well explained, and I think that this has contributed to the reluctance of researchers to adopt this approach.

The Baron and Kenny article spent about half a page explaining how one might conduct multiple regression analyses to construct a path model like this, and this lengthy and complicated explication may scare some users away from trying this approach. My advice is to use path modeling in LISREL or some other SEM program to do these analyses, and they will prove to be much quicker and simpler.

Baron and Kenny briefly mention *mediated moderation* and *moderated mediation* in the context of Figure 2.4. They point out that this model is an example of mediated moderation because the moderation term is included in a mediation-based path model. Their example of moderated mediation, on the other hand, is quite opaque, and I suspect that most readers probably throw in the towel at this point. They cite the 1984 article by James and Brett in passing but do not present a clear example in any detail. Later in this book I discuss how to conduct both mediated moderation and moderated mediation (see Chapter 7), and hopefully this section will clear up any remaining confusion about these issues. In my experience, I find that many beginning researchers need to have clarity about basic mediation and moderation before they are prepared to forge on into the murky territory of combinations of these two techniques. That is the rationale for the way I have laid out the present book in the hope that the beginning user will be able to navigate the complicated terrain of hybrid techniques in due course.

9. The final issue concerns how to refer to the IV-to-DV relationship. Baron and Kenny's diagram and text referred to it only as *c*. Most other researchers (e.g., MacKinnon, 2008) make a distinction between the original IV-to-DV relationship and the IV-to-DV relationship after the MedV is included in the model. I adopt MacKinnon's usage, which is that the original IV-to-DV relationship is referred to as *c*, whereas the same relationship with the MedV included is referred to as *c'* (*c prime*). This distinction is helpful because it allows us to discuss the size of the indirect and direct effects. Refer to the beginning of the next chapter for a clear delineation of this practice.

Summary

The Baron and Kenny (1986) article was immensely helpful when it first came out, and what is truly remarkable about this article is its longevity and continued relevance today. As you can tell from my detailed description of the article's points, the authors accurately captured the main issues concerning mediation and moderation and did a good job of explaining how to distinguish between cases of mediation and moderation, how to conduct these basic techniques, and how to approach more complicated cases of combined mediation and moderation. They identified areas that still today are incompletely explicated (e.g., quadratic moderation), and they appropriately identified SEM and latent variable modeling as useful future directions.

Looking back at the article from a vantage point informed by more than 20 years of statistical program development and research, it is amazing that I did not identify more problematic issues than I did. The vast majority of articles from the 1980s have been superseded by subsequent work that has identified errors, faulty assumptions, and incorrect prognostications for the future in the original work. From my reading of the literature on mediation and moderation, I would argue that the Baron and Kenny article contains no error of significant merit and that the authors were remarkably prescient about future directions; the only criticisms of the article would be those noting instances of omission (e.g., lack of clarity about the Sobel formula). Despite the fact that the paper was published in a journal devoted to personality and social psychology, it has been cited by a wide variety of disciplines, and it has been taken to heart by many disciplines outside of psychology. Possibly the authors underestimated the reach of this article when they submitted it to *JPSP* in 1986, but that is a specious criticism and one that I would not make. One of my purposes in writing the present book is to promote the basic message that Baron and Kenny so ably conveyed in 1986 to a wider audience than readers of a subdisciplinary journal in psychology.

I think it's interesting to note that, against the backdrop of the stunning success that this article has achieved, David Kenny (2008) remarked in a review article about mediation that "for most of my career, I have felt that mediation is not all that interesting a topic. I was obviously wrong" (p. 354). It's humbling (and heartening in a perverse sort of way) to know that individuals who explicate a particular approach are not always certain of its impact and value. I recommend that interested readers find Kenny's short and illuminating account of his history with mediation (and the related articles in this special issue of *Organizational Research Methods*, Vol. 11, 2008), because his account fleshes out some of the scant history on mediation and moderation and also because these articles stand as useful current directions in this field.

CLARIFICATION OF MEDIATION AND MODERATION SUBSEQUENT TO BARON AND KENNY'S ARTICLE

Much has happened since Baron and Kenny's article was published in 1986, and I devote the rest of this chapter to describing the key articles and innovations of which the informed researcher should be aware.

Writings That Make the Baron and Kenny Proposals Relevant and Known to a Particular Discipline

Following the seminal article of Baron and Kenny, which was chiefly directed at researchers in social and personality psychology, a number of researchers have also written about the mediation and moderation approaches in relation to their own particular fields. For example, Holmbeck and colleagues (Holmbeck, 1997, 2002; Rose, Holmbeck, Coakley, & Franks, 2004) have published a series of articles from the perspective of child clinical and pediatric psychology. Similarly, Frazier, Tix, and Barron (2004) wrote an article for counseling psychology research. And Hayes (2009) has written a nice update for communication researchers. I am confident that there are other papers that I've failed to identify that do something similar in other fields. In these cases, the authors use examples of extant work in the discipline to illustrate both mistakes and exemplary instances of how mediation and moderation analyses are conducted.

Several issues are worth noting in the present context. First, both Holmbeck (1997) and Frazier et al. (2004) note a large amount of confusion about the distinctions between mediation and moderation among researchers in their respective fields. On balance, however, from my experience I would say that these egregious errors are diminishing in number. Second, the most striking development in the time since Baron and Kenny's article came out is that there is increasing interest in and facility with SEM approaches to data analysis. Although Frazier et al. (2004) focused on regression techniques as the most readily available statistical approach, Holmbeck (1997) emphasized that SEM offers many advantages to the analysis of mediation and moderation effects. Many of these issues are drawn out and demonstrated in later chapters.

Bootstrapping the Indirect Effect in Mediation

Considerable attention has been given to evaluating the various ways in which one can estimate the indirect effect in mediation. Sobel's z for the size of the indirect effect is one of these; in fact, it is the best-known and most widely used method. MacKinnon et al. (2002) recently evaluated 14 methods that have been used to evaluate the statistical significance of an intervening variable in a mediation analysis. They concluded that different approaches possess more or less statistical power and are more or less susceptible to Type 1 error depending on the characteristics of the dataset. In general, the Baron and Kenny approach was deemed to have low statistical power, and Sobel's (1982) approach (testing $a*b$), although useful in providing an estimate of the size of the indirect effect, is vulnerable to biased error.

A possible way forward that has been vigorously explored recently (e.g., Shrout & Bolger, 2002) is to estimate the indirect effect ($a*b$) through bootstrapping. Preacher and Hayes (2004) reviewed the MacKinnon et al. (2002) article and expressed concern that the Sobel test is commonly used with non-normal distributions that may yield biased estimates. Their suggestion is that researchers may wish to estimate the indirect effect through the bootstrapping technique, which is robust for small and/or non-normal distributions. More is said about this approach in Chapter 4, but let me say briefly here that bootstrapping is a method of resampling subsets of data from a given dataset, performing the relevant statistical tests on these subsets, and then summarizing the results of these numerous resamplings. Conclusions based on these distributions of resampled data are more robust than typical or standard statistical tests, especially with small datasets and/or non-normal distributions. The prevailing opinion in the literature is that data should be analyzed with bootstrapping to obtain the optimal estimate of the indirect effect, and this method, according to published reports of research, is increasingly being used. It must be said, however, that beginning researchers often are unfamiliar with this technique and, if and when they do become acquainted with it, often experience difficulty in finding a statistical platform on which to conduct these analyses. More needs to be done to make this type of analysis more easily accessible.

Testing Mediational Models with Longitudinal Data

Cole and Maxwell (2003) published a striking article in the *Journal of Abnormal Psychology* that took on the issue of testing mediation with longitudinal data. The impetus for their article is the question of whether mediation can be convincingly demonstrated with cross-sectional data. Let me back up a bit. Baron and Kenny, as you read earlier, were unspecific about the nature of data needed for mediational analyses. If you read the Baron and Kenny article closely, you can note that they imply that temporal sequence of variables assists the researcher in arguing for mediation; however, they do not come out and explicitly say that one should use longitudinal data. They do mention the utility of using the mediational approach with experimental data, and this line of research has been fruitfully exploited by David MacKinnon in a series of articles illustrating mediation within the context of intervention studies (e.g., Krull & MacKinnon, 1999; MacKinnon & Dwyer, 1993).

But if one is not using an experimental method, then the matter of whether one can or should use concurrent data (gathered at one point in time) or longitudinal data (gathered on the same individuals across time) in mediational designs has been ambiguous. In fact, I would like to emphasize that this is quite a controversial issue in that a great deal of published evidence about mediation is based on concurrent data, yet there are methodologists (such as Cole and Maxwell, 2003) who warn against this practice.

David Kenny, near the top of the mediation page on his website (2007), says this: "Note that a mediational model is a causal model. For example, the mediator is presumed to cause the outcome and not vice versa." He goes on to say that the IV should be temporally and logically the starting point in the causal chain. In the case of an experiment, the IV is manipulated, and there is no ambiguity about the origin of causality. However, the MedV and DV are typically measured later, and it is possible that reverse causation or reciprocal causation may cloud the relationship between these two variables. Kenny suggests reversing the order of the MedV and DV in an additional analysis to see whether this altered pattern of variables yields the same result. If it does, then it is questionable whether the MedV-to-DV relationship is unidirectional. The closest Kenny (2007) gets to discussing concurrent versus longitudinal data is this text: "Design considerations may also weaken the plausibility of reverse causation. Ideally, the mediator should be measured temporally before the outcome variable." Clearly, the best way to obtain the MedV temporally before the DV is to conduct a longitudinal study in which a significant amount of time has elapsed between the MedV and the DV.

Most people make the assumption that a significant mediational result obtained with concurrent data will generalize reasonably well to longitudinal data. Cole and Maxwell (2003) douse cold water on this assumption by saying "In reality, testing mediational hypotheses with cross-sectional data will be accurate only under fairly restrictive conditions. Furthermore, *estimating mediational effect sizes* will only be accurate under even more restrictive circumstances. When these conditions do not pertain, cross-sectional studies provide biased and potentially very misleading estimates of mediational processes" (p. 560). They go on to present persuasive arguments to support their unwelcome contention and end by recommending that researchers analyze longitudinal data with sophisticated SEM approaches. The beginning user will find many of their arguments to be opaque and confusing, but I present many of their suggestions in Chapter 4. This issue is far from settled, and I would like to encourage users to be aware of the critical issues raised about direction of causality in mediational analyses. Reading the Cole and Maxwell (2003) article is a good place to start.

David MacKinnon's Book on Mediation

During the writing of this book, I was pleased to see that one of the major figures in the field of mediational analyses, David MacKinnon (2008), published a book titled *Introduction to Statistical Mediation Analysis*. I would strongly recommend this book to researchers because of its definitive explication of mediation and its detailed presentation of examples. He touches on the topic of moderation as well, but the emphasis is clearly on mediation. The level of his book, in my view, is a notch or two above the one adopted for the present book, so the reader who finds my book lacking in specificity and detail will be amply rewarded by perusing David's book.

Other New Directions

Although Baron and Kenny discussed how mediation and moderation could be combined and gave a couple of examples, much more needs to be explored with regard to how these analytical techniques can be usefully combined, overlapped, or used in conjunction with each other. Many of the writings on this topic have been technical (e.g., Preacher, Rucker, & Hayes, 2007), which is necessary, but there has also been more theoretical work with regard to the philosophical and empirical questions of how causality can and should be measured. Pearl (2000), writing from a philosophical–econometric point of view, has laid out a number of models, obviously involving mediation, that he views as fundamental in the assessment of causality. In a similar vein, Spencer, Zanna, and Fong (2005) have argued that constructs or manipulations that differ in assessment difficulty should be tackled with different mediational and/or moderational approaches. Space does not permit a thorough discussion of these points, but these articles represent continuing interest by philosophers, psychologists, economists, and researchers and theorists in other fields who are continuing to examine how research designs that obtain empirical data can elucidate abstract theories and models—and methods involving mediation and moderation are often at the center of these discussions.

SUMMARY

As noted at the outset of this chapter, no well-elaborated and authoritative history of the mediation and moderation approaches seems to exist. How and why the common words *mediation* and *moderation* came to be applied to the statistical techniques of partial correlations and interactions in the regression format still remains to be definitively determined, but my reading of the literature suggests that these terms were imported into psychology from biology and/or philosophy of science during the 1950s. In any case, we can see that the burgeoning interest in psychology during the '50s and '60s in process models (i.e., x leads to z, z leads to y, etc.) provided the impetus for the field to grapple with issues of intervening and mediating variables. The advent of high-speed computing capabilities of machines led to a wider awareness of cybernetic linkages and feedback loops and provided the capability of analyzing and modeling complex interconnections among variables with computers. Over the past 20–30 years we have witnessed an explosion of different analytical techniques made possible by a variety of different statistical programs, and these have resulted in an outpouring of exciting and new possibilities within mediation and moderation. A primary goal of this book is to document where we are at the present moment and to consolidate our knowledge about what techniques work to give us useful information. In 10 years' time, this book will be hopelessly outdated, because the rate of development is, if anything, increasing, so read this book now and make use of what we know now.

FURTHER READING

If you read only one extra reading, this should be it:

> Baron, R. M., & Kenny, D. A. (1986). The moderator–mediator variable distinction in social psychological research: Conceptual, strategic, and statistical considerations. *Journal of Personality and Social Psychology, 51,* 1173–1182.

Following are several other key readings that I mentioned in this chapter. In order to more fully appreciate the history and current trends in mediation and moderation approaches, it would be helpful to read some or all of these.

> Cole, D. A., & Maxwell, S. E. (2003). Testing mediational models with longitudinal data: Questions and tips in the use of structural equation modeling. *Journal of Abnormal Psychology, 112,* 558–577.

Hayes, A. F. (2009). Beyond Baron and Kenny: Statistical mediation analysis in the new millennium. *Communication Monographs, 76*, 408–420.

Hyman, H. H. (1955). *Survey design and analysis.* Glencoe, IL: Free Press.

James, L. R., & Brett, J. M. (1984). Mediators, moderators, and tests for mediation. *Journal of Applied Psychology, 69*, 307–321.

Kenny, D. A. (1979). *Correlation and causality.* New York: Wiley.

Kenny, D. A. (2008). Reflections on mediation. *Organizational Research Methods, 11*, 353–358.

MacKinnon, D. P. (2008). *Introduction to statistical mediation analysis.* Mahwah, NJ: Erlbaum.

McClelland, G. H., & Judd, C. M. (1993). Statistical difficulties of detecting interactions and moderator effects. *Psychological Bulletin, 114*, 376–390.

Preacher, K. J., & Hayes, A. F. (2004). SPSS and SAS procedures for estimating indirect effects in simple mediation models. *Behavior Research Methods, Instruments, and Computers, 36*, 717–731.

Rozeboom, W. W. (1956). Mediation variables in scientific theory. *Psychological Review, 63*, 249–264.

Wright, S. (1921). Correlation and causation. *Journal of Agricultural Research, 20*, 557–585.

3

Basic Mediation

This chapter describes the basic procedures for conducting mediation with multiple regression. This approach is based on the Baron and Kenny (1986) recommendations, and it is the conventional technique that most researchers use today. The sections are as follows:

1. Review of basic rules for mediation
2. How to do basic mediation
3. An example of mediation with experimental data
4. An example of null mediation
5. Sobel's z versus reduction of the basic relationship
6. Suppressor variables in mediation
7. Investigating mediation when one has a nonsignificant correlation
8. Understanding the mathematical "fine print": Variances and covariances
9. Discussion of partial and semipartial correlations
10. Statistical assumptions

The reader who perseveres through all of this material will achieve one of the chief goals of the present book, namely, to learn how to perform a mediational analysis with multiple regression. This method is referred to as "basic mediation" because it is the simplest form of mediation that one can perform. Further, if you read all of the auxiliary material that follows (points 6, 7, and 8 in the preceding list), you will understand at a deeper level the mathematical underpinnings of this analytical technique. I suppose that this order of topics to some extent gives you "the dessert before the vegetables," but I present the material this way to give you a chance to enjoy the thrill of conducting mediation before moving on to the more mundane issues of understanding the statistical details. In my experience, students are more interested in the latter details if they can actually perform the mediation analysis. And I would strongly encourage you to "eat your vegetables" and learn or review the statistical foundation for this technique.

REVIEW OF BASIC RULES FOR MEDIATION

This chapter is devoted to describing in great detail how to perform a basic mediational analysis. I begin with a straightforward example, progress through several other instances of mediation, show how to make an interpretation of a mediation result, discuss problems and pitfalls with conducting mediational analyses, and conclude by describing the statistical assumptions that must be satisfied in order to perform a valid mediational analysis.

To "mediate" something is to stand in between two other things and pass on the effect of one to the other (see Chapter 1), and that is the meaning that we explore now. In this chapter I describe a mediational hypothesis about several variables drawn from a dataset made available to me by my colleague Aaron Jarden, a Lecturer in psychology here in New Zealand on the topic of positive psychology. An example of the accepted way to depict a mediational hypothesis is presented in Figure 3.1.

There are a number of important features of this figure that deserve notice. First, I refer to the relationship between the predictor variable (or IV) and the outcome variable (or DV) as the *basic relationship* because this is the

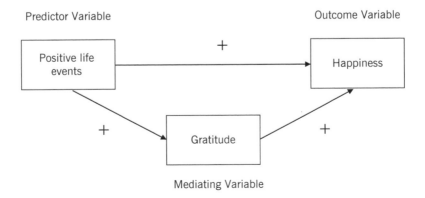

FIGURE 3.1. Depiction of a mediational hypothesis.

association that we are trying to understand in greater depth. This relationship is what we suspect is being mediated by a third (or more) variable(s).

Second, researchers should predict all three relationships depicted here. I have inserted plus signs to indicate my hypotheses about the direction of these relationships. (Minus signs can be used to indicate a negative relationship.) In this particular case, I believed that the basic relationship would be positive in sign: The more one experiences positive life events (e.g., getting a promotion), the happier one is likely to be. I also believed that higher numbers of positive life events would positively predict a sense of gratitude, and I believed that gratitude, in turn, would positively predict happiness. Taken together, these several hypotheses compose a single mediational hypothesis. The last thing I would like to say about this hypothesis may seem a bit subtle, but it lies at the heart of what mediation is about: The proposed indirect path is anticipated to reduce the strength of the basic relationship once it is included in the analytical model. I return to this essential point several times in this chapter.

HOW TO DO BASIC MEDIATION

Before we examine the empirical data, I need to lay out the customary nomenclature for mediation (following MacKinnon, 2008, and others) that will help you make connections between this treatment of mediation and other descriptions. The first model (see Figure 3.2) to consider is the "basic relationship" I referred to before. The regression equation that describes this relationship is

$$Y = i_1 + cX + e_1 \tag{3.1}$$

The important information here is that c refers to the coefficient of the relationship between the IV and the DV and that e_1 refers to the variance in Y that is not explained by X (i.e., the residual). The i_1 term refers to the intercept, and it will not figure in our discussion at this juncture. Now we add in the third variable and create the mediational triangle (see Figure 3.3). The two new regression equations that describe this model are

$$Y = i_2 + c'X + bM + e_2 \tag{3.2}$$

$$M = i_3 + aX + e_3 \tag{3.3}$$

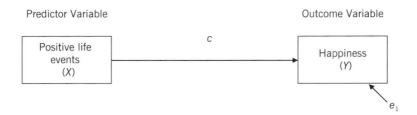

FIGURE 3.2. First model with statistical notation.

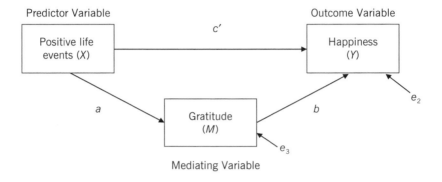

FIGURE 3.3. Second model with statistical notation.

The most important elements of these three equations are *a, b, c,* and *c′,* and I now focus on what they mean. Note that the coefficient for the X-to-Y relationship (*c*) in the first model becomes *c* prime (*c′*) in the mediated model to represent the fact that it is *adjusted for the inclusion of the mediating variable.* In other words, this latter *c′* coefficient is different from the original *c* coefficient because we now have an indirect path in the model that is likely to reduce the strength of the basic relationship. The original relationship, *c,* is usually termed the *total effect,* and it is the starting point of the mediation analysis. The *c′* coefficient, in contrast, represents the X-to-Y relationship after removing the indirect effect that goes through the mediating variable, and it is termed the *direct effect.* You will note that the X-to-M coefficient is named *a* and the M-to-Y coefficient is named *b,* and together they lay down the path of what we refer to as the mediated (or "indirect") effect. How does one determine the size of this mediated effect? There are two methods, and they yield the same result in basic linear regression: $a*b$ or $c - c'$. The first method, $a*b$, relies on the *multiplicative rule* of path analysis, which I think is one of the most underappreciated aspects of mediation: One simply multiplies a by b to obtain the indirect effect. (We revisit the mechanics of this later, when we have actual results.) You now have the basic facts of these mediation equations, so we press on to an empirical analysis, and you will see how to compute mediation.

The first step is to determine whether the preconditions set down by Baron and Kenny (1986) are met, namely, (1) the predictor variable (X) is significantly associated with the outcome variable (Y); (2) X is significantly associated with the mediating variable (M); and (3) M is significantly associated with Y when X is also included in the regression equation. I generated a Pearson correlation matrix involving these three variables to check the first two preconditions; it is presented in Table 3.1. The last precondition is checked when one computes a multiple regression with X and M as joint predictors of Y (see Table 3.3 presented later).

These data, by the way, were taken at one point in time from respondents to the International Wellbeing Study (IWS) devised by Aaron Jarden and five other positive psychology researchers (including myself). For more information, visit: **http://www.wellbeingstudy.com/index.html**. An international sample of 364 adults between the ages of 17 and 79 went online to respond to a collection of positive psychology measures taken at five times of

TABLE 3.1. Zero-Order Correlations among the Three Variables Included in a Mediation Analysis

	Subjective Happiness Scale	Gratitude Survey	Positive Life Events
Subjective Happiness Scale			
Pearson correlation	1	.549[**]	.338[**]
Sig. (two-tailed)		.000	.000
N	364	364	364
Gratitude Survey			
Pearson correlation	.549[**]	1	.306[**]
Sig. (two-tailed)	.000		.000
N	364	364	364
Positive Life Events			
Pearson correlation	.338[**]	.306[**]	1
Sig. (two-tailed)	.000	.000	
N	364	364	364

[**]Correlation is significant at the .01 level (two-tailed).

measurement separated by 3 months each. The data analyzed here all came from Time 1. For the first measure, individuals responded to five questions such as "your living conditions improved" on a 5-point Likert scale from "none" (0) to "a lot" (4). Responses were summed to create a total score for "positive life events." The second measure was the Gratitude Questionnaire by McCullough, Emmons, and Tsang (2002). Six questions, such as "I have so much in life to be thankful for," were answered on a 7-point Likert scale, from "strongly disagree" (1) to "strongly agree" (7). These responses were summed as well to create a total score. The third measure was the Subjective Happiness Scale (Lyubomirsky & Lepper, 1999) in which four questions such as "In general, I consider myself: [not a happy person] to [a very happy person]" were answered on a 7-point Likert scale. Again, a summed total was generated among these four items.

> **Helpful Suggestion:** It would be helpful if you pulled up the dataset "mediation example.sav" (see **www.guilford.com/jose-materials**) and conducted the following analyses on it as you go through this chapter. I recommend that you do so because, as I argued in the first chapter, I think statistics is one of those activities that is best learned by doing it.

It should be noted at this juncture that in this example X, M, and Y are all continuous variables. To use garden-variety linear regression-based mediation, both the MedV and outcome variable must be continuous in nature, and in most of the analyses that researchers do, the predictor variable is continuous as well. One can use a dichotomous predictor variable in mediation (e.g., gender or experimental condition), but the MedV and outcome variable must be continuous. (If you have dichotomous MedVs or outcomes, then you will wish to read in Chapter 4 about logistic mediation; it involves the use of logistic regression, which is required of categorical outcomes. But for now, we stay with the standard method of computing mediation, so let us go back to our example.)

As just noted, if we have conducted an experimental (or quasi-experimental) study, the X variable is likely to be categorical (e.g., 0 = control; 1 = experimental). This is not a problem with regard to the regression analyses involved in the mediation analyses described later, but sometimes description of this dichotomous variable creates special requirements. I give an example of this type of data later in this chapter.

Another issue is whether the data conform to permissible statistical standards. One should evaluate first whether the distributional requirements are met for these variables, so I ran descriptive statistics to determine whether problems with skewness or kurtosis would be found. I found that gratitude evidenced slight negative skew (i.e., the scores were more bunched to the right side of the distribution); it also manifested slight kurtosis (peakedness). Neither problem was significant, so I left the variables in their raw form. On occasion, these analyses will yield significant problems, and the researcher is urged to transform his or her variables in a manner to reduce skewness or kurtosis (see Tabachnick & Fidell, 2001, for procedures for doing so) before conducting the mediation analysis.

As I noted before, all three correlations turned out to be significant. And it does *not* matter whether the direction of association is positive or negative. The results of the Pearson correlations verify the directional predictions that I made, which is good, but this pattern alone does not tell us whether gratitude mediated the basic relationship. This determination requires a special treatment of the data using multiple regression (or other statistical techniques to be described later in the book).

We are now ready for the specific definition of mediation that Baron and Kenny (1986) have popularized: *a variable has mediated the relationship between two other variables when the basic relationship is reduced when the mediating variable is included in the regression equation.*

This definition is often confusing to the beginning user, because she or he does not know how to tell whether the basic relationship is reduced or not. To assess this critical matter, one must conduct two regressions. The first regression (see Table 3.2 and Figure 3.4) documents the basic relationship: "Positive life events" is the predictor, and "happiness" is treated as the outcome. This SPSS output shows that the positive life events measure significantly predicted happiness in this multiple regression. One might notice in passing that the standardized regression coefficient of .338 (or "beta weight") is identical to the Pearson correlation obtained previously. However, notice

TABLE 3.2. Statistical Output Verifying the Basic Relationship

Model	Unstandardized coefficients		Standardized coefficients		
	B	Std. error	Beta	t	Sig.
1. (Constant)	4.008	.156		25.752	.000
Positive Life Events	.485	.071	.338	6.843	.000

Note. Dependent variable: Subjective Happiness Scale.

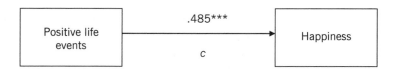

FIGURE 3.4. First model with statistical output.

that I am using the *unstandardized regression coefficient* in the path model here rather than the beta weight because most associated computations involving the indirect effect in mediation use this type of coefficient, and this will be evident later when I describe the computation of Sobel's z-score.

This step merely demonstrates in a regression format that we have a significant basic relationship. The next step is to perform a simultaneous inclusion regression in which the predictor (positive life events) and the mediating variables (gratitude) are both included in the analytical model as predictors of happiness. In essence, all we are doing is adding the mediating variable to the previous equation. Table 3.3 presents the results.

Notice that gratitude is a significant predictor of happiness and that positive life events, which previously was a significant predictor by itself, is now reduced in its strength as a predictor. The previous definition says that mediation occurs when the basic relationship is *reduced* when the mediating variable is added. Did it occur? If you compare the initial .338 beta weight with the subsequent .188 beta weight, or the initial .485 *B* with the subsequent *B* of .269, it certainly looks as though mediation occurred; that is, the basic relationship between the predictor and the outcome was reduced.

TABLE 3.3. Statistical Output of the Independent and Mediating Variables Predicting the Dependent Variable

Model	Unstandardized coefficients		Standardized coefficients		
	B	Std. error	Beta	t	Sig.
1. (Constant)	−.056	.397		−.141	.888
Positive Life Events	.269	.065	.188	4.168	.000
Gratitude Survey	.123	.011	.492	10.902	.000

Note. Dependent variable: Subjective Happiness Scale.

Size of Reduction

So on the basis of these two regressions, can I assert that mediation occurred? Actually, I cannot. Who is to say that this reduction was *significantly large enough* to qualify as a statistically significant reduction? As it turns out, Sobel, a statistician, has come up with a way to determine whether it is sufficiently large. Sobel published a paper in 1982 that laid out a statistical test that researchers can use to verify whether the reduction is statistically significant or not. I should mention in this context that it is a test of the size of the indirect effect, that is, the amount of the basic relationship that "goes through" the indirect path from X to MedV to Y. The numerator is the estimate of the indirect effect, and the denominator is the standard error of this estimate. And it might help to be aware that the null hypothesis that the Sobel test is testing is $a*b = 0$, namely, that the size of the indirect effect is very small.

$$z\text{-value} = \frac{a*b}{\text{SQRT}(b^2*s_a^2 + a^2*s_b^2)} \tag{3.4}$$

To make sense of this equation, you need to know (see Figure 3.5) that *a refers to the unstandardized regression coefficient (the B, not the beta) for the path from X to the MedV, b refers to the unstandardized regression coefficient for the path from the MedV to Y in a simultaneous inclusion regression involving X and MedV as predictors of Y, s_a refers to the standard error of the a path, and s_b refers to the standard error of the b path.*

Does anyone want to compute this equation by hand? Although I have hand-computed this equation dozens of times, I find it tedious to do. A great

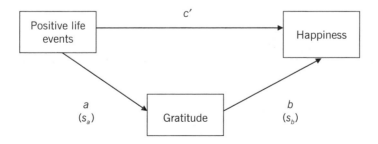

FIGURE 3.5. Second model with specification of the indirect path with B's and standard errors.

alternative is to visit Kristopher Preacher and Geoffrey Leonardelli's helpful website (**http://www.quantpsy.org/sobel/sobel.htm**) and plug in output values from two regressions in order to compute Sobel's z. Let me hasten to point out that one needs to compute the regressions somewhat differently from what I just did. In particular, in the first regression X predicts the *mediating variable* (MedV), and the second regression is the same as the second regression described previously (i.e., X and MedV predict Y). Take an unstandardized regression coefficient and a standard error (SE) from each equation and then plug them into this interface. The first regression yields the output in Table 3.4. Write down the B and SE for the IV: These would be 1.752 and 0.287, respectively. I repeat the output from Table 3.4 for the second regression (Table 3.5) to show you where we obtain the last two bits of additional information.

The two values obtained here are the B and *SE for the MedV* (gratitude): 0.123 and 0.011, respectively. (Note that in practice you should double-click on values in SPSS output presented as .000 because these values are not exactly zero, and it would be inaccurate to input them into further macros and programs as 0 or .000. In the present case, 0.011 is good enough.)

TABLE 3.4. Statistical Output of the Independent Variable Predicting the Mediating Variable (First Regression)

Model	Unstandardized coefficients		Standardized coefficients	t	Sig.
	B	Std. error	Beta		
1. (Constant)	33.056	.630		52.468	.000
Positive Life Events	1.752	.287	.306	6.111	.000

Note. Dependent variable: Gratitude Survey.

TABLE 3.5. Statistical Output of the Independent and Mediating Variables Predicting the Dependent Variable (Second Regression)

Model	Unstandardized coefficients		Standardized coefficients	t	Sig.
	B	Std. error	Beta		
1. (Constant)	−.056	.397		−.141	.888
Positive Life Events	.269	.065	.188	4.168	.000
Gratitude Survey	.123	.011	.492	10.902	.000

Note. Dependent variable: Subjective Happiness Scale.

Now you have all of the necessary information. Go ahead and find this website and input these values. I assume that you did visit this site and correctly input the values. You should have obtained the output in Table 3.6.

Excellent! We now have a result. We have a significant Sobel z-value (the p-value, presented as 8e-8, is given in scientific notation, and it tells us that we move the decimal point eight positions to the left, that is, .00000008; as you can see, this value is hugely less than .05), and this result tells us that we have obtained a statistically significant mediation.

Just for the sake of completeness, I insert here a short-hand computation of the Sobel equation to demonstrate that it yields the same answer (within rounding error) as obtained in this website. The equation is

$$z\text{-value} = \frac{a*b}{\text{SQRT}(b^2*s_a^2 + a^2*s_b^2)}$$

$$= \frac{(1.752)*(.123)}{\text{SQRT}(.123^2*.287^2 + 1.752^2*.011^2)} = \frac{.215496}{\text{SQRT}(.015*.082 + 3.07*.0001)}$$

$$= \frac{.215496}{\text{SQRT}(.00123 + .000307)}$$

$$= \frac{.215496}{\text{SQRT}(.001537)} = \frac{.215496}{.03920} = 5.497$$

So, yes, we did obtain the same answer (to a reasonable degree). If you did this by hand, what you would have to do next is to consult a z-score table in a statistics textbook or go online to use an applet that will convert z-scores into p-values. In either case, you will find that the p-value is close to .00000008. Thus you have a choice of whether you want to compute this equation by hand or to use the handy Preacher website.

TABLE 3.6. Output from Preacher's Online Sobel Test

	Input		Test statistic	Standard error	p-value
a	1.752	Sobel test	5.35806025	0.04021903	8e-8
b	.123				
s_a	.287				
s_b	.011				

Let me emphasize at this point that 0.215 is the "size of the mediated effect" or "size of the indirect effect." It was obtained here by multiplying a by b, and note that these are the unstandardized regression coefficients, not the betas. Further, the value of 0.039 is referred to as the "standard error of the mediated effect."

If you are disturbed by the difference between the hand-computed 5.497 and the online calculator z-score of 5.358 (as I am), then there is another equation you can use to hand-calculate the z-score. MacKinnon (2008) helpfully suggests the following equation (Equation 3.5), which is based on t-scores (easily found in the SPSS output), and it is more accurate because it does not involve squaring very small numbers.

$$SE = \frac{a*b \; \text{SQRT}[(t\text{-score of } a)^2 + (t\text{-score of } b)^2]}{(t\text{-score of } a)*(t\text{-score of } b)} \qquad (3.5)$$

$$= \frac{(1.752)*(.123) \; \text{SQRT}[(6.111)^2 + (10.902)^2]}{(6.111)*(10.902)}$$

$$= \frac{.215496 \; \text{SQRT}[37.3443 + 118.8536]}{66.622}$$

$$= \frac{.215496 \; \text{SQRT}[156.1979]}{66.622} = \frac{.215496 * 12.4979}{66.622} = \frac{2.69325}{66.622}$$

$$= .04043$$

Sobel's z = indirect effect/SE = .215496/.04043 = 5.3307

You can see that it yields the same basic answer as obtained previously. The reason that all of these values fail to converge on a single precise answer to 3 or 4 decimal points is that these computations are based on numbers with varying numbers of decimal points; that is, rounding distorts the true values through the various calculations. In order to derive the best hand-computed values, you should use initial values of at least 5 and preferably 10 decimal points (instead of the 3 decimal points that I reported earlier) and retain resulting values to about 10 decimal points. Note that SPSS defaults to 3 decimal points in its output, but by clicking on the output, one can obtain more precise information of initial values, and if this precision is retained, then the resulting hand-computed values will be much closer to the actual values. One last issue of note is that if one inputs imprecise values into Preacher's or my macros, then the resulting values will reflect this imprecision. In practice, enter values at least to 5 decimal points, preferably to 10 decimal points.

Confidence Interval Information

It is useful to know whether the obtained indirect effect is statistically significant with the computation of a confidence interval (CI; these can be computed in addition to Sobel's formula), and here is how to do this. Once you know the size of the estimate of the indirect effect and the *SE* (computed previously), you can insert these values into the following lower and upper CI equations and determine whether the range includes the value of zero or not (see Table 3.7). I use the *SE* determined from the *t*-score method, as I trust it more than the other method.

Putting all of this information together, one can say this: "The size of the indirect effect was found to be 0.215, *SE* = 0.04, with 95% CI values of 0.14 to 0.29. Because the CI did not include zero, one can conclude that this mediation result is statistically significant. Therefore, it seems that gratitude functioned as a significant mediator between positive life events and happiness."

MacKinnon (2008) points out that an indirect effect computed from the product term (*a**b) would more validly be evaluated with *asymmetrical* confidence limits (instead of 1.96 as in Table 3.7, they would be −1.6175 and 2.2540, respectively, for lower and upper limits, adjusting for the distribution of multiplied values). Recomputing these equations, I obtained the new values shown in Table 3.8.

Thus, by adjusting for a slight shift in the distribution caused by multiplying these two values together, the resulting CI boundaries move slightly upward. In the present case, both symmetrical and asymmetrical CIs yield

TABLE 3.7. Calculation of the Symmetrical 95% Confidence Interval

	Estimate of indirect effect	±	(95% CI coefficient	×	Standard error)
Lower limit	.215496	−	(1.96	×	.0404)
	.215496	−		.07918	
	.136312				
Upper limit	.215496	+	(1.96	×	.0404)
	.215496	+		.07918	
	.294676				

TABLE 3.8. Calculation of the Asymmetrical 95% Confidence Interval

	Estimate of indirect effect	±	(Asym. 95% CI coefficient	×	Standard error)
Lower limit	.215496	–	(1.62	×	.0404)
	.215496	–		.065448	
	.150048				
Upper limit	.215496	+	(2.25	×	.0404)
	.215496	+		.09090	
	.306396				

a significant result, but you are advised to use the asymmetrical confidence limits when you obtain the indirect effect by multiplying a by b. And one last issue: The 95% CI is standard because most users adopt the traditional $p < .05$ cutoff rule, but of course one may adopt different values. A symmetrical 99% CI ($p < .01$) would use a value of 2.575 instead of 1.96.

For more information about the derivation of asymmetrical confidence limits for mediated effects, read MacKinnon, Fritz, Williams, and Lockwood's (2007) article on PRODCLIN, a stand-alone program devoted to this topic. The program allows the user to input values for a and b, their standard errors, the correlation between a and b, and the Type I error rate. The program then generates the asymmetric confidence limits, which can be used to identify whether the indirect effect is statistically significant or not. You may also be interested in an R program named RMediation, which can perform similar functions (Tofighi & MacKinnon, 2011).

KNOWLEDGE BOX. Controversy: Calculation of Whether Significant Mediation Has Occurred

The approach described in this chapter is based on the original Baron and Kenny formulation set down in 1986, and I have focused on it simply because it seems to have been adopted by the largest number of people and the widest range of disciplines. It is not the only way to compute whether significant mediation has occurred, however.

Let me be clearer on this point. The so-called "Baron and Kenny causal steps model" enunciated herein is the simplest approach; if the beta weight for the basic relationship goes down when the MedV is included in the regression equation, then significant mediation is assumed to have happened. Many researchers and statisticians are dissatisfied with this method because (as I noted previously), it is not clear how much of a decrease is necessary.

That's where Sobel's test comes in. Baron and Kenny described the use of Sobel's z-test in their article, and many (but not all) researchers have adopted this additional criterion in order to be more certain that the observed decrease is "statistically significant." This approach is the basic level of mediation analysis that I want to see from a researcher.

But it is not the final answer. As MacKinnon and colleagues (e.g., Fritz & MacKinnon, 2007; MacKinnon et al., 2002) have pointed out, there are many other options, including the Aroian computation (see Kris Preacher's website for this computation), the joint significance test (determining whether both the a and b paths [X to MedV and MedV to Y] are significant), various confidence limits approaches (see MacKinnon, Lockwood, & Williams, 2004), and a number of different bootstrapping methods.

Which is best? Considerable controversy still exists on this issue, but it seems that the prevailing direction of movement is away from multiple-regression-based mediation analyses toward bootstrapping methods (see Kenny, 2008; MacKinnon, Fairchild, & Fritz, 2007). So why am I teaching Sobel's z-test approach here? The answer is that informed users need to begin with this basic approach, learn it thoroughly, and, when they have acquired sufficient statistical knowledge and expertise with various statistical platforms (e.g., SEM, multilevel modeling, bootstrapping), then they will naturally move on to the more powerful techniques. (You will find a description of bootstrapping in the next chapter, which will take you to this next level, if you are interested and committed.) This book is written to acquaint you with the history and the basics of both mediation and moderation and hopefully to prepare you for a career-long exploration of new developments in these areas over time.

Strength of Indirect Effect

Here is an additional question for you to consider: *How strong of a mediational effect did you obtain?* You are able to answer that it was statistically significant, but you are not able to say whether the amount of mediation (indirect effect = 0.215) was small, medium, or large. Baron and Kenny (1986) say that *perfect mediation* is obtained when the basic relationship is reduced to zero, and *significant mediation* is obtained when the Sobel z-value is significant but the basic relationship is not reduced to zero. As noted in Chapter 2, Baron and Kenny acknowledged that perfect mediation is very unlikely in the social sciences, in which probabilistic data are gathered. That leaves considerable ambiguity about the size of the effect. MacKinnon (MacKinnon, 2008;

MacKinnon, Warsi, & Dwyer, 1995) argues that we need to have a metric for the ratio between the direct and indirect effects because it would clarify the issue about the strength of the mediation effect.

MacKinnon, in his book on mediation (2008), states that there are three different (but related) ways to measure the effect size of the mediated effect: (1) ratio and proportion measures; (2) R^2 measures; and (3) standardized effect measures. The first approach computes various ratios between different effects. For example, Sobel (1982) suggested that one could divide the indirect effect by the direct effect; in the present case, it would be 0.215/0.269 = 0.80. Another ratio computation is to determine the proportion of the total effect that is mediated: $[1 - (c'/c)]$ or $[ab/c]$, which in the present case would be 0.44. (See Kenny's discussion of these two ratios at **http://davidakenny. net/cm/mediate.htm**.) Problems arise, however, if one has both negative and positive estimates. Absolute values are recommended for use in these equations. The second approach, R^2 measures, requires the computation of the amounts of variance in Y explained by X alone (variance of the direct effect) and by X and MedV together (allowing identification of the variance of the indirect effect). The most useful index, perhaps, from this approach is the proportion of the variance of the indirect effect to the variance of the total effect. In the present case, it is 0.728 (see the upcoming section on semipartial correlations for instructions about how to compute this ratio). A ratio of 0.73 suggests that almost three-fourths of the variance in the total effect is composed of the indirect effect, a sizable proportion. And the third and last approach yields an effect size in standardized units, dividing the indirect effect by the standard deviation of the DV. In the present case, this is 0.215/1.344 = 0.159. Which of these indices is the best? My view is that they *all* tell us something useful about the relationships in the mediational triangle, but they illuminate different aspects of the mediational triangle. I think two indices are particularly illuminating: (1) the ratio of the indirect effect to the total effect based on standardized regression coefficients and (2) the same ratio using R^2 measures. On the other hand, these two methods yield differing estimates of the "size of the indirect effect," so one must be careful in explaining which method one is reporting in a given context.

It is probably helpful to point out at this juncture that recent work by Preacher and Kelley (2011) suggests several more effect size indices that should be considered by the research community. One new effect size index is an index based on residuals; in particular, it is based on the amount of variance explained in both the mediator and the outcome. The other new effect size index assesses the indirect effect as a proportion of the maximum possible indirect effect that could have been obtained given the variables involved. Although these are new developments, these indices are promising and deserve attention in future work.

I created a website in 2004 that I designed to provide a graphical depiction of the mediational triangle to the user and to provide information on effect sizes. Let us consider output generated by MedGraph on the present mediational pattern, and in this fashion you can see how these effect size values are generated. Go to **http://www.vuw.ac.nz/psyc/staff/paul-jose/files/ medgraph/medgraph.php** and input the necessary output values into Med-Graph. You will notice that it asks for more information than the previous website does, and the reason for this is that these other sources of information are needed to create a full graph or figure of the mediational triangle. In particular, you need to provide the correlation matrix, the size of the sample, the B's and standard errors stipulated previously, and the altered betas in the final regression. If you input all of these values, you will obtain a figure that looks like Figure 3.6.

Type of Mediation			Significant
Sobel's z-value	5.35806		$p < 0.000001$
95% Symmetrical Confidence interval			
Lower			.14
Upper			.26
Coefficients: Unstandardized		Stand.	R^2 estimates (variances)
Total:	.485	.338	.114
Direct:	.269	.188	.032
Indirect:	.215	.150	.083
Indirect/Total ratio: .443		.443	.728

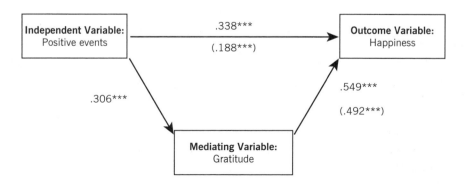

FIGURE 3.6. MedGraph output for example.

My intent was to create a website that would provide the user with more information than just Sobel's z-score so that he or she would be able to make a more appropriate interpretation of the finding. Beyond Sobel's z-score, this website also reports the associated significance level and the 95% symmetrical CI. Also in the figure, output provides information to allow the user to determine the strength of the mediational effect in three ways. The first is based on unstandardized regression coefficients, and the total effect refers to the original bivariate relationship between the IV and the DV, 0.485 in this case. (You should take absolute values of these estimates, rendering negative numbers positive.) The total effect is partitioned into two components: direct and indirect effects. The direct effect is the regression coefficient after inclusion of the MedV, 0.269 in this case, and the indirect effect is the total effect minus the direct effect, 0.215 in this case. The indirect/total ratio computed on the basis of unstandardized coefficients refers to 0.215/0.485, or 0.443. The ratio value varies from 0 to 1 and tells the user how much of the original basic relationship is explained by the indirect effect; in this case it turned out to be somewhat less than half (i.e., 44%).

The second column reports the same values in terms of standardized regression coefficients (see also the values reported in the mediational triangle, which are the same). You should notice that the indirect/total ratio (0.150/0.338 = 0.443) is identical, whether one computes it with unstandardized or standardized coefficients.

The last set of values report the R^2 estimates (based on variances), which allows a different (but related) way to identify the size of the indirect effect. These values are generated by using the semipartial correlations of the predictor variable and MedV with the outcome. In addition to other statistical output described before, MedGraph asks the user to input "part correlations" (also known as semipartial correlations) generated by the hierarchical regression analysis described earlier in this chapter. This analysis enters the predictor on the first step and then adds the MedV on the second step. The resulting semipartial correlations are used in several simple computations (see pp. 82–86 later in this chapter that describe these conversions) that yield these three reported values in the MedGraph output. It is important to notice—and it is fairly obvious—that these values differ from the estimates of effect sizes generated by standardized regression coefficients, but let me assure the reader that they are based on the same statistical outputs. The values in the left column are perhaps easier to understand because they refer to relative sizes of regression coefficients, whereas the values in the right column are more opaque because they are based on relative amounts of explained variance in the outcome, which are not obvious and apparent. I have designed MedGraph to report all three types because all are valid ways to examine the mediational results, and I leave it to the user to decide which of these two approaches best suits his or her particular mode of explanation.

And last, below these outputs is the graph of the mediational triangle, and it succinctly tells the researcher everything that he or she needs to know about the dynamic interplay of these variables. I suppose the graph is not entirely necessary, but I am a very visual person, and I like to see the entire mediational triangle laid out in its entirety to facilitate my understanding of what the result means. It forces the researcher to double-check that he or she has entered the data correctly (which does not always happen).

Did the Multiplicative Rule Work?

Remember that I said that $a*b = c - c'$? How did that work out? Focusing on the unstandardized regression coefficients, the numbers I obtained are: 1.752 * 0.123 = 0.215 and 0.485 − 0.269 = 0.216, which are close, given rounding errors. The same computations with standardized regression coefficients are: 0.306 * 0.492 = 0.150 and 0.338 − 0.188 = 0.150. Thus the multiplicative rule works regardless of whether you use unstandardized or standardized coefficients, but it should be clear that the two methods yield different absolute values for the size of the indirect effect. I have focused on computing the indirect effect with unstandardized regression coefficients because this is the customary way to derive it and because this value is used in other equations (such as computation of the confidence intervals). I showed you the numbers generated by the standardized coefficients only to point out that the indirect/total ratio is identical for these two sets of numbers.

Interpretation of the Result

I think we are ready to interpret the outcome. The results generated by Med-Graph tell us that gratitude acted as a significant mediator between positive life events and happiness. The statistical output, after being transformed by several equations, tell us that the basic relationship was significantly reduced by the introduction of a third variable (unstandardized indirect effect = 0.215; ratio of indirect/total = 0.44). The ratio tells us that the path through the mediating variable accounted for almost half of the basic relationship between the predictor and the outcome, and the R^2 estimate of the indirect effect tells us that about three quarters of this relationship was explained by the indirect effect.

ɔw might we interpret this result? I would say the following. "The
s show that if someone experiences a high level of positive life events,
then he or she is likely to report greater happiness. This relationship can
be partially explained by detailing the involvement of gratitude. In essence,
individuals who reported higher levels of positive life events reported feeling more grateful, and, in turn, grateful individuals reported higher levels
of happiness." These results make intuitive sense, and I am not aware of any
published report that includes all three of these particular constructs in this
particular fashion, so this may be a unique finding. Nevertheless, researchers
(Emmons & McCullough, 2003; Watkins, Woodward, Stone, & Kolts, 2003)
have noted that gratitude is positively associated with happiness, one link in
this triangle.

The estimates of direct and indirect effects tell us how strongly this mediator operated. In this particular case, the indirect effect was relatively large
compared with the direct effect. The ratio tells us that almost half (in the case
of regression coefficients) of the effect of positive life events on happiness
was "explained by" the intervening variable of gratitude. In other words, a
considerable amount of the shared variance between positive life events and
happiness was explained by the indirect route through gratitude. Researchers say that mediation tells us about the "operating mechanism" that exists
among three variables, and this interpretation is relevant here in that we can
say that we have discovered that gratitude seems to explain a significant part
of the relationship between positive life events and happiness.

AN EXAMPLE OF MEDIATION WITH EXPERIMENTAL DATA

The previous example was based on survey data collected at one point in
time (often called "concurrent"), and some of you will have data of this type.
However, in the social and physical sciences, a researcher often will have
experimental or quasi-experimental data. MacKinnon has written exten-
sively about this subject (2008; MacKinnon & Dwyer, 1993), and reading his
various papers will provide a more detailed treatment of this topic than I can
present here, but I would like to briefly touch on this method. The two chief
differences from the mediation example presented here are:

1. The IV is often a dichotomous categorical variable that represents the
   enactment of an intervention.
2. Temporal order of the variables allows for an unambiguous placement of the variables within the mediational triangle.

On the first point, I noted at the outset of this chapter that an experimental manipulation will usually yield a categorical dichotomous variable in which 1 = experimental group and 0 = control group. The values should be 0 and 1, not 1 and 2, because this variable is technically a dummy code (see a fuller explanation concerning dummy codes in Chapter 5). If we create more than two groups, as can happen when we are manipulating dosage levels of an intervention, then the IV will be more complex and can be composed of several dummy codes. In the present case, I keep it simple and focus on a single dichotomous categorical IV.

On the second point, let me note that when we have three concurrent variables, as in the previous mediation example, we can juggle the order of the variables in the three slots in the mediational triangle; but when we have experimental data, the design constrains the placement of variables. Presumably the IV is enacted at the outset of the study, so it would naturally be located in the leftmost slot. The mediation variable is obtained subsequent to the manipulation and would come next in order; and finally, the outcome, usually temporally obtained last, would fall into the final slot. Sometimes the researcher measures the mediating and outcome variables simultaneously at the end of the study, and this may create problems (see Baron & Kenny, 1986, on this point).

> **Helpful Suggestion:** If you access the dataset titled "experimental mediation example.sav," you can perform the analyses that I report next.

The present dataset came from a quasi-experimental study of resilience in 13-year-old adolescents conducted by one of my PhD students, Olivia Notter. She enacted a positive psychology-based program named PAL that sought to orient these teenagers to identify strengths, savor pleasant experiences, find flow in their lives, and practice feeling gratitude about the positive things in their lives. We predicted that students who participated in the PAL program would, as a consequence, report greater life satisfaction. Further, we expected to find a mediational pathway through increased gratitude that would lead to greater life satisfaction. The predicted mediational pattern is depicted in Figure 3.7.

We screened a large group of 13-year-olds and selected individuals with mildly to moderately elevated depression scores (i.e., individuals who were "at risk"). We solicited students in this range to volunteer for a program to help with living skills. Those who volunteered were randomly assorted into either the experimental or the control group. Pretest depression scores

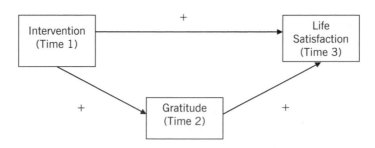

FIGURE 3.7. Predicted mediational pattern for the experimental mediation example.

indicated that the two groups did not differ significantly. Due to the time-consuming and extensive nature of the program, the two groups ended up with relatively small numbers (compared with other datasets described in this book). The experimental group constituted 38 teenagers, and the control was composed of 30 teenagers. The program ran for 12 weeks, 1 hour per week, and at the conclusion of the program (time 2) various measures were taken, including self-reported gratitude. Life satisfaction was assessed at this point as well as 6 months later, at time 3. We used the equations described earlier to conduct the analyses:

$$Y = i_2 + c'X + bM + e_2 \quad \text{[Life satisfaction} = c'(\text{Intervention}) + b(\text{Gratitude})]$$

$$M = i_3 + aX + e_3 \quad \text{[Gratitude} = a(\text{Intervention})]$$

The correlations and the two regression equations yielded the outputs presented in Tables 3.9, 3.10. 3.11, and 3.12 and in Figure 3.8. Selecting values from these outputs, one can compute Sobel's test by hand in this fashion:

$$z\text{-value} = \frac{a*b}{\text{SQRT}(b^{2}*s_a^2 + a^{2}*s_b^2)}$$

$$= \frac{(3.781)*(.376)}{\text{SQRT}(.376^2*1.333^2 + 3.781^2*.133^2)} = \frac{1.42166}{\text{SQRT}(.141*1.78 + 14.296*.0018)}$$

$$= \frac{1.42166}{\text{SQRT}(.25098 + .25288)} = \frac{1.42166}{\text{SQRT}(.50386)} = \frac{1.42166}{.70983} = 2.003, p = .045$$

Table 3.13 shows how you would calculate the 95% symmetrical CI.

TABLE 3.9. Zero-Order Correlations of the Three Variables Used for the Experimental Mediation Example

	Treatment	T2Gratitude	T3LifeSat
Treatment			
Pearson correlation	1	.330[**]	.233
Sig. (two-tailed)		.006	.056
N	68	68	68
T2Gratitude			
Pearson correlation	.330[**]	1	.380[**]
Sig. (two-tailed)	.006		.001
N	68	68	68
T3LifeSat			
Pearson correlation	.233	.380[**]	1
Sig. (two-tailed)	.056	.001	
N	68	68	68

**Correlation is significant at the .01 level (two-tailed).

TABLE 3.10. Statistical Output for the Basic Relationship of the Experimental Mediation Example

Model	Unstandardized coefficients		Standardized coefficients		
	B	Std. error	Beta	t	Sig.
1. (Constant)	21.347	1.134		18.820	.000
Treatment	2.957	1.517	.233	1.949	.056

Note. Dependent variable: T3 Life Satisfaction.

TABLE 3.11. Statistical Output for the Relationship between the Independent Variable and Mediating Variable of the Experimental Mediation Example (First Model)

Model	Unstandardized coefficients		Standardized coefficients		
	B	Std. error	Beta	t	Sig.
1. (Constant)	24.667	.996		24.754	.000
Treatment	3.781	1.333	.330	2.836	.006

Note. Dependent variable: T2Gratitude.

TABLE 3.12. Statistical Output for the Relationship between the Independent and Mediating Variables and the Dependent Variable of the Experimental Mediation Example (Second Model)

Model	Unstandardized coefficients		Standardized coefficients		
	B	Std. error	Beta	t	Sig.
1. (Constant)	12.069	3.459		3.489	.001
Treatment	1.535	1.528	.121	1.004	.319
T2 Gratitude	.376	.133	.340	2.823	.006

Note. Dependent variable: T3 Life Satisfaction.

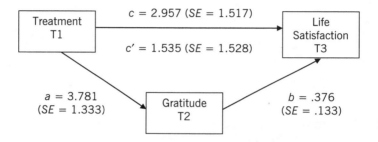

FIGURE 3.8. Depiction of mediational triangle with statistical outputs.

TABLE 3.13. Calculation of the Symmetrical 95% Confidence Interval for the Experimental Mediation Example

	Estimate of indirect effect	±	(95% CI coefficient	×	Standard error)
Lower limit	1.42166	−	(1.96	×	.710)
	1.42166	−		1.3916	
	0.03006				
Upper limit	1.42166	+	(1.96	×	.710)
	1.42166	+		1.3916	
	2.81326				

Taken together, these results tell me that I obtained significant mediation with these three variables across this period of time. The interpretation would be:

"Support was found for the hypothesis that gratitude significantly mediated between the treatment effect of the PAL program and resulting life satisfaction 6 months after the conclusion of the program. Specifically, a measurable treatment effect was greater gratitude among the experimental group participants noted at the conclusion of the 12-week program, and this difference differentially predicted greater life satisfaction 6 months later. The mediational analysis yielded a Sobel z-score of 2.003, $p = .045$, asymmetrical 95% CI was .03 to 2.81. The standardized effect size indicated that about 48% of the total effect of the treatment on resulting life satisfaction was explained by the indirect effect through gratitude."

AN EXAMPLE OF NULL MEDIATION

According to Baron and Kenny, one should not examine a mediation triangle in which at least one of the three relationships is statistically nonsignificant. According to this rule, the easiest example of null mediation that you will run across is a dataset in which at least one of the three preconditions is not met. (People have questioned whether this is a sound procedure, though, so see the upcoming section "Suppressor Variables in Mediation" for a reexamination of this assumption.)

However, there is a slightly more interesting example of null mediation—if there is such a thing—in which the three variables display significant zero-order correlations with each other but Sobel's z-score is nonsignificant. Following is an example of this latter type of no (or null) mediation that I found in a dataset supplied to me by my colleague, Dr. Taciano Milfont, in my home institution (i.e., the School of Psychology, Victoria University of Wellington, New Zealand). He has described these variables and this dataset (Milfont, Duckitt, & Wagner, 2010), but for obvious reasons he did not describe this particular relationship—I had to go looking for it to find it.

Helpful Suggestion: Just as I suggested earlier with basic mediation, if you would like to analyze the present dataset and conduct the following analyses on it as you go through this section, find and download "null mediation example.sav."

Taciano is interested in how personal values inform and affect attitudes and behaviors concerned with preservation and protection of the environment. The hypothesis to be tested was that the effect of altruism on environmental values (the degree to which individuals endorsed items measuring unity with nature, protecting the environment, and respecting the Earth, taken from the Schwartz Value Scale; Schwartz, 1994) would be mediated by the value of self-enhancement. In essence, one's general altruism should predict concern for nature, and it might be mediated by a general orientation toward doing things to enhance one's own self. I thought this might make sense insofar as an altruistic person might be motivated by self-enhancement to be concerned about nature. The researchers obtained data from three countries (South Africa, New Zealand, and Brazil), but in this particular case I focused only on the South African group ($N = 257$). I proceeded to compute the regressions and obtain the MedGraph result (see Figure 3.9). The correlation matrix that I obtained is presented in Table 3.14.

Type of Mediation	Null	
Sobel z-value	1.537598 significance p =.124147	
Standardized coefficient of Altruism on Concern for Nature		
Direct:	.488	
Indirect:	.019	
Total:	.507	
Ratio:	.037	

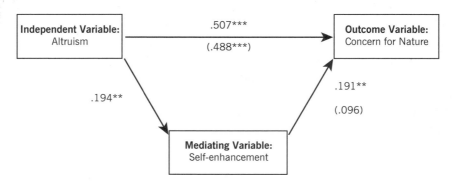

FIGURE 3.9. MedGraph output for the null mediation example.

TABLE 3.14. Zero-Order Correlations among the Variables for the Null Mediation Example

	Self-enhancement	Concern for nature	Altruism
Self-enhancement			
Pearson correlation	1	.191[**]	.194[**]
Sig. (two-tailed)		.002	.002
N	257	257	257
Concern for nature			
Pearson correlation	.191[**]	1	.507[**]
Sig. (two-tailed)	.002		.000
N	257	257	257
Altruism			
Pearson correlation	.194[**]	.507[**]	1
Sig. (two-tailed)	.002	.000	
N	257	257	257

**Correlation is significant at the .01 level (two-tailed).

The indirect path through self-enhancement was very small (0.02); inclusion of the mediating variable did *not* reduce the basic relationship to a significant extent. What is notable here is that the beta for the basic relationship does not significantly decrease (i.e., Sobel's test is nonsignificant). That result by itself tells the user that mediation did not occur. A nonsignificant Sobel z tells the user that only a small reduction in the beta for the basic relationship was obtained.

The ratio index yielded a value of 0.037, suggesting that only a very small amount (about 4%) of the total effect was explained by the indirect path through self-enhancement. The nonsignificant Sobel value ($p = .12$) with the minuscule indirect/total ratio tells us that no significant mediation occurred with this particular arrangement of three variables. In this case, the researcher should accept the null hypothesis and say that the involvement of self-enhancement did not explain any significant portion of the basic relationship between altruism and concern for nature.

[margin handwritten note: null Hypo]

SOBEL'S z VERSUS REDUCTION OF THE BASIC RELATIONSHIP

What do you have when Sobel's z-value is nonsignificant but the basic relationship is reduced to nonsignificance? I have had several MedGraph users raise this issue. In essence, what happens is that the beta for the basic relationship is initially statistically significant, but when the mediating variable is included, the basic relationship decreases to nonsignificance. At the same time, Sobel's z-test yields a *non*significant z-value. According to some people's thinking (based on reading Baron and Kenny, I think), the reduction of the basic relationship to nonsignificance suggests that one has obtained significant mediation. However, I think that most mediation cognoscenti (that means "people in the know") would agree that the Sobel test takes precedence in this case: if Sobel's z is nonsignificant, then one has obtained null mediation. End of the story.

This situation is usually obtained when the original basic relationship is barely significant, for example, $p = .04$, and although the subsequent Sobel test might show that the mediating variable explains a small portion of the basic relationship—for example, the p-value for the Sobel test might be .08— Sobel's z will not be sufficiently large to obtain that all-important "p less than .05" outcome. My advice in this situation is to acknowledge the nonsignificant Sobel test and admit that null mediation was obtained. A result such as this can be frustrating to the researcher, and she or he may be inclined to ignore Sobel's z result, but its use has been adopted into general practice now, and I do not think it can be ignored. The researcher may wish to report this result as "suggestive of a possibility that a trend might have happened" or such, but there are some statisticians who would say that even that is too bold. My advice: Be honest about what you found. Do not overinterpret the result, even if it is very enticing for you to find a significant result.

SUPPRESSOR VARIABLES IN MEDIATION

Can the strength of the basic relationship *increase* when the mediating variable is included? Yes. Occasionally we find the paradoxical situation in which we obtain significant mediation (as determined by the Sobel test) but the beta for the basic relationship actually goes *up* when the mediating variable is included. Following is a case in point. I am again using the dataset provided by my colleague Taciano Milfont, which was described in the previous section on "null mediation." Although he has published a report from these data (see Milfont et al., 2010), he did not report this particular aspect of the data. I found this relationship when I began examining the mediational relationships among the variables. As deep background, you may wish to read their report to obtain a greater understanding of what these variables measure and why I might have obtained a suppressor effect in this case. They obtained data from three countries (South Africa, New Zealand, and Brazil), and the present analyses were performed only on the South African data.

Helpful Suggestion: Find the dataset "suppressor mediation example.sav" if you would like to analyze this dataset, and conduct the following analyses on it as you go through this section.

In this case, altruism is the predictor variable (the degree to which individuals endorsed items measuring a desire for equality, a world at peace, and social justice, taken from the Schwartz Value Scale; Schwartz, 1994), the mediating variable is self-enhancement (the degree to which individuals endorsed being wealthy, wielding authority, and being influential, also taken from the Schwartz Value Scale), and the outcome is a summed score of generalized environmental attitudes (assessed by the Milfont & Duckitt *Environmental Attitudes Inventory*, 2010). The basic correlations are presented in Table 3.15. Right away the astute researcher should be able to note that something is out of the ordinary. There is an implicit logic to correlation matrices in that variables that are correlated in a positive direction with each other should generalize that direction of correlation to a new variable. In other words, if X and Y are positively correlated with each other, then a third vari-

TABLE 3.15. Zero-Order Correlations for the Variables in the Suppressor Variable Example

	Altruism	Self-enhancement	General Environmental Atts
Altruism			
Pearson correlation	1	.194[**]	.132[*]
Sig. (two-tailed)		.002	.034
N	257	257	257
Self-enhancement			
Pearson correlation	.194[**]	1	−.230[**]
Sig. (two-tailed)	.002		.000
N	257	257	257
General Environmental Atts			
Pearson correlation	.132[*]	−.230[**]	1
Sig. (two-tailed)	.034	.000	
N	257	257	257

*Correlation is significant at the .05 level (two-tailed).
**Correlation is significant at the .01 level (two-tailed).

able Z should be "consistent" and correlate in the same direction with both X and Y. This pattern is not found in the previous example. Altruism and self-enhancement are positively correlated, but when I add the third variable, I find that although altruism is positively correlated with general environmental attitudes, surprisingly self-enhancement is *negatively* correlated with general environmental attitudes.

In this case I consider altruism to be my predictor, self-enhancement to be my MedV, and general environmental attitudes to be my outcome. I run my mediational analysis, and Figure 3.10 presents what I obtained. Hmmm, that's interesting. MedGraph tells me that I have obtained significant mediation, yet the basic relationship becomes *stronger*. And note that the direct, indirect, and total effects (and ratio) do not make sense because the indirect effect has a different sign than the direct effect. So what is going on here? What we have here is a *suppressor variable* (Conger, 1974; Darlington, 1968; Horst, 1941; Krus & Wilkinson, 1986; Paulhus, Robins, Trzesniewski, & Tracy, 2004). A suppressor variable is defined differently by different authors, but Conger defines it as "a variable that increases regression weights and, thus, increases the predictive validity of other variables in a regression equation" (Conger, 1974, pp. 36–37). One can notice that both the X-to-Y and the

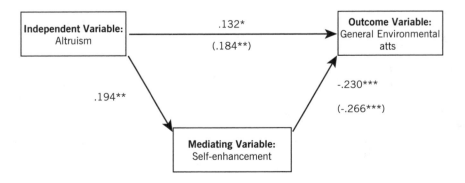

Type of Mediation	Significant
Sobel z-value	-2.553226 significance p = .010673
Standardized coefficient of Collectivism on Depression	
Direct:	.184
Indirect:	-.052
Total:	.132
Ratio:	-.394

FIGURE 3.10. MedGraph output for the suppressor variable example.

MedV-to-Y relationships are increased here. Several types of suppressor variables have been identified (see Krus & Wilkinson, 1986, or Gaylord-Harden, Cunningham, Holmbeck, & Grant, 2010), but this discussion is not pursued here because of a concern for space.

Some authors argue that this phenomenon reveals spuriousness, that is, false or misleading correlations, but some writers (and I agree with this point of view) think that these relationships may reveal important information about the ways in which these variables are related. For example, in the mediational triangle in Figure 3.10 we see that self-enhancement has a paradoxical (enigmatically termed "quasiparadoxical" by Cohen & Cohen, 1975) relationship with the other two variables. Altruism positively predicts self-enhancement, suggesting that an altruistic person is enjoying some self-enhancing aspect of being altruistic ("Aren't I a good person for helping out others?"), but self-enhancement, in turn, is a *negative* predictor of general environmental attitudes, suggesting that a person high in self-enhancement is relatively uninterested in helping the environment. These two relationships suggest that there is a counterintuitive indirect path between the X and Y relationship—namely, that being altruistic is positively predictive of having more positive environmental attitudes through the intervening variable of self-enhancement.

Some people think that suppressor relationships are false and spurious, and maybe some are, but I do not think that there is anything false or spurious about the present set of relationships. I think that they make perfect sense, in that self-enhancement is related to altruistic impulses in some people, and this psychological dynamic seems to work against a person having more proenvironment attitudes. I would suggest in the present case that this obtained finding is potentially valuable because it points out the danger of making altruism a salient reason for people to care for the environment: Some may espouse altruistic views to enhance their own sense of self, but this strategy might not increase positive environmental attitudes. By the way, these data were concurrent, taken at one point in time, and the present set of findings cries out for a longitudinal study to be done to probe the causal relationships hinted at by this mediation result.

In sum, I think that evidence of a suppressor variable is a marvelous motivation to probe the relationships more closely and identify the hidden currents swirling below the surface. I recommend that if and when you find evidence of a suppressor effect you take the opportunity to examine the relationships more closely in order to unpack the reasons that the X-to-Y beta weight increased. In my experience one is more likely to find a suppressor effect when one obtains either one or three negative correlations (in the case of three-variable mediation), when the researcher is using a large sample size, and when the measures involved are composed of multiple items.

INVESTIGATING MEDIATION WHEN ONE HAS A NONSIGNIFICANT CORRELATION

Is it feasible to examine mediation when one does *not* have three significant relationships? As it has been laid out by Baron and Kenny, the dogma (repeated by me at the beginning of this chapter) is that one must have three significant correlations before one can examine mediation. However, I also noted that this stipulation is controversial, and MacKinnon (2008), among others, has argued that mediation can be found in triads of variables in which the X-to-Y relationship is not statistically significant.

Let me present an example. In this case, we have a sample of 1,774 adolescents who responded to a survey asking them about their views on social support and connection to different institutions and groups. I focus on three variables: susceptibility to social pressure (*X*), perceived social support (MedV), and sense of being part of a school community (*Y*). I expected teenagers who reported high susceptibility to social pressure to be more isolated because they probably lack social skills. Thus an adolescent high in susceptibility to social pressure would be likely to report lower school connectedness and lower social support. Further, I anticipated that social support would mediate between susceptibility to social pressure and school connectedness. The triangle would look like Figure 3.11.

The obtained zero-order correlations in the dataset are presented in Figure 3.12.

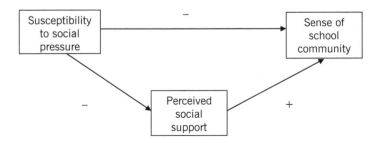

FIGURE 3.11. Predicted mediational pattern for an example when all three paths are not statistically significant.

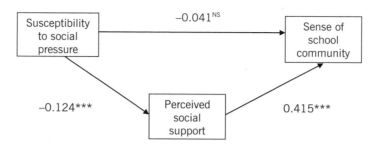

FIGURE 3.12. Depiction of statistical output for example in which the basic relationship is not statistically significant.

By the usual rules of the game, I should stop at this juncture and go off and try to find another set of variables. However, for the sake of argument, let us pursue this analysis and see what I obtained. After computing the two regressions and inputting values into MedGraph, Figure 3.13 depicts what I obtained. This result seems to argue against the knee-jerk reaction not to examine triads of variables in which at least one correlation is nonsignificant. I will echo what MacKinnon and others have argued: Even in cases in

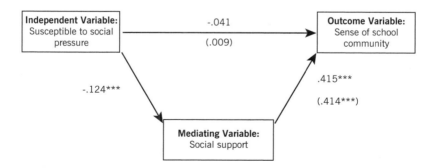

FIGURE 3.13. MedGraph output for example in which the basic relationship is not statistically significant.

which one obtains a nonsignificant relationship, significant mediation *might* be found. In my experience, significant mediation is sometimes found in cases in which the *X*-to-*Y* relationship (*c*) is weak but the *a* and *b* links are strong (as in the preceding case).

You have now seen a case in which three significant correlations did not yield significant mediation (pp. 67–69), juxtaposed against this example in which significant mediation was obtained in a case in which a nonsignificant correlation was manifested in the mediational triangle. These examples should highlight to you that significant mediation is likelier to be found in cases in which the *a* and *b* links are strong, and it is likelier *not* to be found in cases in which either (or both) of the *a* and *b* links are weak.

UNDERSTANDING THE MATHEMATICAL "FINE PRINT": VARIANCES AND COVARIANCES

I have found that it is easier to teach students how to conduct mediational analyses than it is to teach them how to make clear and unambiguous interpretations of the mediational findings. And one of the murky issues that students typically struggle with is the matter of what the indirect effect actually measures. I tell them helpful things such as "Well, the size of the indirect effect tells you the amount of variance in the total effect left over after you take out the direct effect." The point I have gotten to now is to say "You know, you need to learn the mathematical stuff underlying the computations of hierarchical regressions." And then I begin with Venn diagrams to ease them into the process. If you are interested in learning about some of the underlying foundation for mediational analyses, then I would recommend that you try to make it through the rest of this chapter, because I think that learning this material will make you a more informed user of mediation, and it will enable you to make clearer interpretations of your findings.

Before We Get to Venn Diagrams: Learning about Variances and Covariances

I think it might be useful to digress for a brief journey into the world of *variance* and *covariance* for a moment, because many people (including seasoned researchers, if truth be told) do not precisely understand what these terms mean. Here is a definition of variance: "the total amount of distribution of obtained values around the mean." In the three following sets of numbers, the mean is 10, but you will see that there is more "spread" of values around the mean in the second set of numbers than in the first or third.

Set 1: 10, 10, 10, 10, 10
Set 2: 0, 5, 10, 15, 20
Set 3: 8, 12, 9, 11, 10

The equation for computing the sample variance is

$$\text{Variance} = \Sigma_i(x_i - \bar{x})^2/N - 1 \tag{3.6}$$

where Σ_i is the sum of all elements in a particular set, N is the number of elements in the set, x_i is the ith element of the set of elements, and $\bar{x}$ is the mean of the set of all elements. The variance for the first set of numbers is 0 because there is no spread of values around the mean. If one sums up five instances of $10 - 10$, one will obtain a variance of 0. For the second set of numbers:

$$
\begin{aligned}
\text{Var} &= [\Sigma_i(x_i - \bar{x})^2]/(N - 1) \\
&= [(0 - 10)^2 + (5 - 10)^2 + (10 - 10)^2 + (15 - 10)^2 + (20 - 10)^2]/(5 - 1) \\
&= (100 + 25 + 0 + 25 + 100)/(5 - 1) \\
&= 250/4 \\
&= 62.5
\end{aligned}
$$

For the third set of numbers:

$$
\begin{aligned}
\text{Var} &= [(8 - 10)^2 + (12 - 10)^2 + (9 - 10)^2 + (11 - 10)^2 + (10 - 10)^2]/(5 - 1) \\
&= (4 + 4 + 1 + 1 + 0)/(5 - 1) \\
&= 10/4 \\
&= 2.5
\end{aligned}
$$

This equation yields the *sample variance*, and it varies between 0 (as in the preceding set 1) and very large positive numbers. Most researchers, however, when they wish to report how much variation exists in a given variable, do not tend to report variance of a given variable; instead, they report the standard deviation. You may already know that the *sample standard deviation* is the square root of the sample variance. So in the case of the second set of numbers, the standard deviation (*SD*) is the square root of 62.5, or 7.91, and in the case of the third set of numbers, it is the square root of 2.5, or 1.58.

Let us turn to *covariance* now. Covariance is an index of the degree to which two variables covary, or are related to each other. That sounds a lot like a correlation, so it is important to detail how these two constructs are similar and different. They are mathematically related, so it will probably be instructive to define each before we move on. Here is the usual definition of covariance in equation form:

Where $\bar{x}$ and $\bar{y}$ are the means of two variables:

$$Cov(x, y) = \frac{\Sigma(x_i - \bar{x})(y_j - \bar{y})}{N - 1} \tag{3.7}$$

Using the second and third sets of values identified earlier, we have the values in Table 3.16 to consider. The sum of the products, 15, is divided by $N - 1$ (i.e., 4), which yields a covariance of 3.75. This result by itself is not very illuminating, but let's move on to correlation now.

A definition of correlation, jumping off from the previous derivation of a covariance, is the following:

$$\rho_{x,y} = \frac{Cov(x,y)}{\sigma_x \sigma_y} \tag{3.8}$$

This equation is not meant to be daunting, and in fact it's quite simple. What it means is that the correlation (ρ is the Greek letter *rho*) between variable x and variable y is equal to the covariance between two variables divided by the product of the two *SD*s (σ is the Greek letter *sigma*, which commonly rep-

TABLE 3.16. Calculation of Covariance

	x_i	y_i	$x_i - \bar{x}$	$y_i - \bar{y}$	Products
Subj. 1	0	8	−10	−2	20
Subj. 2	5	12	−5	2	−10
Subj. 3	10	9	0	−1	0
Subj. 4	15	11	5	1	5
Subj. 5	20	10	10	0	0
Mean	10	10			$\Sigma = 15$
Standard deviation	SQRT(62.5) = 7.91	SQRT(2.5) = 1.58			

resents the *SD*). What this conversion accomplishes is to place the obtained values for correlations between the values of +1.0 and –1.0, thereby putting them on a metric that is easy to understand and appreciate. Most beginning statistics students readily grasp that positive correlation values indicate that things go along together, that negative correlation values indicate that things go in opposite directions, and that values near zero indicate that things are not associated very much at all. In the case given here, the covariance (3.75) is divided by the product of the two *SD*s (7.91 * 1.58 = 12.4978), which yields a correlation of .30. Most of us can understand how these two columns of numbers are related to each other with a correlation of .30 better than we can if we are told that they manifest a covariance of 3.75. But it is important to realize that the correlation is merely the covariance divided by the product of the two *SD*s.

Let's consider a larger dataset. In this case I've correlated two variables, individualism and collectivism. Collectivism is the tendency to value one's participation in groups and collectives and to be interdependent with others, and, in contrast, individualism describes the tendency to value competition, self-reliance, and independence (see Triandis, 1995). The analysis I requested yielded a covariance value of –.017 between individualism and collectivism in a sample of about 1,900 New Zealand adolescents. If I reported this statistic in a paper, most readers would be confused and would want to know what the Pearson correlation value was. One can see in Table 3.17 that the correlation is –.05, and with a sample of this size, this correlation is deemed to be statistically significant at $p < .05$, although it is obviously not very strong.

TABLE 3.17. Example of Correlation and Covariance between Individualism and Collectivism

	Individ.	Collect.
Individ.		
Pearson correlation	1	–.050*
Sig. (two-tailed)	·	.029
Covariance	.417	–.017
N	1921	1921
Collect.		
Pearson correlation	–.050*	1
Sig. (two-tailed)	.029	
Covariance	–.017	.288
N	1921	1921

*Correlation is significant at the .05 level (two-tailed).

TABLE 3.18. Descriptive Statistics of Individualism and Collectivism

	N	Mean	Std. Deviation	Variance
Individ.	1921	3.0013	.64574	.417
Collect.	1921	3.7967	.53693	.288
Valid N (listwise)	1921			

I have also appended descriptive statistics (see Table 3.18) for the two variables in question. SPSS generated the variance and *SD*s of both variables, and these are reprinted in Table 3.18. You may notice a curious inconsistency between these two tables of findings. The *covariance* of individualism is reported to be .417 in Table 3.17, and the *variance* of the same variable is reported to be .417 in Table 3.18. So which is it? The answer is that the covariance of a variable with itself is known as the variance. It is customary to refer to the variance of a variable by itself but to covariances among pairs of variables.

What does all of this have to do with mediation? I want to make sure that you understand what the Venn diagrams in the next subsection depict as I go through this explanation. In essence, *the circles represent variances of variables, and the graphical overlap between two variables defines the size of the covariance between any two variables.*

Graphical Depiction of Mediation with Venn Diagrams

Now that we have a clearer idea of what covariance, correlation, and variance are, we can now delve into the illuminating world of Venn diagrams. John Venn, a British philosopher and mathematician, introduced his system of diagrams in 1881 to illustrate set theory, that is, making clear distinctions about membership of unique or shared elements among sets. More than 100 years later, we are still using his invention to good effect. Venn diagrams are a good way to understand the various strengths of correlation, and Figure 3.14 presents four depictions of different-sized correlations.

Now we are ready to depict mediations, which require three variables. There are essentially two types of these: null and significant mediations. We begin with a typical example of significant mediation based on the example given at the outset of this chapter. We assume that the relationship between positive life events and happiness described earlier would look something like Figure 3.15, which depicts a moderate relationship. The area of overlap represents the shared variance between these two variables, and the fact

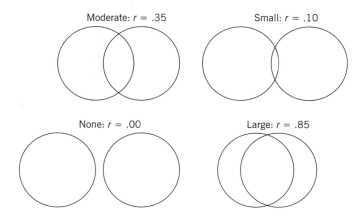

FIGURE 3.14. Graphical depiction of different correlation strengths with Venn diagrams.

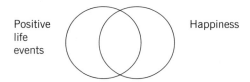

FIGURE 3.15. Moderate correlation between positive life events and happiness.

that it is of moderate size indicates that a moderate correlation was obtained between these two variables.

When we add in the variable of gratitude (the mediating variable; see Figure 3.16), notice that this new variable partially overlaps the shared variance between the X and Y variables. In fact, it covers about half of the overlapping area between positive life events and happiness. You may recall that the ratio indicated that the indirect effect accounted for about 44% of the total effect, so I have depicted this percentage about right in the figure. This figure signifies that we have mediation in which about half of the basic relationship between positive life events and happiness is explained by the involvement of this third variable, gratitude.

The case of null mediation is fairly clear (see Figure 3.17), because you can see that the third variable covers only a very small amount of the overlap between the X and Y variables. Further, in the "very strong" mediation case, you can see that the third variable covers the majority of the overlapping area between X and Y.

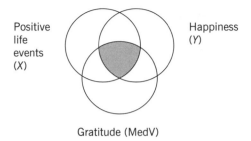

FIGURE 3.16. Venn diagram depiction of mediation.

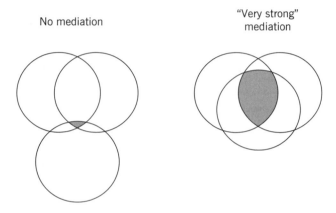

FIGURE 3.17. Venn diagram depictions of null and very strong mediation.

What I hope that these Venn diagrams show is that significant media-tion occurs when a substantial amount of the shared variance between the *X* and *Y* variables is also covered by the third variable, the proposed mediator (MedV). And I hope that these pictures demystify for the reader the process of identifying whether a third variable significantly shares variance with two other variables.

DISCUSSION OF PARTIAL AND SEMIPARTIAL CORRELATIONS

For those of you who have had a good grounding in correlational methods, the preceding discussion will remind you of the terms *partial correlation* and *semipartial correlation*. If you would like to review these concepts or to learn them for the first time, read this section. For the beginning student of statistics, this section may pose a bit of tough going, but an understanding of both mediation and moderation is undergirded by this foundation, so it is definitely worth learning.

When one is interested in examining the ability of two predictor variables to predict an outcome (as in the case of mediation), one needs to be concerned about the potential overlap between the two predictors. In common-sense language, if we want to know how positive life events and gratitude predict happiness uniquely, then we need to consider how positive life events and gratitude are correlated. If they are significantly correlated (which will necessarily be the case in mediation), then there is a part of each that uniquely predicts happiness and a part in common with the other predictor that predicts happiness. Looking at Figure 3.18, the reader can discern that area *b* reflects the shared variance of positive life events and gratitude that also predicts happiness, whereas area *a* is the unique variance in happiness predicted by positive life events, and area *c* is the unique variance in happiness predicted by gratitude.

Tabachnick and Fidell (2001) present a nice exposition of these issues in their book (see also Cohen, Cohen, West, & Aiken, 2003). Tabachnick and Fidell examined the issue of two *X* variables predicting a single *Y* variable, which is exactly the case that we are considering here. They noted that "The total relationship of the IV with the DV and the correlations of the IVs with each other are given in the correlation matrix. The unique contribution of an IV to predicting a DV is generally assessed by either partial or semipartial correlation" (p. 139). (*Note*: The term *semipartial correlation* is considered to

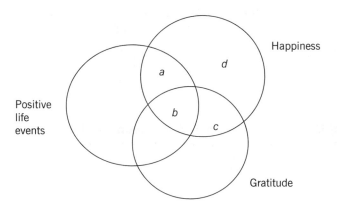

FIGURE 3.18. Shared and unique variance in mediation: the role of semipartial correlations.

be equivalent to the term *part correlation*, and statisticians and researchers use these terms interchangeably.) So it looks as though it would be useful to understand what semipartial correlations involve.

If I run a hierarchical regression in which happiness is the DV, positive life events is the first IV, and gratitude is the second IV, I obtain useful information about the ability of these two IVs to predict the DV. Specifically, I find that positive life events alone (in the first step) yields an R^2 value of .115. This tells me that positive life events accounts for 11.5% of the variance in happiness by itself. The areas *a* and *b* together in the figure would represent 11.5% of the variance in happiness. Let us consider the second step: I find that the second IV gives us an R^2 *change* value of .219. This means that area *c* in the figure represents 21.9% of the variance in happiness that gratitude explains above and beyond positive life events. In other words, gratitude uniquely explains 21.9% of happiness. But what about the ability of positive life events to uniquely explain happiness?

To determine this fact, we run the hierarchical regression with a reverse order of IV entry: gratitude first and positive life events second (see Table 3.19). This regression tells me that 30.2% of the variance in happiness is explained by gratitude in the first step (areas *b* and *c*), and in the second step positive life events uniquely predicts only 3.2% of the variance in happiness (area *a*). We now know the sizes of *a* (3.2%) and *c* (21.9%), and we can now mathematically determine the size of *b* by subtracting these two values from the total R^2 (33.4%). After doing this computation, we obtain a value of 8.3% for area *b*.

That is well and good, but how does this tell us anything useful about semipartial correlations? This discussion is germane because SPSS and other statistics programs derive R^2 values from squaring semipartial correlations. The R^2 values tell the researcher about amounts of variance in the DV explained by the IVs, so this knowledge is helpful in determining the relative sizes of the direct and indirect effects in mediation. How does one obtain semipartial correlations, and what do they mean? Let us take a closer look at our data.

TABLE 3.19. Derivation of the Amount of Shared Variance between the Two Predictor Variables (Area *b*)

	Predictor	Change in R^2	Areas
1st regression	Positive life events	11.5	*a* and *b*
	Gratitude	21.9	*c*
2nd regression	Gratitude	30.2	*b* and *c*
	Positive life events	3.2	*a*

I now return to the first step of the regression reported at the beginning of this chapter: Happiness is the DV and positive life events is the IV. I ask SPSS under STATISTICS for "part and partial correlations." This option allows me to see these estimates in the output. (As noted earlier, terminology about semipartials is somewhat confusing, so it is important to know that SPSS uses "part" for what other writers refer to as "semipartial.") Table 3.20 is what I obtained.

The partial and part (semipartial) correlations in the second step are illustrative in our current discussion. The partial correlation is the value we get when we hold constant some third variable from two other variables. Thus positive life events is correlated .214 with happiness, holding gratitude constant; and gratitude is correlated .498 with happiness, holding positive life events constant. However, our emphasis at this juncture is on the part (semipartial) correlation, and we can see that the part correlation for positive life events decreases from .338 on the first step to .179 on the second step. If we square these values, we see that positive life events goes from explaining 11.5% of the variance (area $a + b$) in happiness to 3.2% (area a) of the variance. Gratitude, entered at step 2, yields a part correlation of .468, and that value squared tells us that it uniquely explains 21.9% of the variance in happiness (area c). The remaining portion of variance explained in happiness by the two IVs, 8.3%, refers to area b, that portion explained jointly by the two IVs. We know that the total variance explained is .334, so removing .032 and .219 from the total yields .083. Thus positive life events and gratitude jointly explain about 8% of a person's happiness.

TABLE 3.20. Statistical Output Displaying Part (Semipartial) Correlations in a Hierarchical Regression

Model	Unstandardized coefficients B	Std. error	Standardized coefficients Beta	t	Sig.	Zero-order	Partial	Part
1. (Constant)	4.008	.156		25.752	.000			
Positive Life Events Total	.485	.071	.338	6.843	.000	.338	.338	.338
2. (Constant)	−.056	.397		−.141	.888			
Positive Life Events Total	.269	.065	.188	4.168	.000	.338	.214	.179
Gratitude Survey Total	.123	.011	.492	10.902	.000	.549	.498	.468

Note. Dependent variable: Subjective Happiness Scale Total.

TABLE 3.21. Use of Part (Semipartial) Correlations in Determining R^2 Estimates of the Size of the Indirect Effect

Areas	Part correlations	Variances	R^2 estimates
$a + b$	.338	.114	Total effect
a	.179	.032	Direct effect
c	.468	.219	
b		.083	Indirect effect

What is important to learn from this? The semipartial correlations provide another way to derive the R^2 values necessary for computing the amounts of variance depicted in Figure 3.18. And by extension, they allow us to compute the R^2 size of the indirect effect (see Table 3.21).

STATISTICAL ASSUMPTIONS

Now let us take up the issue of whether your data are appropriate for the linear regression analyses specified herein. One should not launch into these analyses without first determining whether one's dataset satisfies a number of preconditions.

Power

Is your sample sufficiently large to give you enough statistical power to find a result of a reasonable size? To answer this question, according to Cohen (1992), four interrelated variables must be determined simultaneously: (1) the significance criterion (i.e., the alpha, usually set at .05 or .01); (2) sample size; (3) effect size; and (4) power level (usually set at 0.80). Using Cohen's tables, one can determine a reasonable range for one's sample size given values for the other three dimensions. For example, if I were to compute a linear regression for a mediational analysis—I'm trying to be relevant here—I would have two independent variables (the IV and the MedV), I would choose an alpha level of .05, I would assume a power level of 0.80, and I would assume that I would be looking for a medium effect size (based on previous analyses with the same variables). Looking through the table provided by Cohen, I would find that a sample of 67 should be sufficient. However, note that if I were seeking to obtain information for a *small* effect size, the sample size would swell to 481. Consequently, it makes a huge difference what types of assumptions one makes for these analyses. In addition to Cohen's tables in his article (1992) and his book (1988), there are other books that discuss this important issue (e.g., Kraemer & Thiemann, 1987), as well as online applets (e.g., G*Power, 2011; **http://www.psycho.uni-duesseldorf.de/aap/projects/ gpower/**). I would also recommend that interested readers examine two key articles written specifically about power in mediation analyses: MacKinnon et al. (2002) and Fritz and MacKinnon (2007). The essential conclusion of these latter investigations into various ways to compute mediation is that most studies of this type are underpowered (i.e., the sample is too small). In general, I recommend that researchers use samples that are somewhat larger than the "minimum number required" by these sources to give themselves some protection against this criticism.

Distributions of Mediator and Outcome Variables

Tabachnick and Fidell (2001) have written a good chapter on "preparing one's data," and they argue that researchers need to examine their data to determine whether the variables adequately display normal distributions. The key issues are whether the distributions are skewed (i.e., the bulk of the scores are "smushed" against the left side or the right side of the scale) and whether they are kurtotic (i.e., the shape of the "hill" of scores is too flat or too peaked). They provide several equations that can be used to determine skewness and kurtosis, as well as a number of suggested transformations that can be used to normalize non-normal distributions. Severely skewed or kurtotic data can yield biased estimates when one performs statistical operations; that is, regression analyses for mediation or moderation might be "inefficient" or provide erroneous results. Word to the wise: Check your data to see whether they conform to basically normal distributions, and correct them if they do not.

Bivariate Assumptions

Even if you have verified that individual variables exhibit characteristics of a normal distribution, you are not necessarily out of the woods yet. Statisticians have identified a number of problems that can occur when one uses these variables in correlation or regression analyses. I briefly mention two issues of which a researcher should be aware: (1) Is there a linear relationship between the IV and DV? and (2) Are there normally distributed errors? When one computes a linear regression one is testing for a *linear* relationship, a fact that is sometimes lost on the beginning researcher. In practice, nonlinear relationships are infrequently investigated. Examples of nonlinear relationships are quadratic (U-shaped) or cubic (S-shaped) patterns, and these can be probed by including additional terms in the basic regression equation (x^2 and x^3, respectively). See the section on quadratic moderation in Chapter 6 for more information. I believe that researchers should more often investigate whether nonlinear relationships between predictors and outcomes occur in their data, and this can be done by inspecting the pattern of residual versus predicted values (one should see a symmetrical pattern, not a bowed pattern).

The other issue mentioned concerns the distribution of residual errors. Just as with distributions of individual variables, there can also be outliers in the scatterplot of X-by-Y values of a correlation/regression. These outliers, if sufficiently extreme, have the power to significantly distort or bias obtained estimates, and we can identify them because they yield non-normal distributions of residual errors. In particular, if we obtain a normal probability plot of the residuals, we should see a normal distribution of residuals; but if the pattern is bow-shaped or s-shaped, then we may have a problem. These issues typically arise when the base distributions of individual variables are problematic and/or the relationship between them is not solely linear. So the way forward is simple: Make sure that the distributions of your individual variables are reasonably normal, and make sure that the relationships between predictor(s) and the outcome are principally linear.

SUMMARY

We have covered a lot of ground in this chapter. I have related how to compute the regressions necessary to test mediation (using the Baron and Kenny approach); I have laid out a number of examples; I have identified the potential problem of suppressor variables; and I have given the reader considerable information about the mathematical and statistical underpinnings of these regressions. Hopefully this chapter gives you a clear path forward in terms of accurately performing these analyses and drawing valid conclusions from the findings.

FURTHER READING

I would suggest that the key readings to extend your understanding and knowledge in basic mediation analytical techniques would be the following:

Baron, R. M., & Kenny, D. A. (1986). The moderator–mediator variable distinction in social psychological research: Conceptual, strategic, and statistical considerations. *Journal of Personality and Social Psychology, 51,* 1173–1182.

Holmbeck, G. N. (1997). Toward terminological, conceptual, and statistical clarity in the study of mediators and moderators: Examples from the child-clinical and pediatric psychology literatures. *Journal of Consulting and Clinical Psychology, 65,* 599–610.

MacKinnon, D. P. (2008). *Introduction to statistical mediation analysis.* Mahwah, NJ: Erlbaum.

MacKinnon, D. P., Fairchild, A. J., & Fritz, M. S. (2007). Mediation analysis. *Annual Review of Psychology, 58,* 593–614.

IN-CHAPTER EXERCISES

1. *Significant mediation.* If you would like practice in computing basic linear regression-based mediation analyses, go to **www.guilford.com/jose-materials** and download the dataset named "mediation example.sav." This is the first dataset described in this chapter; it concerns three variables from the positive psychology subdiscipline, namely positive life events, gratitude, and happiness.

2. *Experimental mediation.* The chief difference with experimental data, usually, is that the IV is a dichotomous categorical variable, and one can logically place variables into the three slots on the basis of temporal occurrence.

3. *Null mediation.* Again, if you would like to practice conducting mediation, and in this case obtain null mediation (how exciting!), you can download the dataset named "null mediation example.sav" and hopefully obtain the same results that I detailed herein.

4. *Mediation with a suppressor variable.* If you download the dataset named "suppressor mediation example.sav," you can have a go at duplicating the results obtained in this chapter.

ADDITIONAL EXERCISES

1. Examine the following correlation matrix. Obviously, gender is a dichotomous categorical variable (1 = females; 0 = males), and the remainder are continuous variables. These variables were all measured at a single point of measurement (i.e., concurrent), and no variable was manipulated in an experimental fashion. How many and which specific possible mediational

relationships could be tested with this particular group of variables? Assume that a significant relationship must be noted between variables for them to be included in these models. (Bonus point: If we loosen the assumptions to allow for a nonsignificant IV-to-DV relationship, do any more mediation analyses become possible?)

	Happiness	Intelligence	Extraversion	Stress
Gender	.15^{NS}	.03^{NS}	−.23*	.37**
Happiness		.14^{NS}	.34**	−.53***
Intelligence			−.08^{NS}	.05^{NS}
Extraversion				.24*
Stress				

NS, nonsignificant p; *$p < .05$; **$p < .01$; ***$p < .001$.

2. What can we conclude from this result? In this case, Sobel's $z = 2.02$, $p < .05$, beta weights are reported, and coefficients in parentheses were taken from the X, M predicting Y regression.

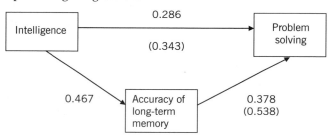

3. Given the standardized regression coefficients depicted in the following figure, identify the values for (a) the direct effect, (b) the indirect effect, (c) the total effect, and (d) the ratio of the indirect/total for standardized regression coefficients.

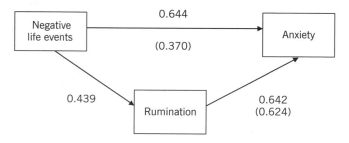

4. Given the following result, compute all of the same values as in question 3, as well as the value of the IV-to-MedV relationship.

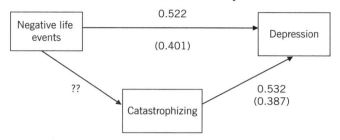

5. Which of these two sets of numbers (variables x and y) has the larger variance?

	x_i	y_i
Subj. 1	1.00	17.00
Subj. 2	6.00	14.00
Subj. 3	7.00	11.00
Subj. 4	2.00	12.00
Subj. 5	4.00	16.00

6. Which area (or areas) in the following figure refer to (a) the total effect, (b) the direct effect, and (c) the indirect effect? Bonus point: What does area d refer to?

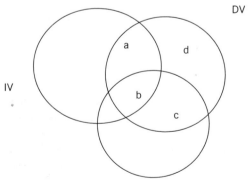

7. In the following mediation example, I have set negative life events (stress) to be the X variable, hope the potential mediating variable, and happiness

the *Y* variable. From the semipartial correlations, work out the sizes of the areas *a*, *b*, and *c*. How much variance in happiness was jointly explained by negative life events and hope?

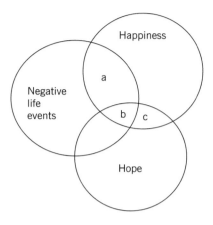

	Unstandardized coefficients		Standardized coefficients			Correlations		
Model	*B*	Std. error	Beta	*t*	Sig.	Zero-order	Partial	Part
1. (Constant)	5.411	.130		41.537	.000			
Negative Life Events	−.387	.097	−.205	−3.976	.000	−.205	−.205	−.205
2. (Constant)	.975	.355		2.748	.006			
Negative Life Events	−.174	.082	−.092	−2.119	.035	−.205	−.111	−.090
Hope	.084	.006	.567	13.108	.000	.585	.568	.556

Note. Dependent variable: Happiness.

8. If you pull up the "mediation problem#8.sav," you will be able to run a mediation analysis on it. The three variables are stressful life events (predictor variable), rumination (mediating variable), and anxiety (outcome variable). Compute Sobel's *z* equation by hand, as well as the 95% asymptotic confidence intervals, and say whether you obtained a significant mediation result or not.

9. Access "experimental mediation problem#9.sav" and determine whether life satisfaction at T2 significantly mediated between the treatment at the outset and gratitude at T3. Report Sobel's *z*-score, as well as both of the 95% symmetrical and asymmetrical CIs. Interpret this result vis-à-vis the result reported previously.

4

Special Topics in Mediation

If you just read through Chapter 3, which describes how to perform basic mediation, you will be primed for this chapter. Here we examine a number of higher order issues and techniques that reflect the efforts of researchers to push the envelope with regard to the technique of mediation. In particular, I cover:

- Model specification: Testing models
- Multiple mediators
- Bootstrapping (resampling)
- Longitudinal mediation models
- Multilevel mediation models
- Categorical mediators and/or outcomes (logistic regression)
- Mediation with quadratic relationships

All of these topics derive from the fact that the variables we often wish to study do not always come in neat three-variable packages that can be optimally examined with multiple regression. The following issues are addressed: How do we choose to specify our model? What do we do if we wish to examine a model with multiple mediators? Can we still do mediation on small samples or datasets with non-normal distributions? What is the best way to examine mediation among variables in a longitudinal dataset? Can one perform mediation analyses in multilevel datasets (i.e., in which data are nested within other data)? And what about the thorny issue of categorical mediators or categorical outcome variables? All of these questions are answered in this chapter and point the way forward to examining mediation in a number of ways other than just with three-variable mediation in multiple regression format.

Before reading further, a gentle warning: As noted at the outset of this book, not all chapters are meant for everyone. The previous chapter on basic mediation was written for the novice student or researcher, and it would likely be too basic and elementary for the experienced researcher. In contrast, this chapter was written for students and researchers who are more knowledgeable and/or experienced but who want to push on to acquire knowledge about the utility of mediation in various platforms such as SEM, bootstrapping, and multilevel modeling (MLM). In fact, and this is where the warning comes into play, if you are unfamiliar with these statistical platforms, then you will find this chapter difficult to read and understand. I have written this chapter with the assumption that those reading it will understand at least the basics of these statistical techniques. I believe that beginners can usefully skim and take away some ideas for future research from this chapter, but if they attempt to perform these analyses before they are familiar with these particular statistical platforms, then errors will be made, and confusion is a distinct possibility. I trust that readers will select material that is appropriate for their interests, level of knowledge, and needs, and in this vein I am recommending that this chapter be read by individuals who know the basics of mediation but want to expand into the cutting-edge areas of SEM, bootstrapping, and MLM.

MODEL SPECIFICATION: TESTING MODELS

I have stated earlier that mediation is the investigation of the correlational (covariance) relationships among three variables. I should probably amend that statement by saying that it is *one* way to examine relationships among three variables. Cohen et al. (2003) have noted that there are at least five ways that one can examine how three variables are related. I think that a short foray into this topic will be helpful, because mediation is a special case of path analysis, and the techniques and procedures inherent in path analysis would lead a researcher to consider several different ways to examine how three variables are related. I think it would be helpful for the typical user to know that he or she is choosing one of several options and, further, to know the basis on which he or she is choosing this option.

Cohen et al. (2003) detailed two model types under the heading of *partial redundancy*. Model A (Figure 4.1) succinctly details a case of having two IVs, a single DV, and an expectation that the two IVs are significantly correlated. If the two IVs are significantly correlated, then the researcher strives to partial out the shared variance (*b*) between them in the process of predicting

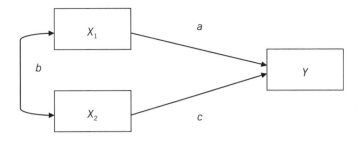

FIGURE 4.1. Model A.

the DV. The discussion in the previous chapter concerning part and partial correlations is very relevant for this type of model. Note that the model does not stipulate a *directional* path between X_1 and X_2, and that is the chief difference between this model and the classic mediational model described in the preceding chapter. Instead of a directional path between the two X variables, in the preceding case we have a directionally unspecified correlation between the two predictor variables. This model is typical and common in multiple regression analyses (see Chapter 1's discussion of additive effects), although regression of this sort does not specifically explore the association that may exist between the two X variables. Model B (Figure 4.2) does this more explicitly.

Model B clearly represents the situation that we are trying to explore with the classic mediational approach. A directional path is stipulated between each pair of variables, flowing from the IVs to the DV. X_1 is considered to be the starting point in the model (the technical term for this variable is *exogenous* variable), and it is seen to have a direct effect on the DV, as well as an indirect effect on the DV through the second IV, X_2.

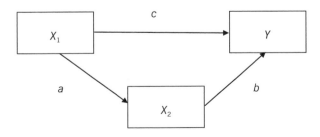

FIGURE 4.2. Model B.

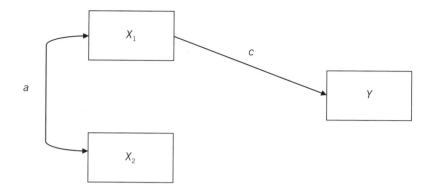

FIGURE 4.3. Model C.

The next three models are considered to be "full redundancy" models because only a single predictor of Y is found in each model. Model C (Figure 4.3) is posited to be an example of a spurious relationship. This pattern can be obtained in the case in which X_2 is a suppressor variable (see Horst, 1941). Cohen et al. (2003) argued that this model demonstrates spuriousness insofar as only X_1 predicts the Y outcome, but X_1 and X_2 are related. If the two IVs share common variance, then one might expect that X_2 would also predict Y, but it does not seem to do so in this model. The effect of X_2 on Y may be suppressed by the presence of the X_1 variable. Model D (Figure 4.4) is considered to be an example of spuriousness, too, for similar reasons.

Finally, we have Model E (Figure 4.5), which is also considered to be an example of full redundancy but not of spuriousness. Cohen et al. (2003) refer to it as demonstrating an "indirect effect," and the astute reader can readily

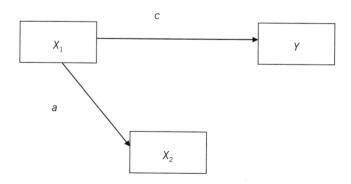

FIGURE 4.4. Model D.

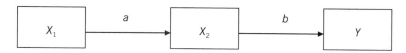

FIGURE 4.5. Model E.

appreciate that it displays the situation of complete mediation of the X_1-to-Y relationship through X_2. One can consider it to be a variation of Model B in that the X_1-to-Y relationship (c) is removed from the model because it is trivial in size. This model can be considered to be a representation of what Baron and Kenny refer to as "perfect mediation."

Three of the five models just described may be obtained through mediational analysis. Model B is the best representation of classic mediation wherein both a significant direct effect and a significant indirect effect are displayed; complete mediation is represented by Model E; and Model D would yield null mediation because it is missing one of the three necessary relationships (i.e., the MedV to the DV path). Models A and C opt not to examine a directional relationship between the two IVs, and in contrast, models B, D, and E all posit a possible indirect relationship from the exogenous X variable to the outcome through a potential mediating variable.

The useful information that I would like the reader to glean from this discussion is that there are a number of different models available to the researcher to consider when she or he is interested in examining the relationships among three variables. Some of these models conform to the classic mediational triangle, and some do not. In particular, one should note that the option of allowing the predictor variables to freely covary (but not to structurally predict one another) is posed by Cohen et al. (2003) as a possible fruitful direction. Mediational analysis will not elucidate this type of model, but multiple regression or path analysis with an SEM program will.

Choice of Model

So how does one come up with a model to test? In the first approach, which is espoused by statisticians (Duncan, 1975; Kenny, 1979), the researcher poses a mediational model from theory, previous findings, or experience. Let us say that I know that the variable of positive life events has been shown to be predictive of happiness. In addition, I have seen, either in my own data or in other researchers' data, that positive events lead to higher levels of gratitude, and that gratitude, in turn, is positively predictive of happiness. I might envisage that these findings constitute pieces of a mediational triangle and consequently propose that gratitude mediates the relationship between positive life events and happiness. This hypothesis would be motivated by my own or other people's findings and would constitute a reasonable and defensible hypothesis. This approach is *deductive* because one proposes a specific hypothesis from theory and then tests it.

A second way, which I have seen students and other people employ, is not deductive; instead, it would be called *inductive*. A researcher of this type would gather data on numerous variables and then sit down to test systematically a large number of possible mediational relationships. The first step would be to find three variables that are significantly correlated with each other. The second step would be to test for significant mediation among them. This approach is inductive because the researcher is consciously attuned to a variety of possibilities in his or her data rather than focusing on one specific possible mechanism. Researchers and statisticians who promote "data mining" (Kantardzic, 2003) would endorse an approach similar to what I just described. If a researcher employs this technique, then he or she should refer to it as "exploratory" and be honest in saying that many possible relationships were examined before any significant relationships were identified. However, it should be noted here that many researchers and statisticians consider this type of inductive approach to be "bad science," primarily because one can capitalize on chance by examining so many relationships; so if you use this approach, be aware of this criticism and limitation. I might also point out that a data mining approach in which one uses the qualifying precondition that all three relationships must be significant might miss some interesting and/or important mediations because, as authors have noted (e.g., MacKinnon, 2008), one can obtain significant mediation in cases in which the initial predictor-to-outcome (or IV-to-DV) relationship is nonsignificant.

Another issue that comes up with regard to testing models—and this is especially relevant for deductive testing—is that a researcher typically examines only a single mediational model for a set of three variables. For example, at the beginning of the preceding chapter, I reported my efforts to determine whether gratitude mediated between positive life events and happiness. I found evidence to say that it served as a significant mediator. And I stopped with that finding. A critic could come along and say "Why did you stop? Why is that particular arrangement of three variables the best one? Why not test alternative models with the same variables?" and after reflection I would have to admit that this irritating and nettlesome critic has a point. Why should I claim that gratitude is the mediator in this case? I might posit a different model; for example, the one in Figure 4.6.

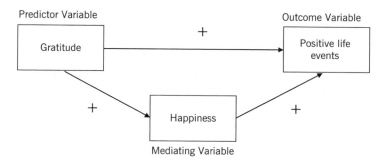

FIGURE 4.6. An alternative ordering of these three variables creates another mediation model.

This model suggests that a sense of gratitude is predictive of a tendency to report higher levels of positive life events. Maybe grateful people just notice more positive events happening around them and to them? Further, happiness is seen to operate here as a mediator between gratitude and positive life events, such that higher gratitude leads to higher happiness and higher happiness leads to reporting higher levels of positive life events. Does this model hold water? Let's test it. When I did, I obtained the result in Figure 4.7. This

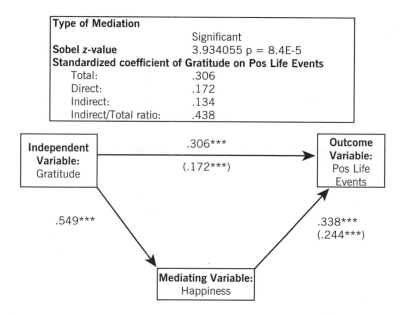

FIGURE 4.7. MedGraph output for the alternative ordering of the three variables.

result also yields significant mediation. What might this result mean? I can tell you that the average researcher is typically able to derive a reasonable hypothesis to fit almost any result, and I am no different. My post-hoc explanation: In this case, people who feel grateful report higher levels of positive life events generally, and this basic relationship can be explained by saying that individuals with high gratefulness levels are happier and that consequently they report higher levels of positive life events. Voila! I came up with a reasonable explanation for an unexpected result. Most clever and motivated researchers are able to produce an explanation after the fact, but we should think long and hard about whether this is good science.

As noted here, this second mediational model seems to yield a significant mediational pattern, too. One might become quite excited about this and say "Bonus: two mediations!" Or a more cynical person might begin to wonder about whether this is an ominous trend. To be specific, how many mediational triangles are possible with any three concurrent variables? The answer is precisely six. You can systematically substitute three variables among these three placements and determine that I am correct. Then you can systematically test each of these six mediational triangles. And what will you find if you do this? I have done precisely this with these three variables (and you can as well, with the dataset provided for Chapter 3), and what I have found is presented in Table 4.1.

The troublesome question that may suggest itself to you, then, is, Which of these six possibilities is the correct one? The somewhat disturbing answer, I conclude, is "all of them." With concurrent data (i.e., data collected at one point in time), it is not possible to determine whether one or several of these models are more valid than others. Baron and Kenny (1986), West and Aiken (1997), and MacKinnon and Dwyer (1993) have tackled this model specifica-

TABLE 4.1. Summary of Systematic Examination of All Six Models Possible with Three Concurrent Variables

IV	MedV	DV	Type of mediation
PLE	Gratitude	Happiness	Significant
PLE	Happiness	Gratitude	Significant
Gratitude	Happiness	PLE	Significant
Gratitude	PLE	Happiness	Significant
Happiness	Gratitude	PLE	Significant
Happiness	PLE	Gratitude	Significant

Note. PLE = positive life events.

tion problem by focusing on the causal and temporal placement of variables in experimental paradigms. In particular, if I set up an experimental study in which I first manipulate levels of positive life events (let's say high, medium, and low levels of positive events), and then later in the study I assess both gratitude and happiness, then I have constrained the temporal order of the variables to some degree (positive life events [PLE] must be the IV), and I have a reasonable avenue for arguing that the effect of PLE on happiness may have been mediated by gratitude. In this particular design, I cannot argue conclusively that gratitude caused higher happiness, because this relationship is not temporally constrained. To clarify these situations, Baron and Kenny (1986) suggested that the researcher manipulate two IVs—one that is presumed to affect the mediator but not the DV, and the other presumed to affect the DV but not the mediator. Although this is a creative solution, it is not always practical. For example, are there positive events that create gratitude but not happiness, and others that create happiness but not gratitude? Perhaps, but I cannot think of any. For a detailed discussion of experimental tests of mediation, see MacKinnon, Fairchild, and Fritz (2007); the article takes up this thorny issue of feedback loops in mediational designs, as well as several other critical issues in this vein.

The point that I am striving to make here is that the researcher should be thoughtful about proposing a particular mediational hypothesis, and if he or she did not utilize an experimental approach, he or she should probably examine several possible alternative models, too. Researchers need to have another tool in their toolbox to clarify which of these six models is likely to be correct. Singular tools for doing precisely this are the obtaining of longitudinal data and the examination of mediation across time. This approach is discussed later in this chapter. Another approach is to conduct an experimental study and order one's variables temporally and causally. This approach was described in the previous chapter, and another example of this approach is discussed under the topic of bootstrapping in this chapter.

Specification Error

The development of path modeling techniques since Sewall Wright's initial paper in 1921 has brought to our awareness the issue of "specification error," which we should discuss in the present context. Duncan (1975) parses the term *specification error* as "using the wrong model." What he and other path modelers are trying to point out is that a researcher's proposed model may or may not fit the data well. Let me give you an example to demonstrate this

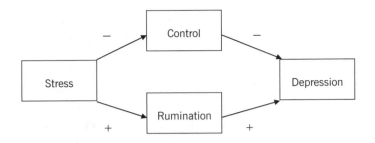

FIGURE 4.8. Hypothesized model: Issues in model specification.

issue. Let us say that a researcher has measured four variables—stress, control, rumination, and depression—and that she proposes the path model in Figure 4.8.

What this model suggests is that stress affects depression through a lessened sense of control and separately through the dynamic of worrying or ruminating about one's problems. The model depicted in the figure is a *hypothetical* model, and we need to find out whether obtained data confirm or disconfirm this proposed model; that is, we are using a deductive approach.

What happens when one tries to fit this proposed model to actual data? As a point of fact, my former student Kirsty Weir has done precisely that (see Weir & Jose, 2008). She collected data from 310 children ages 9–13 years, and she resultantly tried to fit the aforementioned model to the data using the SEM package LISREL 8.54 (Joreskog & Sorbom, 1998). In short, she found that this proposed model did *not* fit the data very well. One might ask, How would one know whether the model fit the data well or not? That is the nub of the matter. LISREL, as well as other well-known and widely used SEM programs such as EQS (Bentler, 2005) and Amos (Arbuckle, 2007), produce model fit indices (i.e., statistical indicators) that allow the user to determine how well the covariance patterns stipulated among the variables in the model conform to the actual patterns found in the data. A thorough discussion of this topic is beyond the scope of this book, but the interested reader may wish to examine Byrne (2009), Hoyle (1995), or Schumacker and Lomax (2004) for further explication of this matter. Suffice it to say, indices such as the RMSEA (root mean square error of approximation) tell the researcher whether he or she has obtained a close fit between the hypothesized model and the data. Values lower than 0.07 are considered to be indicative of good fit (Kline, 2004). My student obtained a ratio of 0.11, and consequently this model was rejected (other model fit indices were poor as well; I am just focusing on one specific index here to simplify the description). In essence, she "misspecified" the model. Using the terminology of Duncan (1975), that model was the "wrong model" for the data that were collected. So what is a researcher to do if he or she obtains feedback that a model is misspecified? The answer: Modify it. Hoyle (1995) discusses the pruning technique, in which one removes or inserts paths in the model in an effort to approximate the actual data covariances, and this approach moves us into the arena of inductive investigation. (Again, there is much to tell about this procedure, but I gloss over these steps in order to arrive at my point.) My former student performed these steps, and she derived the model in Figure 4.9.

This model is of considerable theoretical importance because it is different in a significant and interesting way from the initial proposed model. Specifically, it suggests that rumination might have an effect on depression through a lessened sense of control.

The important point to make in the current discussion is that this model is a *good-fitting model*. We know that it is a good-fitting model because the RMSEA index was 0.04 (and other indices were good to acceptable, as well). Does this tell us that we have the *best* model, that is, the model that explains the covariance patterns to an optimal degree? It probably was, because we tested several theoretically reasonable arrangements of these four variables; however, we did not try out *all* possible models, so it is possible that there is another model that we could try that would fit the data better. We are reasonably confident, however, that we obtained *one* of the best fitting models, if not the best, because we included only significant paths, we deleted nonsignificant paths, and our model fit indices were quite good.

Why is this relevant to a discussion of mediation? Let us reconsider the three-variable mediation that I explored earlier in this chapter. Can we level a charge of "misspecification" against any of those six models that I described?

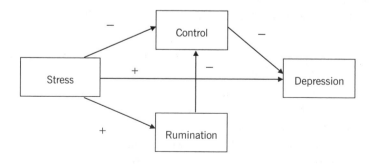

FIGURE 4.9. Empirically supported model based on model specification dataset.

A way to tackle this question is to ask another question: What would various model fit indices, such as the RMSEA, be for these models? If you were to run these models in SEM, you would obtain output saying "model fit is perfect," and the reason for this is that these are all *saturated models*. A saturated model (see Hoyle, 1995) is one in which all possible paths are included in the model and all available degrees of freedom are allocated. In other words, one cannot add another path to the mediational triangle. The model fit was *not* perfect for the two four-variable models presented earlier because they were not saturated; some paths were left out, for example, the direct path between stress and depression in the proposed model. The absence of a single path allows an SEM program to estimate the stipulated paths with a single degree of freedom, and model fit indices are duly computed.

If the mediational triangle does not have a model fit criterion, what *does* it have? As I demonstrated in Table 4.1, we can readjust the placement of variables in the triangle to test six plausible mediational models. What we acquire then is output that tells us whether we have obtained significant or null mediation. Can we use the model specification idea to help us explore these models more fully? The answer to this question is yes.

Is there a way to obtain an unsaturated model? In most tests of mediation, all three paths remain statistically significant, and the researcher will want to retain all of those paths because they explain significant covariance patterns in the obtained data. But in certain cases the basic relationship is reduced to nonsignificance when the mediating variable is included in the equation. That result means that we might be able to delete that path in the model and free up a single degree of freedom to permit model fit indices to be estimated. Let's try it.

> **Helpful Suggestion:** If you access the relevant dataset ("model specification mediation.sav"), you can follow along, not just here but also further along in the chapter when we do some additional analyses.

In the same dataset collected by my former student were three variables that I consider here: rumination, anxiety, and depression. I propose that rumination (excessively mulling over in one's mind one's ineffective efforts to deal with a stressful event) would predict higher depression. Further, I thought that rumination would increase levels of anxiety, which in turn would raise depression levels. In other words, the indirect path from rumination through anxiety to depression is one possible route by which rumination leads to higher depression. If one examines this mediation model first in mul-

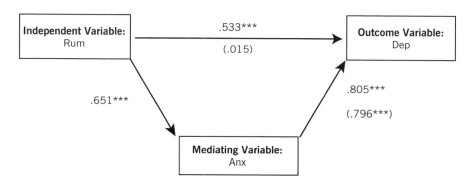

Type of Mediation	Significant	
Sobel z-value	9.177529	p < 0.000001
95% Symmetrical Confidence interval		
Lower	.206	
Upper	.318	
Effect size measures		

Standardized coefficients of Rum on Dep		R² measures (variances)
Total:	.533	.284
Direct:	.015	.000
Indirect:	.518	.284
Indirect to Total ratio:	.972	1.000

Independent Variable: Rum → .533*** / (.015) → Outcome Variable: Dep

.651***

Mediating Variable: Anx

.805*** / (.796***)

FIGURE 4.10. MedGraph output for the model specification example.

tiple regression (see Figure 4.10), one finds that it yields significant mediation and that the indirect effect is large relative to the direct effect.

This type of model is a good candidate for examining what Cohen et al. (2003) refer to as Model E (indirect effect) because the c' pathway is reduced to nonsignificance. Earlier I included the IV-to-DV path (c' when the MedV is included), but when I examined this pruned model in Amos—removing the c' pathway—I found that the model fit indices were excellent: goodness of fit index (GFI) = 1.00; root mean square error of approximation (RMSEA) = 0.0001; comparative fit index (CFI) = 1.00; relative fit index (RFI) = 1.00; Critical N = 10333; standardized root mean square residual (sRMR) = 0.0035; and adjusted goodness of fit index (AGFI) = 0.99 (for an explanation of these additional model fit indices, read Hoyle, 1995). The standardized regression coefficients show that higher rumination predicts higher anxiety and higher anxiety predicts higher depression. The Amos output told me that the size of the indirect path (from rumination to depression) in this pruned model was 0.524, and the same value is obtained by multiplying the *a* and *b* paths (0.651 * 0.805 = 0.524; see Figure 4.11). Although the program does not compute statistical significance for the indirect effect (i.e., no Sobel test), this information can be obtained by asking Amos to perform bootstrapping. This very helpful approach is described later in this chapter. In sum, this result suggests that rumination leads to greater depression through the mechanism of creating anxious symptoms. (As an aside, note that the indirect effect varied slightly from the fully saturated model, 0.518, to the pruned model, 0.524. This will happen only when the *c'* path is reduced to virtually zero.)

What happens if we delete the direct IV-to-DV path for a case in which the direct relationship is still statistically significant when the mediating variable is included? I have performed analyses such as these, and model fit typically is poor and unacceptable, so it is preferable to retain the *c'* path in these models.

What did we learn here? Most mediational triangles that yield significant or null mediation constitute good-fitting models insofar as no path can be deleted; however, some triangles that yield significant mediation (i.e., ones in which the direct effect is reduced to near zero after the MedV is included in the model) can be pruned further to produce good-fitting models in the SEM sense. Does one have to learn SEM to perform mediational analyses? My view is that most users can use multiple regression to derive useful and informative output concerning the relationships among three variables. Classic regression-based mediational approaches are a good place to begin, but a researcher who wants to acquire a more powerful analytical tool should acquire the capacity to perform SEM analyses as well. I sidestepped into a

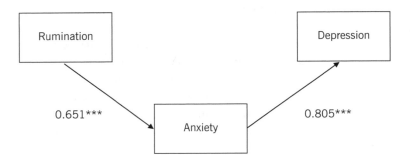

FIGURE 4.11. Obtained statistical output when the basic relationship was deleted.

discussion of path modeling and specification of models to show the interested reader that mediation is a special case of path modeling and that a knowledge of path modeling can be helpful in more fully explicating the relationships among the three variables. Certainly, in the case of trying to examine more than three variables (as in the previous four-variable case), then the logical next step is SEM.

KNOWLEDGE BOX. Another Area of Potential Confusion: Implications for Naming Different Types of Mediation Results

In my career I learned how to do mediation with multiple regression first, and then I went on to learn SEM. I found over time that I naturally wanted to apply SEM concepts to regression-based mediation, and the previous section in this chapter reflects this tendency. I realize that there are certain differences between these two analytical approaches (i.e., regression uses ordinary least squares computations and SEM uses maximum likelihood computations as a default), and these differences mean that we should be careful in drawing parallels between the two approaches. However, I think that there are more commonalities than differences, and the issue of how we label different results and how we determine whether significant mediation has occurred should be talked about and clarified because this constitutes another area of confusion for researchers who use mediation.

In the first case I think that there are several implications of all of this for how we name different types of mediational results. Baron and Kenny's (1986) article has led many people to think about placing their obtained result into one of three identified "boxes": (1) null mediation, (2) significant mediation, or (3) perfect mediation. I have already highlighted the issue raised by Baron and Kenny and others that perfect mediation is not reasonably obtainable in the social sciences, and for this reason I would suggest that we set this "box" aside in these disciplines.

Against this backdrop, we have SEM terminology, which is somewhat at variance with Baron and Kenny's usage. Here's an example: How many and what type of mediational patterns exist in the following model?

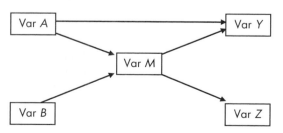

Most people who do path modeling would say that the relationship between *A* and *Y* is *partially mediated* by *M* because there is a direct path from *A* to *Y*, as well as an indirect path through *M*. In contrast, the path from *B* to *Z* is *fully mediated* by *M*. The direct path from *B* to *Z* presumably was removed because it was weak (i.e., nonsignificant). Thus all of the variance that *B* explains in *Z* must be mediated by *M*. The reason I am highlighting this issue is that, if one examined variables *A*, *M*, and *Y* in a regression format, the result would presumably be called "significant mediation," and if one examined variables *B*, *M*, and *Z* in the same format, the result would also be called "significant mediation." Hmm, this would not be as informative as what one obtains in SEM.

(Incidentally, for those of you interested in the answer to the question I posed before: There are four mediations: *A*, *M*, and *Y*; *A*, *M*, and *Z*; *B*, *M*, and *Y*; and *B*, *M*, and *Z*. The first mediation is "partial," and the other three would be considered "full.")

Most people I've talked to about this matter want to leave it alone and just use the term *significant mediation* in regression-based mediation if and only if Sobel's *z*-test yields a significant result. Reluctantly I concur with this stance, because when one is using only multiple linear regression, one cannot conclusively determine whether full mediation has been obtained without pruning the model (i.e., using SEM).

The material in this box is written entirely out of an effort to clarify a major confusion that exists between regression-based mediation and SEM-based mediation. The bottom line of all of this for you is this: (1) in regression-based mediation, use the categories of either *null* or *significant* mediation; and (2) in SEM-based mediation, open your mind to the possibilities of *null*, *partial*, and *full* mediation and construct or prune your models to allow for all of these possibilities. I strongly recommend that you acquire skills in SEM, if you do not have these already, so that you can take your knowledge of mediation to another level. I officially end my lecture/sermon at this point, and we can return to our usual programming. . . .

MULTIPLE MEDIATORS

I have seen that many beginning users become fixated on the Baron and Kenny analytical approach and, due to a lack of familiarity with other techniques, focus exclusively on testing mediation with three variables in the multiple regression format. This approach is fine in and of itself, but as you can tell from the preceding discussion about model specification, an exclusive reliance on a specific temporal order of three variables may be limiting in terms of exploring other possible ways in which the variables are related to each other. As I am fond of saying, "the world has more than three variables operating within it."

One complication that the beginning user may wish to consider is the possibility that more than one mediator may intervene between the predictor and the outcome. Let us consider the following case. I believe that collectivism should be negatively predictive of depressive symptoms due to previous research on this topic. A question that has occurred to me is whether a person who expresses a high level of collectivism uses differential amounts of different types of coping strategies and whether these in turn may predict the outcome measure of depressive symptoms. At the outset I did not know whether I would obtain full mediation or partial mediation, but I proposed partial mediation to be on the conservative side (Figure 4.12; note the direct path from collectivism to depression, as well as the four indirect paths).

The logic of this model is similar to that of the classic mediational triad. In other words, I expected that the predictor variable (collectivism) would exert an impact on the outcome variable (depressive symptoms) through the indirect paths passing through all or some of the four coping strategies. I have also depicted a direct path from the predictor to the outcome because I am proposing to find partial mediation, but of course I may find that this is incorrect. But how does one test this model?

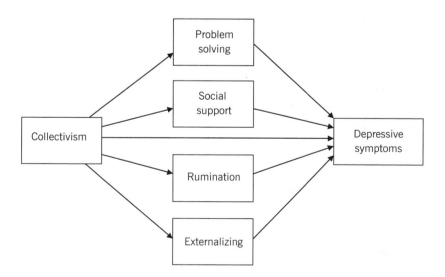

FIGURE 4.12. Hypothesized multiple mediator model.

Instead of three-variable regression, I would be inclined to use SEM (Amos in this case) to conduct this analysis because: (1) I know how to conduct SEM; (2) it is easy to perform in this format; and (3) it is the best way to estimate the various parameters simultaneously. I realize that some readers of this chapter have not acquired this very important analytical skill (yet), so I will keep it simple.

> **Helpful Suggestion:** You can find a copy of the dataset ("multiple mediators.sav") and if you know an SEM program, like Amos in the present case, you can run the same analyses and hopefully obtain the same outputs.

In this case I have self-report data taken from one point in time (i.e., not longitudinal) from 159 Maori (the indigenous cultural group here in New Zealand) adolescents. The first thing that I would like to check is whether my predictor variable predicts my outcome, so I compute a basic regression, and I find that it does, $\beta = -.25$, $p < .001$. I now know that I have something to mediate. (Although, strictly speaking, a significant IV-to-DV relationship is not absolutely necessary.) Then I go into Amos and set up the model as presented earlier. It is a fully saturated model because all possible paths are represented, and I also estimate covariances among the four potential mediators because I expect that they will be significantly related to each other. I run the model asking for output that includes modification indices, direct and indirect effects, standardized regression coefficients, and squared multiple correlations, because these turn out to be handy in pruning and interpreting the model.

Because I have no degrees of freedom (it is a just-identified model), I resultantly obtained no modification indices, but I did obtain estimates. Table 4.2 presents the unstandardized regression weights. Table 4.2 tells me that I likely have two paths that could be deleted (i.e., collectivism to externalization and problem-solving to depressive symptoms). All other paths are statistically significant and should probably remain. Further, two covariances proved to be nonsignificant (see Table 4.3). So what I do is remove these four nonsignificant estimated parameters. Figure 4.13 (on page 112) depicts the results I obtained.

As you can see, mediation occurred between collectivism and depressive symptoms through rumination and social support, but not through problem solving or externalization. I have another choice now: (1) I can stop with this model and discuss what I found, or (2) I can delete problem solving and

TABLE 4.2. Amos Output (Unstandardized Regression Coefficients) for the Multiple Mediator Model

Regression Weights: (Group number 1 – Default model)

		Estimate	S.E.	C.R.	p	Label
ruminate	← col	.465	.195	2.382	.017	
socsup	← col	.408	.143	2.855	.004	
probsolv	← col	.303	.110	2.740	.006	
extern	← col	−.027	.114	−.232	.817	
depression	← col	−.071	.019	−3.770	***	
depression	← ruminate	.036	.010	3.749	***	
depression	← socsup	−.029	.010	−2.767	.006	
depression	← probsolv	−.013	.015	−.835	.404	
depression	← extern	.072	.014	4.983	***	

TABLE 4.3. Amos Output (Covariances) for the Multiple Mediator Model: Group Number 1—Default Model

			Estimate	S.E.	C.R.	p	Label
e1	↔	e2	11.704	4.110	2.848	.004	
e2	↔	e3	6.329	2.321	2.727	.006	
e3	↔	e4	1.305	1.816	.719	.472	
e1	↔	e3	18.811	3.439	5.470	***	
e2	↔	e4	.048	2.344	.020	.984	
e1	↔	e4	18.004	3.509	5.130	***	

externalization and streamline the mediational model. Just for the sake of completeness, I performed the latter option, and Figure 4.14 (on page 113) depicts what I obtained (coefficients are betas and all are statistically significant).

What we have is a case of partial mediation in which two mediators explain a portion of the basic relationship between collectivism and depressive symptoms. This result is actually very interesting from a research point of view because the model contains a maladaptive mediator (rumination) and an adaptive mediator (social support), and their opposite tendencies are evidenced in the direction of the beta weights. To be specific, collectivism was found to be a positive predictor of rumination, which makes sense as other research has shown that people from interdependent societies report higher levels of these constructs than people from independent societies do (Jose & Schurer, 2010). Rumination, in turn, and as expected, was a strong predictor of depressive symptoms. On the other side, we see that collectivism was associated with social support, which makes sense given that collectivist individuals tend to support each other more (Triandis, 1995). Social support, in turn, and as expected, was a negative predictor of depressive symptoms. And the direct path between collectivism and depressive symptoms proved to be a negative relationship; individuals who reported that they consider themselves to be a part of groups or collectives reported lower depressive symptoms.

Let us now examine the statistical outputs generated by Amos. First of all, this is a fully saturated model, so it does not yield any model fit indices. However, all estimated parameters are statistically significant, so it would

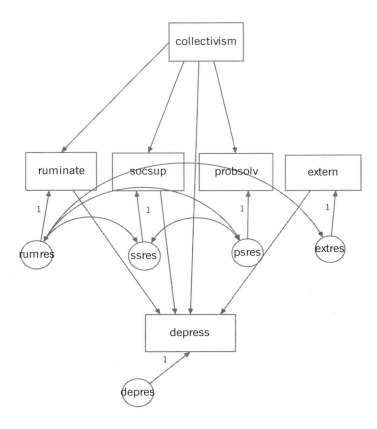

FIGURE 4.13. Amos model after deletion of nonsignificant paths from collectivism to externalization and problem solving to depression.

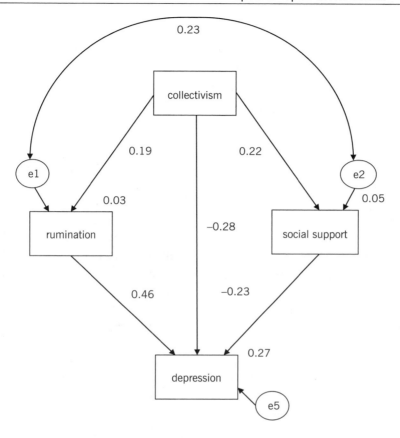

FIGURE 4.14. Obtained Amos output for the simplified multiple mediator model.

seem to be a reasonably good model. Second, the betas and *B*'s are listed in the output and can also be depicted on the graphical model. Third, and most relevant, Amos will generate total, direct, and indirect effects if you ask it to, and these are helpful in the interpretation of the model. It does not generate Sobel's *z*-value to help the user determine whether mediation is significant or not (LISREL, in contrast, tells the user whether indirect effects are significant or not, which is helpful), but the user can surmise whether mediation has occurred by examining the pathways and noting the significance of estimated paths. Let us look at the three pathways. The standardized total effect of collectivism (Col) to depression (Dep) is listed as −0.249, and this will need to be partitioned across the three pathways. The standardized indirect effect of Col to Dep is listed as 0.034 (which includes the two indirect paths), and the standardized direct effect of Col on Dep is −0.283. To compute the size of the two indirect paths, you can use the "multiplicative rule": specifically, you multiply the beta between CoI and the mediator with the beta between the mediator and Dep. In the first case, compute $0.19 \times 0.46 = 0.087$, and in the second case compute $0.22 \times -0.23 = -0.051$. If you add these two values, you get 0.036, which is close to the total indirect effect (0.034). Add that to the direct effect (−0.283), and you get −0.249, which is the total effect. In this way, the researcher can identify exactly how large each component is and calculate the ratios of the three pathways. In this case it is clear that the direct path is much larger than either of the two indirect paths. To learn whether both indirect paths are statistically significant, you can use bootstrapping, which is described in the next section.

Hopefully, this example shows the user the virtues of using SEM in identifying mediation, because one can include more than three variables. I will not go into it, but you can have multiple IVs and multiple DVs as well. The mediation pathways become more tortuous and complicated in these situations, but again models with more variables probably approximate reality closer than models with three variables only. For a further example of multiple mediators, read the following section on bootstrapping, as it is possible to include more than one mediator at a time in this type of analysis, too.

BOOTSTRAPPING (RESAMPLING)

The estimation of the indirect effect in mediation is typically performed in multiple regression, which uses the OLS (ordinary least squares) algorithm, and this approach is deemed appropriate for most cases by most researchers. However, concern has been raised from various quarters (see MacKinnon et al., 2004; Preacher & Hayes, 2004, 2005, 2008; Shrout & Bolger, 2002) that in cases of small sample sizes the OLS approach seems to provide biased estimates. The chief problem with OLS is that even if the raw variables are normally distributed, the product of these variables usually results in non-normally distributed parameters. The Sobel test, which is an example of a Wald test, is based on the assumption of normally distributed parameters, so it is biased in the general case, and particularly so with small samples. As a solution, bootstrapping has been increasingly used in recent years as a method to overcome this problem (Chernick, 1999). In essence, the distributional requirements that I noted near the end of Chapter 3 become less important when one uses bootstrapping; one can analyze small samples (within reason) and have more confidence in a bootstrapped result than in an OLS result. Not to put too fine a point on it, the prevailing opinion in the literature at this juncture is *always use bootstrapping for mediation analyses.*

It is necessary to define bootstrapping at this juncture. A program that bootstraps a particular dataset randomly selects individuals from the original dataset and thereby constructs a new dataset composed of the same number of individuals. The specified statistical analyses are performed on this new dataset, and the outputs are stored. The bootstrap function performs the dataset construction and data analysis steps multiple times (usually in the high hundreds or low thousands), and, by combining all of the generated outputs, more reliable estimates of the analytical outputs are obtained. I now discuss several ways in which one can perform bootstrapped mediation.

Bootstrapping with Macros

Kris Preacher presents several bootstrapping macros on his website (**http://people.ku.edu/~preacher/sobel/sobel.htm**) and provides other additional useful information as well. As of this writing, he offers these services (see **http://www.quantpsy.org/sobel/sobel.htm**):

1. SPSS and SAS bootstrapping macros for simple mediation.
2. SPSS and SAS bootstrapping macros for multiple mediators.
3. SPSS bootstrapping macro for moderated mediation.

The first macros compute the basic IV–MedV–DV mediational analysis that was covered in Chapter 3. However, some people want to examine the possibility of multiple mediators (as noted in the previous section of this chapter), and the second set of macros would allow this type of analysis. And finally, the last macro would allow a researcher to examine how mediation varies across levels of a moderator variable (e.g., gender, SES, or ethnicity).

I present an example of bootstrapped simple mediation using Preacher's method here. The dataset is derived from a small sample ($N = 88$) of adolescents who yielded self-report assessments of stressful event intensity, rumination, and anxiety. The hypothesis I want to test is whether rumination significantly mediates the stress-to-anxiety relationship, that is, whether stress might trigger higher levels of rumination, which in turn might lead to higher levels of anxiety. Figure 4.15 depicts the predicted model.

The first step is to prepare your dataset and have it active in SPSS. Second, download the macro from Preacher's website. I find that the script macro is the easier macro to use. When you go to Preacher's website, you will have a choice between the SPSS syntax and the SPSS script. Download (i.e.,

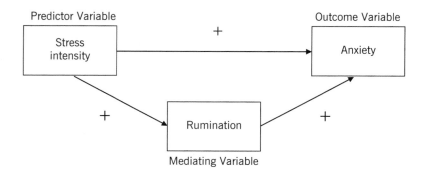

FIGURE 4.15. Predicted mediation model for the Preacher macro bootstrapping example.

save) the script macro. Do not modify the script at all, and in that window click on MACRO and then RUN. This will pull up an SPSS menu in which you can specify your IV, MedV, and DV (and any covariates). You will want to specify 1000 or more resamplings, and then hit OKAY. Then you wait . . . because it will take a while to run through its computations. What it is doing is performing the 1000 (or whatever you specified) regressions and storing the results. Do not lose patience and shut down SPSS; otherwise, you will lose that particular run. At the bottom right of the SPSS window you will see "Running MATRIX," which means that the resampling analyses are occurring. When that message ends, you will find that the bootstrapping output has been created. Table 4.4 presents the output that I obtained from my particular bootstrapping run.

Statistical significance was obtained here. The Z and the Sig(two) under "Indirect Effect" refers to Sobel's z-value—4.326—and the associated significance level is p less than .0001 (two-tailed). The Sobel result, as well, is in agreement with the 99% confidence intervals: .04 to .19. What these results indicate is that there was a significant mediational result in this bootstrapping analysis. An examination of the lines under "Direct and Total Effects" is instructive in terms of understanding what happened here. First of all, the first three lines indicate that the three preconditions of Baron and Kenny were met: All three relationships were statistically significant. The fourth line tells us that the basic relationship (stress predicting anxiety) diminished in strength when the mediating variable, rumination, was included in the equation: The coefficient went from .19 in the first line to .08 in this line.

A common question that I receive is whether bootstrapping yields different estimates than linear regression. If truth be told, sometimes it does

TABLE 4.4. Output from Preacher and Hayes's Bootstrapping for Simple Mediation

VARIABLES In SIMPLE MEDIATION MODEL
Y   cmatot
X   emuch
M   ruminate

DESCRIPTIVES STATISTICS And PEARSON CORRELATIONS

	Mean	SD	cmatot	emuch	ruminate
cmatot	8.7727	5.6847	1.0000	.5510	.6729
emuch	15.3750	16.0969	.5510	1.0000	.6049
ruminate	21.0568	7.5038	.6729	.6049	1.0000

SAMPLE SIZE
   88

DIRECT And TOTAL EFFECTS

	Coeff	s.e.	t	Sig(two)
b(YX)	.1946	.0318	6.1231	.0000
b(MX)	.2820	.0400	7.0454	.0000
b(YM.X)	.4057	.0740	5.4808	.0000
b(YX.M)	.0802	.0345	2.3234	.0225

INDIRECT EFFECT And SIGNIFICANCE USING NORMAL DISTRIBUTION

	Value	s.e.	LL 95 CI	UL 95 CI	Z	Sig(two)
Effect	.1144	.0264	.0626	.16	4.3260	.0000

BOOTSTRAP RESULTS For INDIRECT EFFECT

	Data	Mean	s.e.	LL 95 CI	UL 95 CI	LL 99 CI	UL 99 CI
Effect	.1144	.1124	.0287	.0595	.1734	.0420	.1900

NUMBER OF BOOTSTRAP RESAMPLES
   2000

not. When I analyzed the same dataset with the customary linear regression technique, I obtained a Sobel z-value of 4.330, which is very close to the 4.326 obtained through bootstrapping. The literature on bootstrapping suggests that values can diverge more dramatically when distributions are highly skewed and/or the samples are significantly smaller than 100 individuals. The variables I examined here did not vary from normality in any extreme way, and the sample was large, so I did not expect much difference between these two estimates. Results may vary more when you use skewed or kurtotic variables and/or small samples. It is good to use bootstrapping if your sample violates either power or distributional assumptions, and you might check

)le regression analyses as well. If they agreed, then
s, and if they did not agree, I would be inclined to
:esult. As noted earlier, some researchers and statis-
:xclusive reliance on bootstrapping analyses, which
typical OLS regression-based approach altogether. I
nion; however, be aware that with large samples with
ariables, the two methods will yield almost identical
resu..

Bootstrapping in Amos

I now present three bootstrapping examples in Amos. The first one I considered earlier in the section "Model Specification": Does anxiety mediate
between rumination and depression? (Pull up the "model specification medi-
ation.sav" dataset and follow along, if you wish.) If you review this model,
you will remember that I removed the c' path, obtained a good-fitting path
model, and found that the size of the indirect effect was large. When you
run a path model in Amos and request INDIRECT, DIRECT, AND TOTAL
EFFECTS in the OUTPUT page, you will obtain information about the size
of these effects, but Amos will *not* tell you whether these indirect effects
are statistically significant or not. If you opt for bootstrapping, however, this
information is generated.

First of all, you cannot perform bootstrapping in Amos with missing values in your dataset. Either delete cases for which missing values were obtained
or perform a multiple imputation or expectation-maximization (EM) imputation to prepare your dataset. (The present dataset has no missing values.)

Second, you need to draw the fully saturated model presented earlier in
the Graphics work area in Amos (see Figure 4.16). Include all three paths in
the model; that is, do *not* remove the c' path from the IV to the DV. Third,
under VIEW, and then ANALYSIS PROPERTIES, choose the OUTPUT page
and select INDIRECT, DIRECT, AND TOTAL EFFECTS. Third, choose the
BOOTSTRAP page, and then tick three options: PERFORM BOOTSTRAP,
BIAS-CORRECTED CONFIDENCE INTERVALS, and MONTE CARLO. You
may also wish to modify the default number of bootstrapped iterations. I
often choose 1000, but choose a number that is appropriate for your own
dataset. Now you are ready to run the program, so go ahead and CALCU-
LATE ESTIMATES.

The program will burp and lurch for a period of time, and hopefully
generate usable output. Once you open up the output, follow these steps *precisely*. First, in the upper left-hand box, click on and open up ESTIMATES.

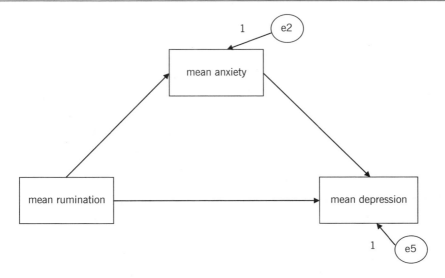

FIGURE 4.16. Amos mediation model: First Amos bootstrapping example.

It will provide three options, but you want to open up MATRICES. It will contain six boxes referring to unstandardized and standardized total, direct, and indirect effects. We focus on the standardized indirect effect. Click on that heading. This box tells me that the size of the indirect effect was 0.518, which we already knew from a previous analysis. However, you will notice that some options previously in gray in the middle left-hand box now appear in black. This means that you can click on those to obtain more information. When I clicked on BOOTSTRAP STANDARD ERROR, the output told me that it was 0.046. This useful information tells me that the estimate of the indirect effect, namely 0.518, varies to some small extent. When I clicked on BIAS-CORRECTED PERCENTILE METHOD, I obtained the results of the bootstrapped analysis. I learned that the lower bound of the 95% confidence interval was 0.451 and the upper bound was 0.602. Because I know that a CI that does NOT include zero is statistically significant, I now have useful information about the significance of the indirect effect: namely, it is significant. The last box is somewhat redundant, but it reports the *p*-value for this indirect effect, and in this case it was reported as .0011, supporting the conclusion I derived from the CI. (Note that you may obtain slightly different estimates from those reported here because each bootstrapping analysis will yield slightly different results from all others.)

Taken together, this information is a very useful addition to the previous run. The bootstrapped CI and associated *p*-value is requisite statistical out-

nen one reports an indirect effect in journals, books, and reports these
. In the present case, I would report that the size of the standardized
indirect effect, 0.518 (standard error = 0.05), was found to be highly statistically significant, 95% CI = 0.45–0.60, p = .0011, supporting the prediction
that rumination led to higher depression through the mechanism of increasing anxiety levels.

Notice that the size of the indirect effect did not vary between the earlier
analysis and the present bootstrapped analysis. Bootstrapping makes a difference in terms of estimating the size of the standard error: Usually bootstrapping yields a smaller standard error, which results in larger Sobel z-scores
and CIs that are boosted by a small constant. That effect was not noticeable
in this case because the data were normally distributed and the sample was
reasonably large (N = 195). But I present a case in which it does make a difference shortly.

Second Amos Bootstrapping Example

I would like to briefly report the results of the bootstrapping analysis on
the second example I have presented in this chapter: "Do coping strategies mediate between collectivism and depression?" (Pull up the "multiple
mediators.sav" dataset, and see whether you can replicate what I report here.)
When I performed the bootstrapping analysis on the model presented in Figure 4.14 (only two mediators: rumination and social support), I obtained the
results shown in Table 4.5.

This result tells me that I obtained a nonsignificant mediation result,
which was disappointing, but I was not terminally deterred. When I performed the multiplicative action on these two indirect paths, I found that the
path through rumination yielded a standardized indirect path of 0.09 and
that the one through social support was –0.05. Could it be that one of these
was significant and the other one was not? After running these two models
separately, I obtained the results shown in Table 4.6.

**TABLE 4.5. Combined Indirect Effect for
the Simplified Multiple Mediation Model**

Standardized indirect effect	.034
Standard error	.04
Lower bound of 95% CI	–.025
Upper bound of 95% CI	.108
p-value of CI	.368

TABLE 4.6. Bootstrapped Estimates of Separate Indirect Effects for the Two Mediating Variables in the Simplified Multiple Mediator Model

	Rumination indirect effect	Social support indirect effect
Standardized indirect effect	.076	−.028
Standard error	.035	.021
Lower bound of 95% CI	.026	−.07
Upper bound of 95% CI	.143	−.002
p-value of CI	.014	.066

Thus it seems that the indirect path through rumination was robust and significant, whereas the indirect path through social support was weak and only marginally significant. I would be inclined to conclude, then, that I obtained evidence of an indirect path only through rumination between collectivism and depression.

Third Amos Bootstrapping Example: Experimental Data

I would like to revisit the experimental mediation example presented in the previous chapter: The dataset was "experimental mediation example.sav," and you can retrieve it again in order to do another analysis on it. Previously I performed regular regression analyses and found significant mediation: Sobel's z = 2.003, p = .045, standardized indirect effect = 0.1122, and the asymmetrical 95% CI interval was 0.02 to 1.41. The question I wish to pose here is: Would we obtain a similar result if we bootstrapped the indirect effect?

If you subject the data to an Amos bootstrapped analysis, you should obtain the outputs shown in Table 4.7. You will notice that the standardized indirect effect is identical to what was obtained in the preceding chapter: 0.1122. The bootstrapping function, however, reduces the size of the standard error, so the CI is narrower and slightly elevated. The obtained p-value of the latter CI, p = .005, is considerably smaller than the one obtained before. As you can see, bootstrapping yielded stronger confirmation of the predicted relationship. None of the variables in this dataset was acutely kurtotic or skewed (although gratitude was moderately skewed); rather, the chief problem was that the sample was very small. Bootstrapping, as you can see, seems to be effective in overcoming this flaw. Authors (MacKinnon et al., 2004; Preacher & Hayes, 2008) have argued that resampling or bootstrapping is a better way to estimate the indirect effect than relying on ordinary least

TABLE 4.7. Amos Output for the Bootstrapped Experimental Mediation Example

	Treatment	T2Grat
Standardized indirect effects (group number 1—default model)		
T2Grat	.0000	.0000
T3LifeSat	.1122	.0000
Standardized indirect effects: Standard errors (group number 1—default model)		
T2Grat	.0000	.0000
T3LifeSat	.0532	.0000
Standardized indirect effects: Lower bounds (BC) (group number 1—default model)		
T2Grat	.0000	.0000
T3LifeSat	.0436	.0000
Standardized indirect effects: Upper bounds (BC) (group number 1—default model)		
T2Grat	.0000	.0000
T3LifeSat	.2247	.0000
Standardized indirect effects: Two-tailed significance (BC) (group number 1—default model)		
T2Grat	. . .	. . .
T3LifeSat	.0051	. . .

squares (OLS) or maximum likelihood (ML) estimation in regression-based analyses. Unfortunately, not all statistics programs make resampling techniques easily available, so users are restricted to programs such as SAS, LISREL, Mplus, EQS, Amos, and other SEM programs. But the day will soon be here when it is widely available and commonly used.

Monte Carlo Estimation of the Indirect Effect

One of the chief drawbacks to conducting bootstrapping for mediation is that it is necessary to have one of these statistical platforms to conduct this computer-intensive technique. (And sometimes it can be fussy to set up the analysis.) A good alternative to bootstrapping is the Monte Carlo test of the indirect effect (see **http://www.quantpsy.org/medmc/medmc.htm**), because the computer-intensive work is done behind the scenes with Rweb. This website by James Selig and Kris Preacher (2008) allows a researcher to enter the same inputs as in Preacher's Sobel website (namely, a, b, s_a, and s_b), and an R program in the background runs a Monte Carlo estimation of the indirect effect based on the provided values. If you run a Monte Carlo analysis of the experimental data presented earlier (the third bootstrapping example), you will obtain the results shown in Table 4.8 contextualized with the OLS and bootstrapping results (all with 95th-percentile CIs).

There is general agreement that the indirect effect is sufficiently large that we can reject the null hypothesis. Several differences are notable among these three estimations. We can see that the OLS lower limit is very near zero. The bootstrapped range is narrower and slightly elevated in values, and the Monte Carlo result, in comparison, yields a larger lower limit than the other two; and the upper limit, similarly, is considerably larger than the other two. At present, researchers do not have a definitive guide as to which of these various approaches is the most valid and reliable, but I suspect that someone will do this work soon and provide us with some much-needed advice on this topic.

But wait—there is one more technique in this vein to consider. Yuan and MacKinnon (2009) describe the nonparametric method of Bayesian estimation of indirect effects in mediation. Still in its infancy with regard to mediation, this method can and should be considered alongside bootstrapping and Monte Carlo approaches, as they all attempt to correct for the bias created by multiplying a by b.

These various examples should motivate the interested researcher to experiment among these cutting-edge methods and ultimately to use one (or several) of these techniques to obtain definitive evidence for or against predicted mediational patterns. Although learning how to perform bootstrapping, Monte Carlo, or Bayesian estimation requires some effort and time, I have found that these analyses become easier, faster, and more satisfying the

TABLE 4.8. Comparison of Confidence Intervals Estimated by Ordinary Least Squares (Regression), Bootstrapping, and Monte Carlo Analyses

	Lower limit	Upper limit
OLS	.02	1.41
Bootstrapping	.04	0.23
Monte Carlo	.24	3.10

more I do them. Regression-based mediation analyses are rapidly becoming obsolete and are being replaced by bootstrapped analyses, and other promising techniques are visible over the horizon, so I would urge readers to learn about and acquire these techniques so that they can obtain the most veridical and accurate mediation results.

LONGITUDINAL MEDIATION MODELS

The preceding chapter laid out the "how to" of mediation with concurrent data, and in the course of judging the validity of findings based on that type of data, I commented that longitudinal data yield much better mediation results. That is all very well and good, but how does one extract better mediation results from longitudinal data? This section lays out an approach in both regression and SEM formats to answer this question.

Many excellent books have been written on the issue of analyzing longitudinal data with an eye toward mediation, and I mention only three in this regard: *Modeling Longitudinal and Multilevel Data* by Little, Schnabel, and Baumert (2000); *Longitudinal Data Analysis* by Bijleveld and van der Kamp (1998); and *Applied Longitudinal Data Analysis* by Singer and Willett (2003). Much can be gleaned from reading these sources. In this section, I primarily focus on suggestions made by MacKinnon (2008) regarding the construction of models and identification of indirect effects.

Causality in Mediation

One of the thorniest issues in mediation concerns the assumption of causality. Based on the findings of the first mediational example presented in the previous chapter, it is very tempting for me to claim that positive life events *cause* greater gratitude and that greater gratitude, in turn, *causes* greater happiness. This "story" makes sense in a theoretical way, and many researchers would be inclined to interpret the findings in such a way. However, there is a significant problem with doing so, and that problem is that these data (like many datasets that researchers examine) were concurrent, not longitudinal.

Concurrent data are collected at one point in time, and although it is technically the case that the PLE data were collected before the gratitude data and that they, in turn, were collected before the happiness data, the passage of time would be mere minutes. I would find it very hard to argue that the occurrence of positive events (which were recollected as having happened to the person over a period of 2 months previously) *caused* the person to feel more gratitude and that more gratitude *caused* the person to feel happier. No, these are concurrent data, and it is a stretch to argue that one variable caused another.

When researchers draw the mediational triangle, they draw arrows with single heads that point in a certain direction. These arrows suggest causal relations between variables, and the unsuspecting reader may fall into the habit of thinking of these relationships as causal. Instead, with concurrent data they are correlational relationships, and as you have been told many times, "correlation is not causality." What, in fact, mediation tells us with concurrent data is the amount of shared and unique variance among three variables (see the discussion on using Venn diagrams in Chapter 3). Causal relations may or may not be lurking among these correlations.

Mediation through Time

Cole and Maxwell (2003; Maxwell & Cole, 2007) have written two excellent papers on the issue of examining mediation with longitudinal data (see also Selig & Preacher, 2009). These authors make several very important points, and one of their chief conclusions is that concurrent mediation results are unlikely to provide good estimates of mediation across time because one must make certain assumptions about stationarity (i.e., causal parameters are constant for all time intervals of equal duration), stability (i.e., the unchanging nature of a variable's mean over time), and equilibrium (i.e., similarity of patterns of variance and covariance over time). They argue that most concurrent mediation results are either overestimations or underestimations of longitudinal path coefficients.

Another issue that they raised concerns the amount of time between times of measurement. The researcher must time the moments of assessment in order to capture mediation that may be occurring. If the times of measurement are too close, they may miss a slow-developing mediational relationship; if the times of measurement are too far apart, they may miss a more transient relationship. This issue comes up in one of my later examples. Clearly, a concurrent mediation analysis does not capture the effects of the passage of time on one's variables, so it would seem to be ill-suited for capturing mediation across time.

Should we then give up computing concurrent mediation? I think that the message that Cole and Maxwell and others are attempting to convey is that one should be wary of claiming too much from concurrent mediation. I would argue that identifying patterns of shared and unique variance among concurrent variables can have value if the researcher does not exaggerate the importance of the results for longitudinal applications.

I now expand on this point by examining the similarities and differences between mediation with concurrent and with longitudinal data. In the present case, as an example, I explore the relationships among the three variables of perceived control, anxiety, and depression. These variables were obtained from a large sample of young adolescents ($N = 926$, ages = 11–16 years) at two points in time separated by 4 months. This subject variable study (described in Jose & Weir, in press) did not manipulate any variable, that is, it was not an experiment or a quasi-experiment. The mediational pattern to be tested in this dataset was whether anxious symptoms would mediate the relationship between perceived control and depressive symptoms. The basic relationship was proposed to be negative in sign: Someone higher in perceived control was expected to report lower depressive symptoms. Further, higher perceived control was expected to predict lower anxiety, which in turn would lead to lower depression. In other words, we predicted that at least a portion of the basic relationship would be explained by examining the indirect path from perceived control through anxiety to depression.

> **Helpful Suggestion:** Again, if you would like to analyze these data side by side with your reading of the book, access the dataset "two wave longitudinal mediation.sav."

The proposed model and the obtained zero-order correlations are presented in Figure 4.17.

Cross-Sectional Mediation Analysis

As a first step in testing this hypothesis, I conducted the suggested mediational analysis only on Time 1 variables, and I found that anxiety operated as a significant mediator, Sobel's $z = -14.43$, $SE = 0.02$, $p < .0001$, direct $= -0.346$, indirect $= -0.290$, ratio = 46%. Similar results were obtained for the concurrent mediation analysis on the Time 2 data: Sobel's $z = -15.54$, $SE = 0.02$, $p < .0001$, direct $= -0.392$, indirect $= -0.302$, ratio = 44%.

It is always a satisfying feeling when the obtained results support the hypothesis. So, can I conclude from these results that perceived control causes lessened anxiety, which, in turn, leads to lower depression? If you

Proposed mediational model

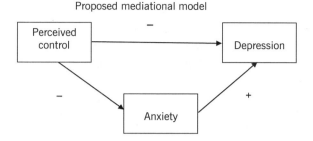

Zero-order correlations at Times 1 and 2

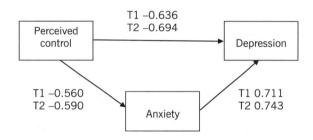

FIGURE 4.17. Proposed longitudinal mediational model and zero-order correlations among the variables at the two times of measurement.

have been paying attention to what I have written before (and I certainly hope that you have been), you will know that the answer is "well, maybe" or something equally equivocal. I would take these concurrent results as suggestive, but we need to examine the longitudinal relationships to say something more definitive in terms of causality over time.

Longitudinal Mediation with Multiple Regression

MacKinnon (2008), in my view, offers an authoritative and helpful view about how to conduct longitudinal mediation, so I relate some of his key points about this method here. The first issue that he notes is the existence of an enduring controversy in methodology and statistics concerning whether one should examine "difference scores" or "analysis of covariance relationships." In the first case, one can subtract Time 2 (T2) scores from Time 1 (T1) scores and analyze the resulting relationships; or, in the second case, one can covary T1 variables from T2 variables and then analyze the relationships. As many readers will know, difference scores have been noted to be unreliable (Cronbach & Furby, 1970), and for this reason many researchers avoid this technique. Rogosa (1988) has shown, however, that change scores are reliable under conditions in which test–retest correlations of variables between time points fall below .50. MacKinnon argues that change scores can be safely used if one's dataset conforms to that precondition. In the present dataset, the stability coefficients for the three variables in turn were found to be .65, .73, and .75, respectively. Due to these relatively high stability coefficients, one would be inclined to use the latter method, shown subsequently. (However, just for comparison I analyzed change score versions of these variables and obtained this result: Sobel's $z = -8.06$, $SE = 0.01$, $p < .0001$, direct = -0.276, indirect = -0.128, ratio = 32%.)

The second consideration is whether one has two- or three-wave data. MacKinnon shows in his book that one can analyze longitudinal mediation with either, but because I have only two-wave data in the present case, that is what I show you first. Following is what MacKinnon refers to as the *autoregressive mediation model* (see Figure 4.18), and it is arguably the simplest place to begin.

> **Helpful Suggestion:** The name of the dataset involved in these analyses is "two wave longitudinal mediation.sav" in case you wish to follow along with the analyses reported next.

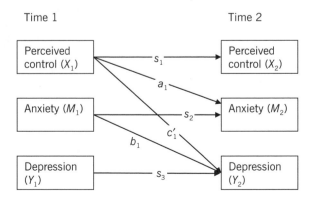

FIGURE 4.18. Statistical notation of longitudinal mediation paths (two-wave model).

As you will recall from Chapter 3, a refers to the relationship between the IV and the MedV, and it does so here between the IV at T1 and the MedV at T2 (a_1). Further, b refers to the MedV-to-DV relationship, and it does so here over time (b_1). And last, c' refers to the changed c relationship, IV to DV, when the MedV is included in the equation or model and we have a direct effect across time (c'_1). These longitudinal estimates map onto the a, b, and c' terms discussed in the previous chapter, and we determine the size of the indirect effect in relation to the direct effect just as we did with the concurrent mediation analysis. Thus researchers will seek to identify the estimate of the longitudinal mediation effect (a_1b_1).

In order to show you how to obtain this numerical information, I must first relate the two critical equations that we use:

$$Y_2 = i_1 + c'_1X_1 + b_1M_1 + s_1Y_1 + e_1 \qquad (4.1)$$

$$M_2 = i_2 + a_1X_1 + s_2M_1 + e_2 \qquad (4.2)$$

To translate these equations within the context of the present variables, we conduct these two regressions (see Table 4.9 and Figure 4.19):

1. depT2 predicted by controlT1, anxietyT1, and depT1.
2. anxietyT2 predicted by controlT1 and anxietyT1.

Although the coefficients suggest support for the hypothesized mediation, one must determine through a Sobel z-score computation whether the mediation effect is statistically significant. To compute this value for the longitudinal mediation (a_1b_1), we should use the following equation (which you have previously seen in Chapter 3):

$$z\text{-value} = \frac{a*b}{\text{SQRT}(b^{2}*s_a^2 + a^{2}*s_b^2)} \qquad (4.3)$$

Taking the relevant values from these outputs (see Table 4.9), one obtains:

$$z\text{-value} = \frac{-.051*.195}{\text{SQRT}(.195^{2}*.019^2 + -.051^{2}*.041^2)} = \frac{-.009945}{.0042543} = 2.33$$

Looking up 2.33 in a z-score table, we find that $p = .02$, yielding a statistically significant mediation result. In addition, taking into account the value for c' (the direct effect), we can determine the values presented in Table 4.10.

TABLE 4.9. Statistical Output from the Two Regressions Performed to Conduct a Longitudinal Mediation Analysis

Model	Unstandardized coefficients		Standardized coefficients		
	B	Std. error	Beta	t	Sig.
1. (Constant)	5.207	1.399		3.722	.000
controlT1	−.051	.019	−.073	−2.699	.007
anxietyT1	.743	.029	.689	25.490	.000

Note. Dependent variable: anxietyT2.

Model	Unstandardized coefficients		Standardized coefficients		
	B	Std. error	Beta	t	Sig.
1. (Constant)	6.493	1.808		3.591	.000
controlT1	−.075	.024	−.088	−3.086	.002
anxietyT1	.195	.041	.147	4.735	.000
depressT1	.610	.035	.586	17.563	.000

Note. Dependent variable: depressT2.

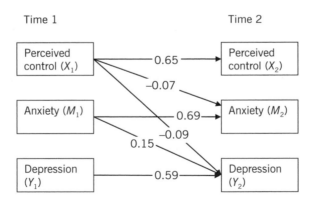

FIGURE 4.19. Statistical outputs (betas) of longitudinal mediation paths obtained from regression analyses.

TABLE 4.10. Computation of Effect Sizes in Two-Wave Longitudinal Mediation Example

	Unstandardized coefficients	Standardized coefficients
a_1	−.051	−.073
b_1	.195	.147
c'	−.075	−.088
Direct effect		.0875
Indirect effect		.0107
Total effect		.0982
Ratio (indirect/total)		11%

Taking all of these findings together, I am now able to argue that my hypothesis that I would obtain longitudinal mediation with this two-wave longitudinal dataset was supported. About one-tenth of the total effect of control at T1 on depression at T2 can be said to be mediated by anxiety. Conceptually, this result suggests that an adolescent at T1 who reports high perceived control experiences lessened anxiety over the next 4 months, and, as a result, he or she reports lessened depressive symptoms at T2.

A variant on this basic model has been suggested by Cole and Maxwell (2003) and described by MacKinnon (2008). Figure 4.20 depicts this model (it is called an *analysis of covariance model* with longitudinal and concurrent mediation), and we can see that it examines longitudinal mediation (a_1b_1),

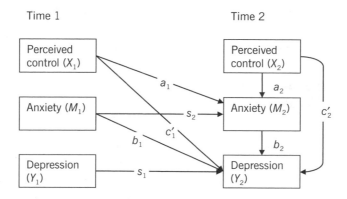

FIGURE 4.20. Statistical notation for Cole and Maxwell's analysis of covariance model with longitudinal and concurrent mediation.

as well as concurrent mediation, at T2 (a_2b_2). The chief advantage is that one can examine both mediations in relation to each other, but a potential drawback to this model is that obtained coefficients may manifest opposite signs from what is expected. For example, when I analyzed my dataset with this model, the a_1 coefficient was positive and the b_1 coefficient was negative. Care must be taken that one is obtaining veridical estimates of these relationships.

Longitudinal Mediation with SEM

MacKinnon (2008) describes three different longitudinal models—all with three waves of data—that can be used in SEM to identify longitudinal mediation. I first present the *three-wave autoregressive model*. The dataset in this case involves three time points separated by 3 months each for a sample of 364 adults. It is the same dataset that was used for the first mediation described in the last chapter, although I have replaced the variable titled "positive life events" with "savoring by counting blessings." The reason I made this replacement is relevant to the current discussion of longitudinal mediation, so I explain this result further. When I conducted a three-wave longitudinal mediation analysis on the three variables used in that initial concurrent mediation, namely PLE, gratitude, and happiness, I found *null longitudinal mediation*. The reason I did not obtain significant longitudinal mediation was that the paths from PLE to gratitude from T1 to T2 and T2 to T3 were nonsignificant. In retrospect, I was not surprised by this outcome, because we have seen in other related research that the impact of daily positive (or negative) life events is transitory. In essence, this result tells me that although PLE had an impact on concurrent data (i.e., the concurrent mediation), that variable did not manifest a lasting effect across 3 months. Now let us examine a situation in which I did identify significant longitudinal mediation.

> **Helpful Suggestion:** The name of the dataset in this case is "three wave longitudinal mediation.sav."

We were interested in whether people who savored the positive events in their lives at one point in time would be more likely to report greater gratitude 3 months later and, further, whether those individuals who felt more gratitude would go on to report greater happiness 3 months later. Figure 4.21 depicts this longitudinal mediation hypothesis with the associated designations of critical estimates.

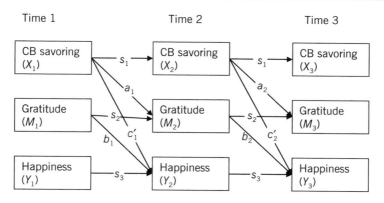

Time 1   Time 2   Time 3

FIGURE 4.21. Statistical notation of longitudinal mediation paths (three-wave model).

The equations that describe this model are:

$$X_2 = s_1 X_1 \tag{4.4}$$

$$M_2 = a_1 X_1 + s_2 M_1 \tag{4.5}$$

$$Y_2 = c'_1 X_1 + b_1 M_1 + s_3 Y_1 \tag{4.6}$$

$$X_3 = s_1 X_2 \tag{4.7}$$

$$M_3 = a_2 X_2 + s_2 M_2 \tag{4.8}$$

$$Y_3 = c'_2 X_2 + b_2 M_2 + s_3 Y_2 \tag{4.9}$$

As before, one can determine the two indirect effects, $a_1 b_1$ and $a_2 b_2$, by identifying the appropriate B's and standard errors from the output and computing Sobel's formula. See Table 4.11 for relevant values taken from the output.

In the case of the first longitudinal mediation (T1–T2), here is the Sobel computation:

$$z\text{-value} = \frac{.146 * .026}{\text{SQRT}(.026^2 * .071^2 + .146^2 * .010^2)} = \frac{.003796}{.0023536} = 1.61$$

Although the mediation pattern was in the right direction, the z-score of 1.61, $p = .11$, indicates that this was a nonsignificant result. Let us consider the second longitudinal mediation, T2–T3:

$$z\text{-value} = \frac{.192*.029}{SQRT(.029^2*.075^2 + .192^2*.010^2)} = \frac{.005568}{.002901} = 1.92$$

Similar to the first mediation, the second mediation result proved to be statistically nonsignificant, $z = 1.92$, $p = .055$, but the result almost reached statistical significance. The pattern is fairly consistent between the two mediations, but in the second one slightly more of the total effect is mediated. Thus, on the basis of these results, I am *not* able to argue that gratitude mediated between counting blessings (CB), a savoring strategy, and resultant happiness for either period of time.

You may have noted that so far we have only tested the two 3-month periods separately. What about the entire 6-month period? To do this, I inserted an arrow between CB savoring at T1 to happiness at T3 to assess the direct effect and reran the model with the intent to assess $a_1 b_2$, the indirect effect between T1 and T3. Table 4.12 shows the values I obtained. The Sobel z-score was found to be .97, $p = .33$, so I did not obtain support for the media-

TABLE 4.11. Computation of Effect Sizes for the Two Time Spans (T1 to T2 and T2 to T3) Separately in Three-Wave Longitudinal Mediation Example

		Unstandardized coefficient	Standard error	Standardized coefficient
T1 to T2	a_1	.146	.071	.082
	b_1	.026	.010	.109
	c'_1	.004	.016	.010
T2 to T3	a_2	.192	.075	.104
	b_2	.029	.010	.117
	c'_2	.006	.016	.013
T1 to T2	Direct effect			.010
	Indirect effect			.009
	Total effect			.019
	Ratio (indirect/total)			47%
T2 to T3	Direct effect			.013
	Indirect effect			.012
	Total effect			.025
	Ratio (indirect/total)			48%

TABLE 4.12. Computation of Effect Sizes for the T1 to T3 Time Span in Three-Wave Longitudinal Mediation Example

	Unstandardized coefficient	Standard error	Standardized coefficient
a_1	.078	.076	.041
b_2	.032	.011	.128
c'_3	−.019	.017	−.042
Direct effect			.042
Indirect effect			.005
Total effect			.047
Ratio (indirect/total)			11%

tion hypothesis over the 6-month period from T1 to T3. It is not uncommon for longitudinal mediation to *not* be found over certain time periods, because variables may have effects on other variables over a different time cycle than the one measured (e.g., days as opposed to months). As I noted earlier for my original mediation hypothesis (with PLE as the X variable), I did not find significant mediation over 3 months, probably because transient events at one point in time are unlikely to exert an influence on psychological outcomes 3 months later. The three mediations examined here suggest that a shorter span of time, perhaps a month, would be better than a longer span of time for these particular variables.

Other, More Complicated Longitudinal Mediation Models

In his book, MacKinnon (2008) began his discussion with the autoregressive model noted previously, and then explicated two other, more complicated versions. As with the two-wave data I showed you, we can examine longitudinal *and* concurrent (termed *contemporaneous* by MacKinnon, 2008) mediations in a single model. I do not lay out this model with a figure, but you would insert paths from X to M and from M to Y at T2 and also at T3. And last, MacKinnon (2008) properly notes that the models described thus far are all focused on a particular X-to-M-to-Y relationship. What about mediations other than the one anticipated? In terms of the last analysis reported previously, is it possible that gratitude at T1 leads to greater happiness at T2, which in turn leads to greater use of CB savoring? It is possible, and MacKinnon's (2008) third model is designed to examine all possible mediations over time. For the sake of space, I do not describe these last two models, as worthy as they are; but I would recommend that interested readers examine these other methods in MacKinnon (2008). And in this same vein, a useful document by Gallagher, Howard, and Stump (2010) might be perused as well.

MULTILEVEL MEDIATION MODELS

A statistical approach increasingly being used in the social sciences is MLM, because it can analyze relationships between variables across different types of nesting. Nesting? Yes, there are two basic types of nesting that researchers can intentionally (or unintentionally) inflict on the data that they collect.

The first type is *nesting within levels of groups*. A doctoral student wishes to examine the relationships between IQ scores and grades that children earn in different subjects, so she collects data from 100 grade-school children drawn from five different schools (numbers of children from each school were 5, 12, 15, 25, and 43). She individually administers a standard intelligence scale, such as the Wechsler Intelligence Scale for Children, to all of the children, because different schools typically employ different measures of IQ. She also obtains information about grades that each child obtained over the previous year. Once she has entered all of her data into the computer, she goes ahead and computes correlations between IQ and grades obtained in four different subjects: mathematics, English, art, and social studies. She presents these findings to her advisor, and her advisor begins to ask some questions about how the data were collected, whether data obtained from different schools were comparable, and so forth. The student admits that she noticed that the grades from some schools were uniformly high or low compared with the mean. The advisor points out that two of these schools emphasize mathematics and that one school is known for its English language enrichment program. In short, the student treated all of the data as identical regardless of the school from which they were obtained, when in fact there may have been differences among the schools that influenced the grades (and possibly the IQ scores). The student then dutifully creates a number of scales that reflect the relative strengths and weaknesses of these schools in terms of their curricula in math, English, art, and social studies. Then she covaries these variables out of the correlations that she computed and presents the new findings to her advisor. Her advisor examines the results and acknowledges that this approach is an improvement, but then the advisor says, "Were the covariates statistically significant?" The student looks at the outputs and says yes. The advisor goes on: "Shouldn't we be interested precisely in the relationship that you just took out?" They agree that differences among schools that affect grades, IQ scores, and relationships between grades and IQ scores might be very interesting to look at, but they are not sure about how to proceed with the analyses. One school contributed 43 children, and another school contributed only 5; if they merely correlate "strength of English curriculum" with English grades, then they will have only five values for the first variable, and numbers of children in the five schools will vary considerably. They instinctively recognize that this would be a poor way to proceed, but they are unaware of any alternative.

This is where MLM can be very helpful. The conundrum just described has bedeviled educational psychology for quite some time, and consequently two scholars by the names of Bryk and Raudenbush (1992) decided to solve the problem by employing MLM to analyze data such as these (see Bryk, Raudenbush, & Congdon, 1996; Raudenbush & Bryk, 2002; Raudenbush, Bryk, & Congdon, 2000, 2004; Raudenbush & Sampson, 1999). They wrote a series of papers and devised a statistics program named HLM (hierarchical linear modeling) in the late 1980s and early 1990s to describe and resolve this type of problem. Other statistics programs have had an MLM subcomponent for a number of years, such as SAS, and SPSS has recently added this capability, so it is possible to find programs other than HLM that perform these types of analyses, but it is probably fair to say that the Raudenbush and Bryk program is the most commonly used MLM program.

I first need to describe how one sets up the data before I can explain how mediation can be examined with HLM. In the preceding example, a dataset, termed the Level 1 dataset, is created in which each individual is represented by one line of data each and the scores from the IQ test plus the various grades are recorded for each person. There will be 100 lines in this dataset. The second dataset, termed the Level 2 dataset, represents the schools; thus there will be five lines, one for each school, in this dataset. Any characteristic of the schools that the researcher would like to include would be listed here, for example, ranking in terms of academic excellence in particular subjects, how much state money is spent per pupil, teacher–pupil ratio, and so forth. What the HLM program can do is examine (1) relationships among Level 1 variables (e.g., Does IQ predict math grades?); (2) relationships between Level 1 and Level 2 variables (e.g., Do the schools that promote excellence in English language skills have students who receive higher grades in English?); and (3) whether any Level 2 variables moderate relationships between two Level 1 variables (e.g., Do schools that promote excellence in academic performance have students that evidence a stronger relationship between IQ scores and grades?). Obviously, this program is very powerful in what it can do, and unfortunately I cannot discuss all of its merits here. (I discuss the third capability in Chapter 6, when I discuss special topics in moderation.) Now I focus on the first capability, which lends itself to analyses of mediation.

You may have forgotten by now that I began this section by saying that MLM addresses two types of nesting. I have laid out one (individuals nested within groups), but let me go on to describe the second so that I can give an example of mediation. The second type of nesting is referred to as "measures within persons," which is not as clear as it should be, in my opinion. What this type of nesting refers to is longitudinal measurements, in the sense that repeated measures are taken and that they are "located" within individuals. Let me hasten to give you an example.

I conducted a study in 2011 in which I obtained daily diary data from 110 university students for three variables. This diary method is an example of nesting of measures within persons, because I asked each individual to fill out a questionnaire (three questions for each of these three variables) once a day for 14 days. The Level 1 dataset had 14 lines for each individual, 1 line for each day, and the Level 2 dataset had 110 lines, 1 line for each individual. The Level 1 variables were those that we repeatedly measured (i.e., stressful events, rumination, and unhappiness), and the Level 2 variables were those that did not change over time (i.e., gender, age, major, and ethnicity).

In this particular analysis of the data, I wished to determine whether rumination might have mediated between the presumed IV of negative events and the presumed DV of unhappiness, all Level 1 variables. Here is an important point to understand: Although we have longitudinal data here, the analysis that we use is like an analysis with concurrent data; there is no way to determine which variable causes any other variable because they are collapsed across the 14 days. In essence, HLM will combine the 14 data points for the Level 1 variables, and the computed regressions between and among Level 1 variables are analogous to Pearson correlations among concurrent variables taken at one point in time.

HLM computes analyses that are essentially regressions (Bickel, 2007), and because of that constraint, one can compute an analysis with only a single DV. (This approach sets it apart from SEM, which allows for multiple DVs.) The other important fact to keep in mind is that only Level 1 variables can be DVs. You might have a Level 2 variable that you would like to predict with other Level 2 variables or even a Level 1 variable, but that is incompatible with the logic of HLM. Level 2 variables tend to be unchanging variables, such as demographic or state variables (i.e., moderators), so by their very nature they should not be considered to be outcomes. For example, it would not make any sense for me to predict gender (a Level 2 variable) from happiness (a Level 1 variable). On the other hand, it *would* make sense to predict happiness levels from gender.

So let us move on to my example. What I have in Level 1 are three variables—stressful events, rumination, and unhappiness—that I think are related. In fact, I think that they might affect each other in a mediational fashion: I predicted that negative everyday life event intensity would lead to greater rumination and that rumination, in turn, would lead to greater unhappiness. This proposal can be seen as a mediational hypothesis, and that is precisely what I examine in the present dataset.

Kenny, Korchmaros, and Bolger's (2003) Method

So how do we do the analyses? Unfortunately, we cannot just run a couple of regressions (as with linear regression on concurrent data) and input the statistical outputs into a graphing program and obtain a result. The chief problem is that when we examine the relationships between three variables all residing at Level 1 (as is true in the present case), causal effects can all be random rather than fixed. ("Fixed" refers to effects involving variables that are stable, such as gender, which is located at Level 2, whereas "random" refers to effects that involve variables that can vary over a continuous scale, such as freely varying Level 1 variables such as unhappiness.) Kenny, Korchmaros, and Bolger (2003) and MacKinnon (2008) have proposed somewhat similar ways to cope with this particular type of analysis, and I present the latter author's proposal in the present context because it is the easiest to follow.

> *Helpful Suggestion:* The multilevel dataset analyzed in the present case is titled "Random effects mediation in MLM.sav," which is saved in SPSS format. Be aware that Mplus prefers .dat files, so I have also saved the same dataset as "Random_effects_mediation_in_MLM.dat." Mplus does not like dataset names with blanks (hence the awkward underlines), and it does not cope with .dat files with variable names in the first line. On this second point, I removed the variable names before saving, and I simply related particular columns to the appropriate names of the variables in the Mplus syntax (see subsequent discussion).

The critical issue is that one must include a covariance between a and b in the computation of Sobel's formula to account for random effects, and most multilevel programs are not set up to generate this statistical output readily. However, as MacKinnon (2008) has shown, the Mplus program is able to generate this information without a great deal of difficulty. In this example,

I have used the Mplus syntax stipulated on p. 269 in MacKinnon's book (see also Appendix A for this Mplus syntax). In contrast to what I said previously concerning the need with HLM to set up two distinct datasets (Level 1 for repeating variables such as stressful events and Level 2 for the stable variables such as gender), in the present case we need only one dataset. The dataset should be set up as in Table 4.13.

In my dataset, as noted in Table 4.13, I had 1,540 lines, 14 days × 110 subjects. The Mplus syntax computes c' (x predicts y), a (x predicts m), and b (m predicts y), and generates coefficients and variances necessary for the computation of the indirect effect. Table 4.14 is the Mplus syntax that I used.

Table 4.15 presents the outputs from Mplus that I obtained (values underlined are used in subsequent computations). A critical bit of statistical information is the covariance between a and b (referred to in Table 4.15 as the "Between level A WITH B estimate"), which was –.001 in my Mplus output, and it is referred to as "cov(ab)" in Table 4.16. These values are inserted into the following equation provided by MacKinnon on p. 213 of his book to get the variance of ab across the individuals. Note that the two values s_b^2 and s_a^2 are used just as they are; one does not need to square them.

$$z = \frac{ab + \text{cov}(ab)}{\text{SQRT } [a^2 s_b^2 + b^2 s_a^2 + s_b^2 s_a^2 + 2ab^*\text{cov}(ab) + \text{cov}(ab)^2]} \qquad (4.10)$$

$$z = \frac{.160 + -.001}{\text{SQRT } [.490^2 *.005 + .327^2 *.004 + .005 *.004 + 2(.160)*(-.001) + -.001^2]}$$

$$z = \frac{.159}{\text{SQRT } [.240 *.005 + .1069 *.004 + .00002 + 2(-.00016) + .000001]}$$

$$z = \frac{.159}{\text{SQRT } [.001201 + .0004277 + .00002 - .00032 + .000001]}$$

$$z = \frac{.159}{[\text{SQRT } .0013297]} = \frac{.159}{.03647} = 4.36, p < .0001$$

Computations of the asymmetric 95% confidence limits are presented in Table 4.17. Thus, since the CI does not include the value of zero, these results suggest that in our 1 – 1 – 1 mediation model, the mediated effect of negative events to rumination to unhappiness significantly differs across the individuals in the study (i.e., there is significant variability in the indirect effect).

TABLE 4.13. Depiction of How the Level 1 Dataset Should Be Set Up for HLM Analyses

Subjid	Day	Neg. events (x)	Rumination (m)	Unhappiness (y)
1	1	7	3	4
1	2	2	4	6
1	3	2	3	2
1	4	1	3	5
1	5	0	2	3
1	6	2	3	4
	and so forth down to the 14th day			
2	1	3	1	3
2	2	5	2	5
2	3	3	2	4
2	4	4	3	4
2	5	4	2	5

TABLE 4.14. Mplus Syntax for Analyzing for Mediation in a Multilevel Dataset

```
title:
  Diary data (2003)
  data:
  file=[path]/[name of dataset];
  variable:
  names=subjid day x m y;
  usevariables=x m y;
  cluster=subjid;
  within = x;
  analysis:
  type=twolevel random;
  algorithm = integration;
  ghfiml = on;
  model:
  %within%
  cprime | y on x;
  a | m on x;
  b | y on m;
  %between%
  a with b;
  output:
  sampstat tech1 tech3 tech8;
```

TABLE 4.15. Output from Mplus for Analysis of Mediation in a Multilevel Dataset

MODEL RESULTS

	Estimate	S.E.	Est./S.E.	Two-Tailed P-Value
Within Level				
Residual Variances				
M	3.996	0.219	18.256	0.000
Y	5.413	0.299	18.083	0.000
Between Level				
A WITH				
B	−0.001	0.001	−0.379	0.705
Means				
M	−0.027	0.226	−0.120	0.904
Y	2.787	0.298	9.352	0.000
CPRIME	0.557	0.028	20.168	0.000
A	0.490	0.018	27.397	0.000
B	0.327	0.037	8.849	0.000
Variances				
M	0.278	0.235	1.183	0.237
Y	0.520	0.271	1.921	0.055
CPRIME	0.005	0.002	2.128	0.033
A	0.004	0.001	3.222	0.001
B	0.005	0.005	1.091	0.275

TABLE 4.16. Identification of the B's, Variances, and Covariance from Mplus Output

	Unstandardized coefficients	Variances
a	.490 (a)	.004 (s_a^2)
b	.327 (b)	.005 (s_b^2)
ab	.490*.327 = .160	
cov(ab) = −.001		

TABLE 4.17. Calculation of the Asymmetrical 95% Confidence Interval for the Multilevel Modeling Mediation Example

	Estimate of indirect effect	±	(Asym. 95% CI coefficient	×	Standard error)
Lower limit	.159	–	(1.62	×	.0365)
	.159	–		.0591	
	.100				
Upper limit	.159	+	(2.25	×	.0365)
	.159	+		.0821	
	.241				

The average estimated mediated effect is often of interest in 1 – 1 – 1 models. The mediated effect is the product of the 'average estimated a' by the 'average estimated b' coefficients plus the covariance between a and b (see the numerator in Equation 4.11). These values are inserted into the following equation provided by MacKinnon on p. 213 of his book *with the addition in the denominator of the variance of the covariance of a and b (Var(cov(ab))*. Also, in the formula below, the standard error of the mean of a (.018) and the standard error of the mean of b (.037) are used in the formula. The formula also uses the covariance between these means of a and b (–.0001, which is not shown in the output above but is included in the tech 3 Mplus output) and the variance of this covariance between the means of a and b (.001, listed as the SE of the A WITH B term in the Mplus output).

$$z = \frac{ab + cov(ab)}{SQRT\ [a^2 s_b^2 + b^2 s_a^2 + s_b^2 s_a^2 + 2ab^*cov(ab) + cov(ab)^2 + Var(cov(ab))]} \quad (4.11)$$

$$z = \frac{.160 + -.001}{SQRT\ [.490^2{}^*.037^2 + .327^2{}^*.018^2 + .037^2{}^*.018^2 + 2(.490)(.327)^*(-.0001) + (-.0001)^2 + .001^2]}$$

$$z = \frac{.159}{[SQRT\ .00033]} = \frac{.159}{.0183} = 8.69, p < .0001, \text{Normal Theory LCL} = .123, \text{UCL} = .196$$

Bauer, Preacher, and Gil's (2006) Method

In addition to the methods suggested by Kenny et al. (2003) and MacKinnon (2008), we also should consider a method proposed by Bauer, Preacher, and Gil (2006). Before we review this method, note that Bauer et al.'s method can handle models such as the 2–1–1 model, in which the IV comes from Level 2 and the MedV and DV come from Level 1. These require special treatment, so if your particular multilevel mediation model is not of the 1–1–1 type, then you will need to do some additional reading.

I wanted first to determine that these three Level 1 variables were significantly and positively related to each other, so I performed three separate regressions in HLM (see Table 4.18). And yes, it seems that they are.

The next step is to use the suggested method proposed by Bauer et al. (2006), and I suggest that you read their article and then visit Bauer's website, which includes instruction manuals for three different statistical platforms (SAS, SPSS, and HLM): **http://www.unc.edu/~dbauer/publications.html**. The instructions tell you how to perform a series of data conversion steps, and although it will not be entirely clear what you are doing in any given step, if you do them correctly, you should end up with a valid and interpretable result. I used the SPSS platform, and after going through the various steps, I obtained 16 specific bits of statistical output that I then put into their Excel macro (downloadable from the website). I obtained the following result.

The random indirect effect was estimated to be 0.97 (SE = 0.33), and the random total effect was estimated to be 2.09 (SE = 0.68). The 95% confidence interval was found to be 0.79 to 1.18, SE = 0.06. Two conclusions can be obtained here: (1) The proposed mediation was found to be statistically significant and (2) the size of the indirect effect was almost half of the total effect. I know that the proposed mediational pattern was statistically supported because the confidence interval did *not* encompass the value of zero. And one can conclude that the indirect effect explained about half of the total effect because both estimated effects are scaled on the same metric. These

TABLE 4.18. HLM Statistical Output for the Three Associations among the Three Level 1 Variables: Multilevel Analyses for Hypothesis 1—Level 1 Variables Predicting Each Other

Predictor variable	Predicted variable	Slope coefficient	Standard error	Significance (p-value)	Intercept coefficient	Standard error	Sig.
Positive events	Savoring	2.49	.08	.001	7.11	.11	.001
Positive events	Happy mood	0.78	.03	.001	3.33	.07	.001
Savoring	Happy mood	0.23	.01	.001	3.35	.06	.001

findings are reported by Jose, Lim, and Bryant (2012), so you can read about them within theoretical context and in greater detail if you like.

I conclude this section by mentioning in passing that Bauer et al.'s (2006) approach is extendable to the examination of moderated mediation, that is, one could ask whether the present mediational result would vary by gender, age, or some other stable moderating variable. I do not take the time and space to go through an example of this powerful and interesting technique, but it is a natural next step to take after one has obtained basic mediation with multilevel data. One last suggestion: Preacher, Zyphur, and Zhang (2010) have proposed the possibility of using SEM to examine multilevel mediation, and this is a very provocative article because it suggests that SEM can be used to analyze a multitude of different types of multilevel mediation models. Just before, I showed you how to do mediation with a 1–1–1 model, but Preacher et al. (2010) propose that many other types of models (e.g., 1–1–2, 1–2–1, and so forth) can be handled with this general approach. This is a worthy proposal, and those individuals familiar with SEM may wish to examine this article.

CATEGORICAL MEDIATORS AND/OR OUTCOMES (LOGISTIC MEDIATION)

I have fielded a lot of questions from researchers concerning the nature of variables in the mediational triangle. Let us briefly review: (1) it is okay to have a dichotomous IV (e.g., gender), but (2) it is *not* okay to have dichotomous mediators or outcome variables. That may seem to be a bit harsh, if not to say a bit capricious, but that is the conventional wisdom. Okay, why?

The literature on logistic mediation is sparse to say the least (for one counterexample, see Huang, Sivaganesan, Succop, & Goodman, 2004), but let me attempt to answer this question by referring to a couple of helpful sources. Nathaniel Herr of UCLA has put up a website that is useful (**http://nrherr.bol.ucla.edu/Mediation/logmed.html**), and I would suggest reading it. He refers to a paper by MacKinnon and Dwyer (1993), and what follows here is based on these two sources of information.

As Herr puts it on his web page, "Logistic regression creates a problem because when outcomes are dichotomous the coefficients in your mediation analyses end up being in different scales," so this means that one *cannot* just appropriate B's and standard errors from regressions performed with dichotomous variables and then plug them into a mediational analysis. They have to be put on the same scale first. Herr has provided an Excel and an SPSS macro for transforming B's and *SE*s so that they are properly comparable, and once this is done, these values can be easily inserted into Preacher's website or my MedGraph website to compute Sobel's value.

So, shall we consider an example? In this case, I consider the case of a dichotomous mediator variable to keep it simple. Also, be aware that three types of logistic mediation are possible: (1) both the mediator and the outcome are dichotomous; (2) the mediator is dichotomous and the outcome is continuous; and (3) the outcome is dichotomous and the mediator is continuous. I illustrate the second possibility here.

Health variables are often dichotomous—for example, diabetic versus not diabetic—and the dichotomous mediating variable that I wish to consider here, I think, fits within this context. My research team and I asked our longitudinal sample of adolescents (see description of sample in Jose, Ryan, & Pryor, 2012) how many days over the preceding month they had had a drink of alcohol. The response format was 1 (*never*), 2 (*1–2 days*), 3 (*3–5 days*), 4 (*6–9 days*), or 5 (*10 or more days*). The resulting distribution of data was highly skewed to the left (thank goodness), and both the median and modal values were 1 (1,645 individuals out of 2,174 said "never"). These data should *not* be analyzed as continuous data because of their highly skewed nature. So we dichotomized this variable as *never* (0) and *some* (1).

> **Helpful Suggestion:** The name of the dataset used here is "Logistic mediation example.sav."

The question that we wished to examine was whether alcohol use might possibly explain some of the negative relationship between stressful events and good health that researchers often find. We asked the participants in other parts of the questionnaire how many stressful events they had experienced in the previous month (measured on a continuous scale), as well as for a global estimation of their good health over the previous month (also measured on a continuous scale). We first sought to determine whether these variables were related to each other in a predictable and significant fashion. The correlation matrix is presented in Table 4.19.

TABLE 4.19. Zero-Order Correlations among the Three Variables for the Logistic Mediation Example

	Alcohol use (dichot)	Good health
Stressful events	.121***	−.147***
Alcohol use (dichot)		−.074***

These results confirmed what we expected—namely, we found a significant and negative relationship between stressful events and good health, and we also found that alcohol use was positively associated with stress and negatively associated with good health. Figure 4.22 illustrates how the mediational triangle would look.

In order to use Herr's Excel macro, we need to derive the 12 values shown in Table 4.20. The standard deviations can be obtained by running a Descriptives analysis in SPSS, and the covariance is easily produced by running a correlation, but be sure that you specify in the Options box that you want the cross-products and covariances. The B's and SEs are produced in the usual

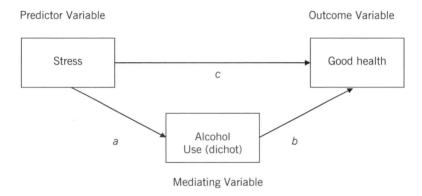

FIGURE 4.22. Predicted model for the logistic mediation example.

TABLE 4.20. Identification of the Critical Statistical Inputs for the Herr Macro

	Standard dev.			Covariance
Stress	3.674	Stress and	.183
Alcohol use	.4103	Alcohol use	
Good health	.8675		

	B	Standard error
a	.076	.015
b	−.124	.051
c	−.035	.006
c'	−.033	.006

way *except* that one must run a *logistics regression where appropriate.* In this case the "*a*" coefficients are obtained from running a BINARY LOGISTIC under REGRESSION in SPSS, where alcohol use is the dependent variable and stress is the independent variable. The B and *SE* are taken from the "Variables in the equation" box, Step 1. The other B's and *SE*s are taken from the usual linear regression analyses that you have already learned how to perform.

If you insert these values into Herr's very handy Excel macro, you see the results from the relevant computations appear before your eyes. Believe me, this is a lot easier than handcomputing these values. In my case, Table 4.21 presents what I obtained. "Sab" means "standard error for the indirect effect" in the first line, and the Sobel z-values are presented in the second line. The three types of formulas follow Kris Preacher's provision of the three variants of the estimation of the indirect effect, but most people will simply choose to report Sobel's value (i.e., Sobel's z = −2.19, p = .028). In conclusion, we have obtained a significant mediational effect.

From the output I could see that the initial negative relationship between stress and good health (β = −.147) was reduced significantly (β to −.139) when alcohol use was introduced as a mediator into the equation. Although this reduction was relatively small (standardized indirect effect = −0.009), Sobel's z-value tells us that this was a significant reduction. Because I had a large sample (N = 1,732, listwise), a very small effect was identified. In theoretical/conceptual language, I would take this result to say something like this:

> "The negative relationship between stressful events and good health was partially mediated by adolescents' use of alcohol; namely, it seems that the experience of stressful events may have precipitated the use of alcohol, which in turn seems to have had a negative impact on good health. However, because these are concurrent data, no firm conclusions about causal direction among these three variables can be made."

I do not take you through the other two variations (continuous MedV and dichotomous DV and dichotomous MedV and DV), but be aware that

TABLE 4.21. Herr's Macro Output for Sobel's Test of Logistic Regression

	Aroian	Sobel	Goodman
Sab =	0.001971866	0.001941	0.0019104
Sobel=	−2.15814399	−2.19204	−2.227594

they are somewhat more involved, because the variance estimate to be used is different than it is for the example I just explained. See MacKinnon, Lockwood, Brown, and Hoffman (2007) for an explanation of this additional complication.

I found that Herr's SPSS macro is easier and faster in doing these analyses than the Excel macro that I have shown here, so I recommend that you examine this option as well. Many researchers have been clamoring for a solution to the problem of a categorical mediator, and I think that Herr has come up with a good answer, so use this approach and spread the word.

MEDIATION WITH QUADRATIC RELATIONSHIPS

I want to mention at the end of this long chapter that another new development that deserves greater attention involves examining mediation in a case in which quadratic relationships are involved in the mediation triangle. Hayes and Preacher (2010) explore this important topic. They note that researchers often overlook the interesting and important case of nonlinear (chiefly quadratic and cubic) relationships that exist among variables. Using a method originated by Stolzenberg (1980), the authors demonstrate how one might capture the nonlinear nature of these relationships in a mediation analysis. They include Mplus, SPSS, and SAS syntax and macros to allow researchers to easily model these relationships.

In my opinion, one of the most unappreciated facts of data analysis is that nonlinear relationships exist in virtually all datasets, yet researchers rarely theorize about or test for them. I encourage readers to read this article and strike out on this path rarely taken.

SUMMARY

What I have attempted to show you in this chapter is that the world of three-variable mediation with multiple regression only cracks the door on a number of powerful mediational approaches that are available. Hopefully, you now have a keen interest in performing mediational analyses on the platforms of SEM, bootstrapping, MLM, and logistic regression. I have shown you only the basics here; there is much more to understand and acquire, and I would recommend a thorough reading of MacKinnon's (2008) excellent book on mediational techniques if you wish to go further.

FURTHER READING

For a thorough discussion of model specification, read Chapter 12 of:

Cohen, J., Cohen, P., West, S. G., & Aiken, L. S. (2003). *Applied multiple regression/correlation analysis for the behavioral sciences* (3rd ed.). Mahwah, NJ: Erlbaum.

To learn more about the application of mediation analysis to experimental designs, read:

MacKinnon, D. P. (2008). *Introduction to statistical mediation analysis*. Mahwah, NJ: Erlbaum.

MacKinnon, D. P., & Dwyer, J. H. (1993). Estimating mediated effects in prevention studies. *Evaluation Review, 17*, 144–158.

MacKinnon, D. P., Fairchild, A. J., & Fritz, M. S. (2007). Mediation analysis. *Annual Review of Psychology, 58*, 593–614.

The following articles are all concerned with the use of bootstrapping in mediation analyses:

MacKinnon, D. P., Lockwood, C. M., & Williams, J. (2004). Confidence limits for the indirect effect: Distribution of the product and resampling methods. *Multivariate Behavioral Research, 39*, 99–128.

Preacher, K. J., & Hayes, A. F. (2004). SPSS and SAS procedures for estimating indirect effects in simple mediation models. *Behavior Research Methods, Instruments, and Computers, 36*, 717–731.

Preacher, K. J., & Hayes, A. F. (2005). *SPSS and SAS macros for estimating and comparing indirect effects in multiple mediator models*. Retrieved December 6, 2006, from **http://www.comm.ohio-state.edu/ahayes/SPSS%20programs/indirect.htm**.

Preacher, K. J., & Hayes, A. F. (2008). Asymptotic and resampling strategies for assessing and comparing indirect effects in multiple mediator models. *Behavior Research Methods, 40*, 879–891.

Shrout, P. E., & Bolger, N. (2002). Mediation in experimental and nonexperimental studies: New procedures and recommendations. *Psychological Methods, 7*, 422–445.

The key reading on mediation in MLM is:

Bauer, D. J., Preacher, K. J., & Gil, K. M. (2006). Conceptualizing and testing random indirect effects and moderated mediation in multilevel models: New procedures and recommendations. *Psychological Methods, 11*, 142–163.

And if you go to the following website, you will find a pdf of this article, as well as a practice dataset and instructions for conducting mediation in HLM, SAS, and SPSS: **http://www.unc.edu/~dbauer/publications.html**.

Several useful sources on basic SEM techniques are:

Hoyle, R. (Ed.). (1995). *Structural equation modeling: Concepts, issues, and applications*. Thousand Oaks, CA: Sage.

Kline, R. B. (2004). *Principles and practice of structural equation modeling* (2nd ed.). New York: Guilford Press.

Schumacker, R. E., & Lomax, R. G. (2004). *A beginner's guide to structural equation modeling* (2nd ed.). Mahwah, NJ: Erlbaum.

IN-CHAPTER EXERCISES

1. What is the size of the direct effect in this path model?

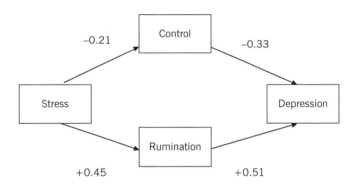

2. Compute the size of the standardized indirect effects in the multiple mediator model presented (beta weights and CIs are shown). Based on bootstrapped CIs, which of these mediational paths is/are statistically significant?

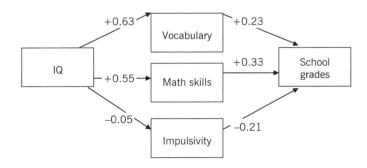

	Vocabulary indirect effect	Math skills indirect effect	Impulsivity indirect effect
Lower bound of 95% CI	0.026	0.071	−0.030
Upper bound of 95% CI	0.143	0.120	0.072

3. The following outputs were generated from a bootstrapped analysis of a mediational pattern in Amos. What can you tell from this output?

Standardized indirect effect	0.103
Standard error	0.052
Lower bound of 95% CI	0.038
Upper bound of 95% CI	0.120

4. Analyses I conducted on a two-wave longitudinal dataset according to the basic autoregressive model yielded the following results. Based on these, was significant longitudinal mediation obtained? Stress is the X variable, social support is the M variable, and depression is the Y variable. Compute Sobel's test to determine statistical significance.

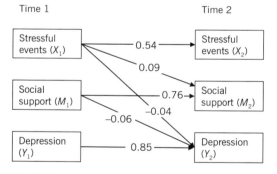

	Unstandardized coefficients	Standard errors	Standardized coefficients
a_1	0.027	0.0147	0.087
b_1	−0.073	0.0505	−0.058
c'_1	−0.015	0.0190	−0.036
Direct effect			0.036
Indirect effect			0.005
Total effect			0.041
Ratio (indirect/total)			12%

5. If you download the dataset "two wave longitudinal mediation problem#5. sav" and examine it for the possibility of longitudinal mediation, what do you obtain? The IV is social support, the MedV is resilience, and the DV is well-being. Compute Sobel's z-score and the 95% asymmetrical confidence interval.

6. Given the values in Table 4.20, work out the total, direct, and indirect effects and the indirect/total ratio based on unstandardized B's. (Base the indirect effect on $a*b$.)

Basic Moderation

In this chapter I describe how to do basic moderation (based on the guidelines laid down by Baron & Kenny, 1986), I give you several examples, and then spend some time explaining how to make interpretations of moderational results. I show the reader how to take the regression results and hand-compute algebraic equations in order to derive means for plotting the graphical depiction of moderation results. This approach follows the guidelines laid down by Aiken and West (1991) and provides anyone who wants to spend the time crunching numbers with the knowledge to do so themselves. I show you how to conduct moderation with a categorical moderator (e.g., gender), as well as with a continuous moderator. And finally I raise the question as to whether the terms *buffer* and *exacerbator* are sufficiently broad to encompass all possible moderational patterns. I suggest that they are not and offer an alternative; namely, that one may want to use the terms *enhancer* and *damper* for those cases in which the outcome is a positive one (e.g., happiness). At the end of this chapter, you will know how to conduct basic moderation, and you will know the basics of interpretation of moderational results. We progress through the following topics in this chapter:

- Categorical variable moderation
    - Data preparation
    - Dummy coding
    - Computation (linear regression)
    - Creating a moderation figure
    - Simple slopes
    - Interpretation
    - Multiple dummy codes

- An example of a continuous moderator
  - Graphing two main effects and the interaction sequentially
  - Simple slopes
  - Buffers and exacerbators
  - Moderational patterns
  - Enhancers and dampeners
  - Things to avoid

CATEGORICAL VARIABLE MODERATION

Moderation refers to the examination of the statistical interaction between two IVs in predicting a DV. One can examine a statistical interaction between two or more IVs in ANOVA or multivariate analysis of variance (MANOVA), of course, but *all* of these IVs will be categorical in nature (e.g., gender, ethnicity, a median split of a continuous variable). In contrast, we are going to focus on moderation within the context of multiple regression. (*Note*: Baron and Kenny [1986] interchangeably used "IV" and "predictor," as well as "DV" and "outcome," and I do the same in this chapter. However, remember that *IV* and *DV* are terms usually reserved for experimental studies, whereas *predictor* and *outcome* are terms used in observational studies. Also, I use the abbreviation *ModV* to refer to the moderating variable.)

Figure 5.1 is the typical graphic depiction of moderation. Notice that there are similarities and differences between this and the mediational triangle depicted in Chapter 3. I first catalog the similarities: (1) three variables are examined at the same time; (2) the focus is on the basic IV-to-DV rela-

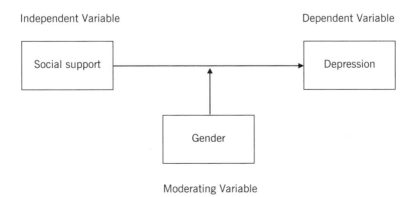

FIGURE 5.1. Typical graphical depiction of moderation.

tionship; and (3) the third variable (a moderator in this case) is seen to be involved with this basic relationship. Now I list the differences: (1) we are *not* interested in the IV-to-ModV relationship; (2) we *are* interested in how the ModV affects the basic relationship (in an interaction with the IV); and (3) these relationships are usually not discussed in causal terms.

To test the moderation hypothesis proposed by this diagram, we perform a multiple regression with three predictive terms: (1) the IV, (2) the ModV, and (3) the interaction term of the IV × ModV. Figure 5.2 is a fair way to represent the relationships in a path model. The regression equation would be

$$Y = i_1 + b_1X + b_2Z + b_3XZ + e_1 \tag{5.1}$$

In short, you can see here that we have three predictor terms: two "main effects" (X and Z) and one interaction (XZ). (We refer to the intercept, i_1, and the residual term, e_1, later as they become relevant.) So, following our labels in Figure 5.2, the basic relationship under investigation is the association between social support (X) and depression (Y), and let us assume that this is significant and negative. Specifically, someone who experiences a high level of social support should also report being less depressed. The ModV (Z) is introduced because we are interested in whether gender might affect this basic relationship. For the moderation hypothesis, someone might envision one of two possibilities: (1) that the association between social support and depression will be greater for males because they report lower levels of both variables than females; that is, the association is more salient, or (2) someone might hypothesize that the association will be greater for females because they are more attuned to the emotional landscape of the psyche. My view was that the former prediction was more likely to be obtained than the latter, so I sought to examine a dataset to determine which of these possible outcomes

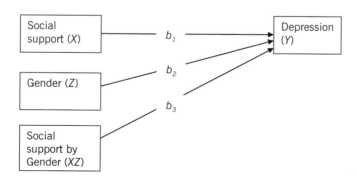

FIGURE 5.2. Path model representation of a moderation analysis.

would be supported. The proposed moderation, if it exists, should be evident in the interaction term (XZ) predicting the outcome (Y).

Why Not Just Perform an ANOVA?

Most of us learned how to do ANOVAs before we were introduced to moderation, and there is a certain overlap between these two techniques, so let us consider this question briefly before getting into moderation. If I were to dichotomize the continuous variable of social support by the median (i.e., those below the median are coded 1 for "low" and those above the median are coded 2 for "high"), then I could just do a simple one-way ANOVA to see whether I would obtain a significant interaction, as presented in Figure 5.3.

So, to answer the question, we certainly could just do an ANOVA, and we would likely obtain a fairly accurate depiction of what the data have to say, but there are two chief reasons that we would choose *not* to take this alternative. First, a great deal of statistical information is lost when we create a dichotomous categorical variable from a continuous variable. In other words, the moderation approach, which retains the continuous information (in social support, in this case), is more sensitive and will yield more accurate results. And second, one might wish to combine this simple moderation analysis with other approaches (e.g., mediated moderation; see Chapter 7), and it would be easier to do so with the moderation technique outlined in the following rather than by using an ANOVA approach.

Helpful Suggestion: As in previous chapters, if you would like to download this dataset and conduct these analyses as I go through this section, download the dataset named "categorical moderation example. sav" and go through what I recommend.

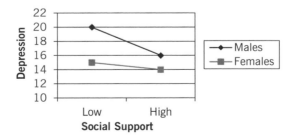

FIGURE 5.3. Predicted interaction between gender and social support on depression.

Preparation of the Data

There are two steps that a researcher must take before performing a moderational analysis.

1. *Dummy-code any categorical predictor variables.* In this case we have one categorical variable, namely gender, so I make sure that it is dummy coded. What does this mean? Refer to Hardy (1993) or the Knowledge Box in this chapter containing a tutorial on dummy coding for more information on how to do this, particularly for variables with more than two levels. In our case, it simply means that one of the genders is coded as 0 and the other gender is coded as 1. It does not matter which is coded 1 or 0, so I arbitrarily code males as 0 and females as 1. My research assistant had originally coded the data 1 for males and 2 for females, so I had to correct this coding.

2. *Create the interaction term.* This step is relatively easy, but conceptually it is a big step for many students. What you do is to go back into COMPUTE and create a new variable that stands for the interaction term. In this case I called it "ssxgend" ("ss" for social support, "x" for multiply, and "gend" for gender), but every user will probably want to adopt his or her own particular system of naming these newly created variables. In the menu box to the right I type "ss * gender," which multiplies the social support variable by the dummy-coded gender variable. I hit "OK" and a new variable is created and placed to the far right of the variable list in the data file.

Centering of IVs?

At this juncture I address a persisting but incorrect belief about how to conduct moderation. Many people believe that the continuous-variable IVs (social support in this case) should be centered before the interaction term is created. Let me address this concern by saying *no, you do not have to center your IVs.* Let me explain why so many people believe the contrary. In the days when researchers would hand-graph the results of regression equations, it proved to be very helpful to center the regression IVs; it simplified the algebraic computations. See advice from Aiken and West (1991) on the graphing of regression and moderation results as an example of this suggestion. The other reason that has been proffered was that it would reduce multicollinearity (excessive correlation among predictor variables). This advice has been repeated by various sources (including myself, I confess) until it passed from "helpful suggestion" to "received wisdom." The only problem is that it's not actually a necessary step in conducting a moderation. Kromrey and Foster-Johnson (1998) have shown that centering does not, in fact, prevent or affect multicollinearity. Centering changes only the intercept (and the size of the conditional main effects) and exerts no influence on the actual shape of the moderation result. I have conducted moderation analyses with and without centering, and I noted that the pattern obtained in both cases was identical. Thus my advice is that centering is not essential, and I would not recommend it unless you wish to create a figure in which the means of the IV and the ModV are 0, enabling certain types of interpretation.

KNOWLEDGE BOX. A Short Tutorial on Dummy Coding

If you do not clearly understand dummy coding, you might wish to spend a few minutes going through this information. Dummy coding is used to convert multilevel categorical variables into variables that can be used in regression and correlation.

Let's take ethnic group status as an example. I frequently collect data from samples in New Zealand composed of members of different ethnic groups, for example, European New Zealanders (also called "Pakeha" down here), Maori, Pacific Islanders, and Asian New Zealanders. Assuming that everyone ticks one and only one option on this variable, then we have a dataset with a single variable called "ethnic identity" with four values. One usually assigns whole numbers to these four categories, in this fashion: 1 = European NZ; 2 = Maori; 3 = Pacific Islander; and 4 = Asian NZ. Do these values mean anything in a continuous variable sort of way? Absolutely not—they are essentially placeholders. Another way to say this is that we could correlate this ethnic identity variable with a continuous variable such as depression, and any result obtained, e.g., $r = .37$, $p < .05$, would be utter nonsense. What one must do is convert the information contained in this variable into a number of dummy codes so that useful analyses can be performed.

Keep in mind this useful rule of thumb: *the number of dummy-coded variables will be one less than the total number of levels in the categorical variable.* So, in the present case of ethnic identity, I end up with exactly three dummy-coded variables because I began with four levels.

The other important bit of information is that one must have a "comparison group" or a "reference group" against which the other groups are compared. In the present case, it makes sense to me to compare European NZers with the other three groups because European NZers are the majority group in New Zealand. So, what I do is assign members of this group a value of 0 for all three dummy-coded variables. Then I insert a value of 1 for the group that is being compared with the comparison group. See the following example.

	Dum1	Dum2	Dum3
Euro NZ (1)	0	0	0
Maori (2)	1	0	0
Pacific Islander (3)	0	1	0
Asian NZ (4)	0	0	1

Thus Dum1 compares Maori individuals with European NZers, Dum2 compares Pacific Islanders with European NZers, and Dum3 compares Asian NZers with European NZers. This set of dummy codes does not compare individuals across the three minority groups, and if someone wanted to accomplish that comparison, then he or she would need to reconfigure the dummy-coded variables using a different group as the comparison group.

The following shows how one would recode the original ethnic identity variable into usable dummy codes in a dataset:

Subject #	Ethnic Identity	Dum1	Dum2	Dum3
1	3	0	1	0
2	1	0	0	0
3	4	0	0	1
4	2	1	0	0
5	1	0	0	0
and so forth				

Once this is done, we can use Dum1, Dum2, and Dum3 as variables in correlations, regressions, mediations, and moderations. Please remember that each dummy code represents a particular comparison, and we must bear that in mind when we attempt to explain a result obtained with a given dummy code.

So what is the implication of using dummy codes for moderation analyses? The researcher must create the proper number of dummy codes (three in this case) and then systematically multiply each of these with the IV to create three interaction terms. Thus the resulting regression will have seven predictors: (1) the continuous IV; (2–4) the three dummy codes; and (5–7) the three interaction terms. If any of the three interaction terms proves to be statistically significant (let's say IV*Dum2), then one would graph that interaction term (with the main effects) to make an interpretation. The graph in this case would include statistical output information for the IV, Dum2, and IV*Dum2. It is possible to find significant moderation for none, one, two, or three of the interaction terms, and, of course, one would graph only the significant relationships.

Computation of the Regression Analysis of Moderation

We are now ready to compute the moderation analysis, and I demonstrate how to do it with a hierarchical regression. (One can do the computation with a simultaneous inclusion regression, and this is discussed later.)

1. Input "depression" in the dependent variable box.
2. Insert "ss" in the independent variable box, and then click NEXT.
3. Insert "gender" in the independent variable box, and then click NEXT.
4. Insert "ssxgend" in the independent variable box.

What this does is create a hierarchical regression analysis; predictors are added one at a time in three individual steps. One more thing: if you click on STATISTICS, and then "R squared change," you will be able to see how much variance each of the three terms explains in the DV. Hit OK to enact the analysis. You will receive five boxes in typical SPSS output. Check the first box to make sure that you entered IVs in the correct sequence and that your expected DV is the correct variable. Now examine the next box, titled "Model Summary" (see Table 5.1). It tells you how much variance in the DV these three predictors explained in each step. The hierarchical nature of the regression allows you to appreciate that social support explained about 9% by itself, gender explained an additional 5%, and the interaction term explained about 3% of new variance above and beyond the two main effects.

Now I skip ahead to the fourth box, which is shown in Table 5.2. This box permits us to make some conclusions about the directions of the main effects. We see that social support yielded a significant negative beta (−0.294) in the first step. This step is considered to be the basic relationship of the moderation, and it tells us that higher social support was associated with lower depression (as we expected). The second step shows that gender was

TABLE 5.1. R^2 change Statistical Outputs in the Model Summary Box

Model	R	R square	Adjusted R square	Std. error of the estimate	R square change	F change	df1	df2	Sig. F change
1	.294[a]	.086	.082	6.53846	.086	19.431	1	206	.000
2	.366[b]	.134	.126	6.37951	.048	11.394	1	205	.001
3	.404[c]	.163	.151	6.28871	.029	6.963	1	204	.009

TABLE 5.2. Statistical Output for the Hierarchical Regression Used to Determine Significant Moderation

Model	Unstandardized coefficients		Standardized coefficients		
	B	Std. error	Beta	t	Sig.
1. (Constant)	17.871	2.074		8.619	.000
Social support	−.390	.088	−.294	−4.408	.000
2. (Constant)	16.620	2.057		8.081	.000
Social support	−.456	.088	−.343	−5.151	.000
Gender	3.607	1.069	.225	3.375	.001
3. (Constant)	8.928	3.551		2.514	.013
Social support (ss)	−.087	.165	−.065	−.525	.600
Gender	14.672	4.324	.915	3.393	.001
ssxgender	−.513	.194	−.816	−2.639	.009

Note. Dependent variable: Depression.

significantly associated with depression after social support is entered first—remember, this is a hierarchical regression, so this beta is not the same as a zero-order correlation between gender and depression (which is .15, $p < .05$, by the way). And finally, on the third step, the interaction term yielded a significant beta in predicting depression. The beta for the interaction term is −0.816. Can we tell from this output what form the moderation took? The simple answer is "no." Most people cannot interpret a result like this. Instead, we should graph it so that we can interpret it.

So let us figure out how to generate the figure from the regression results. Aiken and West (1991) have presented the seminal description of how to do this, and I would recommend that you read this extremely helpful book. Holmbeck (1989) has also presented a good example of how to do this. I learned how to create figures to depict these interactions from these sources, and I now show you how to do this. It involves computing a series of algebraic equations. As I take you through this, I want you to keep in mind that you do *not* have to do this procedure by hand. I have created ModGraph for the express purpose of avoiding these tedious and complicated algebraic computations; it quickly and accurately computes these equations in a fraction of a second. And there are other online programs that do this type of graphing, as well. Nevertheless, you may be reading this book on a desert island, and you may not have access to a computer, so this section will be helpful, and I also think it is instructive to see how one computes these equations by hand.

Creating a Moderation Figure by Computing the Equations by Hand

You will first need to collect a few essential elements of statistical information from your dataset. You will input the eight numerical values in Table 5.3 into six equations (given subsequently) that will create six means that will be used to plot the two lines contained within the figure. Aiken and West (1991) recommended that three means be obtained for each categorical group (males and females, in this case); these means represent the mean, 1 SD above the mean, and 1 SD below the mean. There is nothing sacred about these cut points. You could choose two points (e.g., 1 SD above and below the mean), three different points (e.g., the mean, 0.5 SD below the mean, and 0.5 SD above the mean), four points, and so forth. Most people have adopted Aiken and West's suggestion because it is a useful convention. It is necessary to plot at least two points to create a line, and it is important not to choose points that are too far away from the mean, because those values may not capture the range of values in the actual datasets.

In the following text you see in words where the values come from, and below each of those lines are the substituted values. The unpleasant work comes in systematically writing down all of the values and then carefully computing these simple algebraic functions. I have done many of these. I have found them to be boring and time-consuming, and I am prone to make errors. Nevertheless, let us take a look at these computations.

TABLE 5.3. Summary of Statistical Outputs Necessary to Graph the Moderation Result of Gender on the Social Support-to-Depression Relationship

Variable	Mean	Standard deviation
Social support (ss)	22.8726	5.13719
Gender	N/A 0 = males; 1 = females	N/A

Variable	B (unstandardized regression coefficient)
Social support (ss)	−.087
Gender	14.672
ssxgend	−.513
Constant	8.928

High SS and Male

[B for ss * (ss mean + sd)] + [B for gender * dummy value for males] + [B for interaction term * [(ss mean + sd) * dummy value for males] + constant

–.087(22.8726 + 5.13719) + 14.672(0) + –.513[(22.8726 + 5.13719) * 0] + 8.928 =
–2.4369 + 0 + 0 + 8.928 =
6.4911

Medium SS and Male

[B for ss * (mean)] + [B for gender * dummy value for males] + [B for interaction term * [(mean) * dummy value for males] + constant

–.087(22.8726) + 14.672(0) + –.513(22.8726 * 0) + 8.928 =
–1.9899 + 0 + 0 + 8.928 =
6.9381

Low SS and Male

[B for ss * (mean – sd)] + [B for gender * dummy value for males] + [B for interaction term * [(mean – sd) * dummy value for males] + constant

–.087(22.8726 – 5.13719) + 14.672(0) + –.513[(22.8726 – 5.13719) * 0] + 8.928 =
–1.5430 + 0 + 0 + 8.928 =
7.3850

High SS and Female

[B for ss * (mean + sd)] + [B for gender * dummy value for females] + [B for interaction term * [(mean + sd) * dummy value for females] + constant

–.087(22.8726 + 5.13719) + 14.672(1) + –.513[(22.8726 + 5.13719) * 1] + 8.928 =
–2.4369 + 14.672 – 14.3690 + 8.928 =
6.7941

Medium SS and Female

[B for ss * (mean)] + [B for gender * dummy value for females] + [B for interaction term * [(mean) * dummy value for females] + constant

–.087(22.8726) + 14.672(1) + –.513[(22.8726) * 1] + 8.928 =
–1.9899 + 14.672 – 11.7336 + 8.928 =
9.8765

Low SS and Female

[B for ss * (mean – sd)] + [B for gender * dummy value for females] + [B for interaction term * [(mean – sd) * dummy value for females] + constant

$-.087(22.8726 - 5.13719) + 14.672(1) + -.513[(22.8726 - 5.13719) * 1] + 8.928 =$
$-1.5430 + 14.672 - 9.0983 + 8.928 =$
12.9587

The means obtained for these six equations are presented in Table 5.4.

Incidentally, when I compared my hand-computed values the first time through with those generated by ModGraph, I found that I had made two errors in my hand computations. (Don't worry: I did find the errors and I have corrected them.) I'm not pointing this out to show what a bad mathematician I am, but rather to make the point that anyone who hand-computes these values is likely to make errors along the way. The other serious drawback to doing these by hand is that it takes a lot of time. Even with a fair amount of experience, I spent about 15 minutes doing these. This is time better spent creating innovative approaches to your research, taking a nap, or just about anything else.

The next step is to graph these means. I am using the suggestions of Aiken and West (1991), but also see the book by Kam and Franzese (2007) that lays out other alternatives. We could draw this graph in Word or PowerPoint, or, as I did it in the old days, I could pull out some graph paper. In any case, if you graph these means, Figure 5.4 (on page 166) is what you will obtain.

How does this result compare with the prediction I made earlier? I predicted (erroneously, as it turns out) that males would evidence a stronger relationship between social support and depression, but as one can see in the figure, the pattern supported the other possibility: namely, that females would evidence a stronger relationship between the IV and the DV.

Slopes of the Two Moderation Lines

One way to interpret an interaction is to notice the steepness of slope of the lines. In Figure 5.4 you will notice that the females' line is the steeper of the two and the males' slope is the flatter of the two. This pattern means that the relationship between social support and depression is stronger for females and weaker for males. How do we know this?

TABLE 5.4. Summary of Means Obtained from the Hand Computation of the Moderation Result

	Low ss	Medium ss	High ss
Females	12.9587	9.8765	6.7941
Males	7.3850	6.9381	6.4911

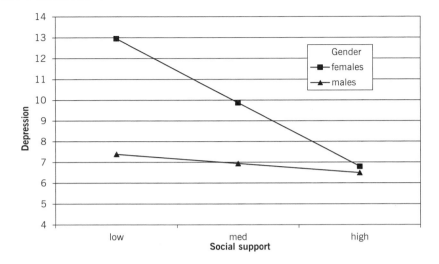

FIGURE 5.4. Graphical depiction of gender moderating the social support-to-depression relationship.

Examining Simple Slopes of Moderation Lines

ModGraph has the capability to compute the simple slopes of these lines. If you input four more items of statistical output obtained from SPSS, the program will generate the simple slopes, their t-values, and the associated significance levels. Before we do this, I need to obtain some additional statistical information. In SPSS, I request the covariance matrix under STATISTICS before I run the regression analysis again, and I obtain in the output a matrix that yields the first three pieces of information (see Table 5.5): the variance of

TABLE 5.5. Statistical Output of the Covariance Matrix Requested in the Regression Analysis

		ssxgender	Social support	Gender
Coefficient Correlations[a]				
Model				
1. Correlations	ssxgender	1.000	−.849	−.970
	Social support	−.849	1.000	.795
	Gender	−.970	.795	1.000
Covariances	ssxgender	.038	−.027	−.815
	Social support	−.027	.027	.566
	Gender	−.815	.566	18.695

Note. Dependent variable: Depression. Necessary values are highlighted in gray.

social support (0.027); the variance of the interaction (0.038); and the covariance of social support by the interaction (−0.027). In addition, the size of the sample is entered (N = 208).

Once this information is entered, the simple slopes are computed, and they turn out to be: males = −0.09, p = .60, and females = −0.60, p < .001 (see Table 5.6). The larger the value for the simple slope, the higher the correlation between social support and depression. One could argue that this is an interesting result, because the simple slopes analysis suggests that males in this sample did *not* evidence a significant correlation between social support and depression at all, whereas females evidenced a strong negative correlation.

Hand Computation of Simple Slopes

Following Cohen and Cohen (1983) and Aiken and West (1991), here is how to do this task. Let us begin with the basic regression equation:

$$Y = b_0 + b_1 X + b_2 Z + b_3 XZ \tag{5.2}$$

Note that Z is actually a dummy code variable and that b_0 refers to the constant. The next step is to restructure the equation in order to simplify the derivation of the simple slopes:

$$Y = b_1 X + b_3 XZ + b_2 Z + b_0 \tag{5.3}$$

The next step removes the common factor X from the first two terms and places it outside of the parentheses.

$$Y = (b_1 + b_3 Z)X + (b_2 Z + b_0) \tag{5.4}$$

TABLE 5.6. ModGraph Output for Simple Slopes of the Two Groups

	Males	Females
Simple slopes	−.09	−.60
Standard errors	.164	.105
t-values	−.529	−5.72
p-values	.597	0

These equations convey identical information; the last equation is just a mathematical restructuring of the first equation. What is important here is that the term $(b_1 + b_3 Z)$ is the simple slope. In essence, the slope of X on Y is conditional on values of Z (which are 0 and 1 in this case). Next I focus on the first term and drop the $(b_2 Z + b_0)$ term just to simplify things.

The next step is to select values of Z in order to draw regression slopes, that is, create simple regression equations. (In the case of a continuous moderator variable, Cohen and Cohen, 1983, recommended using -1 SD, the mean, and $+1$ SD for values of the moderator Z, and I demonstrate this use for continuous variable moderation.) In the present case, we have a dummy-coded variable (0 = males; 1 = females), so we have two groups that will yield two lines. If I had a more complicated dummy-coded situation, for example, if I had four groups, I would have three dummy-coded variables, and I would end up with four lines. See Aiken and West (1991) for examples of how to create simple slopes for analyses involving more than two groups.

For the analysis we are considering here, we substitute in 0 for the male group and 1 for the female group for the variable Z:

General equation: $Y = (b_1 + b_3 Z)X$

Males: $Y = (b_1 + b_3{}^*0)X = b_1 X$

Females: $Y = (b_1 + b_3{}^*1)X = (b_1 + b_3)X$

These equations say that b_1 is the simple slope for males $(-.087)$ and $(b_1 + b_3)$ is the simple slope for females $(-.087 - .513 = -.600)$. These values agree with what I obtained through ModGraph. Now let us consider the standard errors of the simple slopes. The equation for that is

$$SE = SQRT \ [s_{11} + 2(Z)(s_{13}) + Z^2 s_{33}] \qquad (5.5)$$

ere s_{11} is the variance for the main effect $(.027)$, s_{13} is the covariance of the ffect by the interaction $(-.027)$, and s_{33} is the variance of the interac- he computations are presented in Table 5.7, inserting 0 for Z for for females.

dard errors agree with ModGraph, and if one divides ective standard errors with $(n - k - 1)$ degrees of e number of predictors in the equation), one can ed p-values. In this case, degrees of freedom are 4. The hand-derived t-values are similar to what is good.

TABLE 5.7. Calculation of the Standard Errors for the Simple Slopes

	s_{11}	$2(Z)(s_{13})$	$Z^2 s_{33}$	SQRT of sum (SE)
Males	.027	0	0	.164
Females	.027	−.054	.038	.105

Interpretation

Pulling together the results from the regression analysis, discerning the pattern in the figure, and incorporating the simple slope results, I would suggest that the following is a relatively complete and illuminating interpretation of the pattern:

> "It was predicted that males would evidence a stronger negative relationship between social support and depression than females because males' use of social support is less common and may be more salient. A regression analysis was performed to test this moderation hypothesis: Social support was the independent variable, gender was the moderating variable, and depression was the dependent variable. The social support variable was multiplied with the dummy-coded gender variable, and the two main effects and the interaction term were used in a hierarchical regression to predict depression. A significant main effect for gender was obtained ($\beta = .92$, $p = .007$), and it signified that females' depression levels, on average, were higher than males' depression levels. But this main effect was qualified by the significant interaction ($\beta = -.82$, $p = .009$), which was graphed using the techniques recommended by Aiken and West (1991; see Figure 5.4). The figure shows that females manifested a steeper slope between social support and depression than males. Simple slope analyses yielded the result that females manifested a significant negative slope, -0.60, $p < .001$, whereas males evidenced a nonsignificant slope, -0.09, $p = .60$. This result suggests that females' differential use of social support was significantly related to levels of depression, whereas no such association was noted for males. Further, the largest difference in self-reported depression between the genders occurred under conditions of low social support, whereas males' and females' levels of depression were virtually identical under conditions of high social support."

The hypothetical author should go on, of course, to tie these statistical interpretations in with previous findings and theory. Note several things here: (1) I referred to the main effect being qualified by the interaction; (2) I referred to the pattern of lines in the figure; (3) I reported the simple slopes; and (4) I avoided causal language. A moderation result does not claim that the IV and ModV "caused" the DV, but it is implicit in the way that the regression was constructed. The best one can say is something like "males and females who reported high levels of social support did not seem to differ from each other with regards to reported levels of depressive symptoms." I cannot say that high levels of social support *caused* lower depression because these are concurrent data. See the chapter on longitudinal data and mediation (Chapter 4) for more information on the topic of causality.

Multiple Dummy Codes in a Categorical Moderation

When a categorical variable has more than two levels (as discussed earlier), we generate one dummy code less than the number of levels; as an example, five religious groups yield four dummy codes. Then multiply the IV with each of the dummy codes to get IV*dum1, IV*dum2, IV*dum3, and IV*dum4. Set up the regression equation as shown in Table 5.8. I enter these groups of variables in a hierarchical regression and ask for changes in R^2, and by doing this one can see whether the dummy codes as a group and/or the interaction terms as a group yield a significant omnibus R^2 change. If the regression result yields a significant R^2 change value, then follow this up by examining the specific terms. To demonstrate significant moderation, of course, the critical issue is whether any of the interaction terms turn out to be significant predictors of the DV. Let us say that we obtain a significant omnibus R^2

TABLE 5.8. Specification of Entry of Dummy-Coded Variables in a Hierarchical Regression Computed for a Five-Level Categorical Moderator

	Enter
Step 1	IV
Step 2	Dum1
	Dum2
	Dum3
	Dum4
Step 3	IV*Dum1
	IV*Dum2
	IV*Dum3
	IV*Dum4

TABLE 5.9. Separate Regression Analyses Following an Omnibus Regression Which Suggested Significant Moderation by Two Dummy Codes

	1st regression	2nd regression
Step 1	IV	IV
Step 2	Dum1	Dum4
Step 3	IV*Dum1	IV*Dum4

change for the group of interaction terms, and I note that two out of the four interaction terms yield $p < .05$, let us say IV*Dum1 and IV*Dum4. I recommend that one follow this omnibus moderation analysis with two "focused" moderation analyses, as displayed in Table 5.9.

What sometimes happens is that a previously significant interaction term fails to reach statistical significance when it is tested by itself. So, in the preceding example, one might find that IV*Dum1 continues to yield a significant result but IV*Dum4 does not by itself. I would graph the first one and ignore the second one. This is a conservative procedure, ensuring that "significant" interactions within the context of multiple predictors remain significant when they are tested by themselves. A particular interaction may be significant in the omnibus case due to the vagaries of multicollinearity, but not in isolation.

AN EXAMPLE OF A CONTINUOUS MODERATOR

Let me begin this section by saying this: Interpreting interactions is an acquired skill. I have found that beginning students flounder with this task initially, but after some instruction and practice, they begin to be more successful with it. In my experience, teachers of statistics do not do a very good job of explaining this phenomenon chiefly because they underestimate how complex the task is and how unprepared most students are. This section provides both instruction and practice in this technique, and I provide examples of several very common interaction patterns that the user can employ in future interpretations.

Another important point to make at this juncture is to say that the depiction of the interaction in Figure 5.4 includes information about: (1) the main effect of the IV; (2) the main effect of the moderator; and (3) the interaction. Yes, it's true—the figure reflects *all three statistical findings in a single graph*.

Most students do not appreciate this fact, and this is part of the reason that they find it so difficult. Most students think that it depicts *only* the interaction. Knowing this important fact is a useful avenue to easier interpretation. So let us go through an example. The next example involves social support and depression, as in the previous example, but in this case I reorient the variables' relationships and replace gender with stress. The purpose of doing this is to show you how a continuous ModV works.

The data that present here come from a sample of 141 psychology undergraduates at my home institution (Victoria University of Wellington), and I subsequently compare those results with findings obtained from a sample of 267 similar-age undergraduates in Vietnam (students attending one of two Vietnamese universities, one each from Hanoi and Ho Chi Minh City). These data were collected by one of my students, Hang Do, and me in order to conduct a cross-cultural comparison of young adult stress and coping. I do not go into the details of how we made these measures comparable between two dissimilar cultures, but see her thesis (Hang, 2007), if you are interested, for details. Suffice it to say that we obtained comparable measures of stress, social support, and depression from both samples. We begin with the New Zealand sample.

> **Helpful Suggestion:** You can download this dataset and follow along: "continuous moderation example.sav."

I was interested in testing the buffering hypothesis of social support that Cohen and Wills (1985) and others have examined for the past several decades. The prediction is that social support protects (i.e., buffers) the individual from the effects of stress on psychological adjustment. In short, if a person utilizes social support, then they are less likely to show deleterious associations between stress and a measure of adjustment (depression, in the present case). Keep this hypothesis in mind when we examine Figure 5.7 from these data, because our interpretation should speak to this prediction.

Just to remind you, the regression equation is

$$Y = i_1 + b_1X + b_2Z + b_3XZ + e_1$$

where X refers to the IV (stress), Z refers to the ModV (social support), and Y refers to the DV (depression). After we create the interaction term, we are ready to conduct the hierarchical regression. I enter stress on the first step, social support on the second step, and the interaction term on the third step. Table 5.10 presents the SPSS output that I obtained.

TABLE 5.10. Statistical Output of a Hierarchical Regression Used to Assess the Effect of a Continuous Moderating Variable (Social Support) on the Stress-to-Depression Relationship

Model	Unstandardized coefficients		Standardized coefficients		
	B	Std. error	Beta	t	Sig.
1. (Constant)	4.237	1.085		3.906	.000
Stress	.134	.029	.369	4.684	.000
2. (Constant)	12.754	2.521		5.060	.000
Stress	.134	.027	.368	4.874	.000
Social support	−.432	.116	−.280	−3.708	.000
3. (Constant)	1.811	4.774		.379	.705
Stress	.483	.133	1.328	3.626	.000
Social support	.111	.232	.072	.476	.635
strxss	−.017	.006	−1.040	−2.677	.008

Note. Dependent variable: Depression.

Graphing Two Main Effects and an Interaction Sequentially

The first step shows that we obtained a main effect for stress and that it is positive, so we know that more stress was associated with more depression. This is my basic relationship, and it is confirmed. In the second step, social support was found to significantly negatively predict depression, which also makes sense. People who report using more social support are likely to report lower depression. And in the third step, we find that the interaction term proved to be significant. We need to graph it, so we turn to ModGraph . . . but wait, I don't want to do that yet. Instead, I would like to probe the first two steps in sequence so that when I do present Figure 5.7 you will have a better sense of what it means. What I show you over the next several pages is rarely done, but I am doing it here so that you can gain an understanding of what the final graph means.

How do we graph the main effect of stress? We use the information from the first step and plug those values into the following equations (see Table 5.11).

High Stress and High Social Support

[B for Stress * (mean + sd)] + [B for Socsup * (mean + sd)] + [B for interaction term * [(mean + sd of Stress) * (mean + sd of Socsup)] + constant

.134 (32.8652 + 18.88129) + (0) + (0) + 4.237 =

6.934 + 0 + 0 + 4.237 =

11.171

TABLE 5.11. Statistical Outputs Necessary to Graph the Main Effect of Stress on Depression

Variable	Mean	Standard deviation
Stress	32.8652	18.88129
Social support	19.6879	4.44512

Variable	B (unstandardized regression coefficient)
Stress	.134
Social support	not available yet
StressXSocSup	not available yet
Constant:	4.237

High Stress and Medium Social Support

[B for Stress * (mean + sd)] + [B for Socsup * (mean)] + [B for interaction term * [(mean + sd of Stress) * (mean of Socsup)] + constant

.134 (32.8652 + 18.88129) + (0) + (0) + 4.237 =
6.934 + 0 + 0 + 4.237 =
11.171

High Stress and Low Social Support

[B for Stress * (mean + sd)] + [B for Socsup * (mean – sd)] + [B for interaction term * [(mean + sd of Stress) * (mean – sd of Socsup)] + constant

.134 (32.8652 + 18.88129) + (0) + (0) + 4.237 =
6.934 + 0 + 0 + 4.237 =
11.171

Medium Stress and High Social Support

[B for Stress * (mean)] + [B for Socsup * (mean + sd)] + [B for interaction term * [(mean of Stress) * (mean + sd of Socsup)] + constant

.134 (32.8652) + (0) + (0) + 4.237 =
4.404 + 0 + 0 + 4.237 =
8.641

Medium Stress and Medium Social Support

[B for Stress * (mean)] + [B for Socsup * (mean)] + [B for interaction term * [(mean of Stress) * (mean of Socsup)] + constant

.134 (32.8652) + (0) + (0) + 4.237 =
4.404 + 0 + 0 + 4.237 =
8.641

Medium Stress and Low Social Support

[B for Stress * (mean)] + [B for Socsup * (mean − sd)] + [B for interaction term * [(mean of Stress) * (mean − sd of Socsup)] + constant

.134 (32.8652) + (0) + (0) + 4.237 =
4.404 + 0 + 0 + 4.237 =
8.641

Low Stress and High Social Support

[B for Stress * (mean − sd)] + [B for Socsup * (mean + sd)] + [B for interaction term * [(mean − sd of Stress) * (mean + sd of Socsup)] + constant

.134(32.8652 − 18.88129) + (0) + (0) + 4.237 =
1.874 + 0 + 0 + 4.237 =
6.111

Low Stress and Medium Social Support

[B for Stress * (mean − sd)] + [B for Socsup * (mean)] + [B for interaction term * [(mean − sd of Stress) * (mean of Socsup)] + constant

.134 (32.8652 − 18.88129) + (0) + (0) + 4.237 =
1.874 + 0 + 0 + 4.237 =
6.111

Low Stress and Low Social Support

[B for Stress * (mean − sd)] + [B for Socsup * (mean − sd)] + [B for interaction term * [(mean − sd of Stress) * (mean − sd of Socsup)] + constant

.134 (32.8652 − 18.88129) + (0) + (0) + 4.237 =
1.874 + 0 + 0 + 4.237 =
6.111

The means obtained for these nine equations are presented in Table 5.12, and the graph of these results is Figure 5.5.

TABLE 5.12. Summary of Means Generated by Hand Computation of the Main Effect of Stress on Depression

	High social support	Medium social support	Low social support
High stress	11.171	11.171	11.171
Medium stress	8.641	8.641	8.641
Low stress	6.111	6.111	6.111

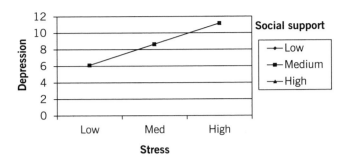

FIGURE 5.5. Graphical depiction of the main effect of stress on depression (without the main effect of social support or the interaction).

TABLE 5.13. Statistical Outputs Necessary to Graph the Main Effects of Stress and Social Support on Depression

Variable	Mean	Standard deviation
Stress	32.8652	18.88129
Social support	19.6879	4.44512

Variable	B (unstandardized regression coefficient)
Stress	.134
Social support	−.432
StressXSocSup	not available
Constant:	12.754

Because we do not have the variable of social support in the equation yet, all three levels of social support fall on top of each other; in other words, the three lines that will depict the three levels of social support lie exactly on top of each other. The main effect of stress on depression is a positive correlation ($r = .37, p < .001$), which is represented by a diagonal line running from lower left to upper right. And that is what we see here.

Let us now consider the second main effect: social support. The information that we use is in Table 5.13 (it is taken from the previous output from the second step).

High Stress and High Social Support

[B for Stress * (mean + sd)] + [B for Socsup * (mean + sd)] + [B for interaction term * [(mean + sd of Stress) * (mean + sd of Socsup)] + constant

.134(32.87 + 18.88) + −.432(19.69 + 4.45) + (0) + 12.75 =

6.9345 + −10.42848 + 0 + 12.75 =

9.256

High Stress and Medium Social Support

[B for Stress * (mean + sd)] + [B for Socsup * (mean)] + [B for interaction term * [(mean + sd of Stress) * (mean of Socsup)] + constant

.134(32.87 + 18.88) + −.432(19.69) + (0) + 12.75 =

6.9345 + −8.50608 + 0 + 12.75 =

11.178

High Stress and Low Social Support

[B for Stress * (mean + sd)] + [B for Socsup * (mean − sd)] + [B for interaction term * [(mean + sd of Stress) * (mean − sd of Socsup)] + constant

.134(32.87 + 18.88) + −.432(19.69 − 4.45) + (0) + 12.75 =

6.9345 + −6.58368 + 0 + 12.75 =

13.101

Medium Stress and High Social Support

[B for Stress * (mean)] + [B for Socsup * (mean + sd)] + [B for interaction term * [(mean of Stress) * (mean + sd of Socsup)] + constant

.134(32.87) + −.432(19.69 + 4.45) + (0) + 12.75 =

4.405 + −10.42848 + 0 + 12.75 =

6.726

Medium Stress and Medium Social Support

[B for Stress * (mean)] + [B for Socsup * (mean)] + [B for interaction term * [(mean of Stress) * (mean of Socsup)] + constant

.134(32.87) + −.432(19.69) + (0) + 12.75 =

4.405 + −8.50608 + 0 + 12.75 =

8.649

Medium Stress and Low Social Support

[B for Stress * (mean)] + [B for Socsup * (mean − sd)] + [B for interaction term * [(mean of Stress) * (mean − sd of Socsup)] + constant

.134(32.87 + 18.88) + −.432(19.69 − 4.45) + (0) + 12.75 =

4.405 + −6.584 + 0 + 12.75 =

10.571

Low Stress and High Social Support

[B for Stress * (mean – sd)] + [B for Socsup * (mean + sd)] + [B for interaction term * [(mean – sd of Stress) * (mean + sd of Socsup)] + constant

.134(32.87 – 18.88) + –.432(19.69 + 4.45) + (0) + 12.75 =
1.875 + –10.42848 + 0 + 12.75 =
4.197

Low Stress and Medium Social Support

[B for Stress * (mean – sd)] + [B for Socsup * (mean)] + [B for interaction term * [(mean – sd of Stress) * (mean of Socsup)] + constant

.134(32.87 – 18.88) + –.432(19.69) + (0) + 12.75 =
1.875 + –8.50608 + 0 + 12.75 =
6.119

Low Stress and Low Social Support

[B for Stress * (mean – sd)] + [B for Socsup * (mean – sd)] + [B for interaction term * [(mean – sd of Stress) * (mean – sd of Socsup)] + constant

.134(32.87 – 18.88) + –.432(19.69 – 4.45) + (0) + 12.75 =
1.875 + –6.584 + 0 + 12.75 =
8.041

The means obtained for these nine equations are presented in Table 5.14.

What we can see in Figure 5.6 is the combination of the two main effects (stress and social support). The three diagonal slopes from lower left to upper right reflect the main effect of stress on depression, and all three lines have the same slope. The three separate lines depict the relationships between stress and depression for the three levels of social support. In this figure, the relationships between stress and depression for the three levels are all

TABLE 5.14. Summary of Means Generated by Hand Computation of the Main Effects of Stress and Social Support on Depression

	High social support	Medium social support	Low social support
High stress	9.256	11.178	13.101
Medium stress	6.726	8.649	10.571
Low stress	4.197	6.119	8.041

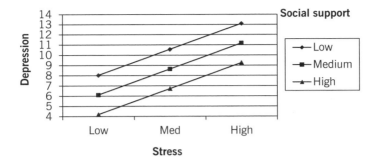

FIGURE 5.6. Graphical depiction of the main effects of stress and social support on depression (without the interaction).

identical, that is, the lines are perfectly parallel. The fact that they are separated now reflects the second main effect: social support on depression. The beta for social support was −0.28, and this means that high social support is associated with low depression. This result is shown by the fact that the line for high social support obtains the lowest depression scores of the three. And low social support garners the highest levels of depression.

One of the truisms of learning how to interpret interactions is that "parallel lines means that you do not have a significant interaction." Clearly, this figure is composed of perfectly parallel lines. In the third and final step, we will include the information for the interaction term, and you will notice that the lines will become distinctly nonparallel.

Let us add in the information for the third term (see Table 5.15).

TABLE 5.15. Statistical Outputs Necessary to Graph the Main Effects of Stress and Social Support and the Interaction on Depression

Variable	Mean	Standard deviation
Stress	32.8652	18.88129
Social support	19.6879	4.44512

Variable	B (unstandardized regression coefficient)
Stress	.483
Social support	.111
StressXSocSup	−.017
Constant:	1.811

High Stress and High Social Support

[B for Stress * (mean + sd)] + [B for Socsup * (mean + sd)] + [B for interaction term * [(mean + sd of Stress) * (mean + sd of Socsup)] + constant

.483(32.87 + 18.88) + .111(19.69 + 4.45) + −.017[(32.87 + 18.88)*(19.69 + 4.45)] + 1.811 =
.483(51.75) + .111(24.14) + −.017[(51.75)*(24.14)] + 1.811 =
25.00 + 2.68 + −.017[1249.245] + 1.811 =
25.00 + 2.68 + −21.237 + 1.811 =
8.25

High Stress and Medium Social Support

[B for Stress * (mean + sd)] + [B for Socsup * (mean)] + [B for interaction term * [(mean + sd of Stress) * (mean of Socsup)] + constant

.483(32.87 + 18.88) + .111(19.69) + −.017[(32.87 + 18.88)*(19.69)] + 1.811 =
.483(51.75) + .111(19.69) + −.017[(51.75)*(19.69)] + 1.811 =
25.00 + 2.19 + −.017[1018.96] + 1.811 =
25.00 + 2.19 + −17.32 + 1.811 =
11.68

High Stress and Low Social Support

[B for Stress * (mean + sd)] + [B for Socsup * (mean − sd)] + [B for interaction term * [(mean + sd of Stress) * (mean − sd of Socsup)] + constant

.483(32.87 + 18.88) + .111(19.69 − 4.45) + −.017[(32.87 + 18.88)*(19.69 − 4.45)] + 1.811 =
.483(51.75) + .111(15.24) + −.017[(51.75)*(15.24)] + 1.811 =
25.00 + 1.69 + −.017[788.67] + 1.811 =
25.00 + 1.69 + −13.407 + 1.811 =
15.09

Medium Stress and High Social Support

[B for Stress * (mean)] + [B for Socsup * (mean + sd)] + [B for interaction term * [(mean of Stress) * (mean + sd of Socsup)] + constant

.483(32.87) + .111(19.69 + 4.45) + −.017[(32.87)*(19.69 + 4.45)] + 1.811 =
.483(32.87) + .111(24.14) + −.017[(32.87)*(24.14)] + 1.811 =
15.88 + 2.68 + −.017[793.48] + 1.811 =
15.88 + 2.68 + −13.489 + 1.811 =
6.88

Medium Stress and Medium Social Support

[B for Stress * (mean)] + [B for Socsup * (mean)] + [B for interaction term * [(mean of Stress) * (mean of Socsup)] + constant

.483(32.87) + .111(19.69) + −.017[(32.87)*(19.69)] + 1.811 =

.483(32.87) + .111(19.69) + −.017[(32.87)*(19.69)] + 1.811 =

15.88 + 2.19 + −.017[647.21] + 1.811 =

15.88 + 2.19 + −11.003 + 1.811 =

8.87

Medium Stress and Low Social Support

[B for Stress * (mean)] + [B for Socsup * (mean − sd)] + [B for interaction term * [(mean of Stress) * (mean − sd of Socsup)] + constant

.483(32.87) + .111(19.69 − 4.45) + −.017[(32.87)*(19.69 − 4.45)] + 1.811 =

.483(32.87) + .111(15.24) + −.017[(32.87)*(15.24)] + 1.811 =

15.88 + 1.69 + −.017[500.94] + 1.811 =

15.88 + 1.69 + −8.516 + 1.811 =

10.86

Low Stress and High Social Support

[B for Stress * (mean − sd)] + [B for Socsup * (mean + sd)] + [B for interaction term * [(mean − sd of Stress) * (mean + sd of Socsup)] + constant

.483(32.87 − 18.88) + .111(19.69 + 4.45) + −.017[(32.87 − 18.88)*(19.69 + 4.45)] + 1.811 =

.483(13.99) + .111(24.14) + −.017[(13.99)*(24.14)] + 1.811 =

6.76 + 2.68 + −.017[337.72] + 1.811 =

6.76 + 2.68 + −5.74 + 1.811 =

5.51

Low Stress and Medium Social Support

[B for Stress * (mean − sd)] + [B for Socsup * (mean)] + [B for interaction term * [(mean − sd of Stress) * (mean of Socsup)] + constant

.483(32.87 − 18.88) + .111(19.69) + −.017[(32.87 − 18.88)*(19.69)] + 1.811 =

.483(13.99) + .111(19.69) + −.017[(13.99)*(19.69)] + 1.811 =

6.76 + 2.18 + −.017[275.46] + 1.811 =

6.76 + 2.18 + −4.683 + 1.811 =

6.07

Low Stress and Low Social Support

[B for Stress * (mean − sd)] + [B for Socsup * (mean − sd)] + [B for interaction term * [(mean − sd of Stress) * (mean − sd of Socsup)] + constant

.483(32.87 − 18.88) + .111(19.69 − 4.45) + −.017[(32.87 − 18.88)*(19.69 − 4.45)] + 1.811 =

.483(13.99) + .111(15.24) + −.017[(13.99)*(15.24)] + 1.811 =

6.76 + 1.69 + −.017[213.21] + 1.811 =

6.76 + 1.69 + −3.62 + 1.811 =

6.64

TABLE 5.16. Summary of Means Generated by Hand Computation of the Main Effects of Stress and Social Support and the Interaction on Depression

	High social support	Medium social support	Low social support
High stress	8.25	11.68	15.09
Medium stress	6.88	8.87	10.86
Low stress	5.51	6.07	6.64

The means obtained for these nine equations are presented in Table 5.16.

Do we have parallel lines now? (See Figure 5.7.) No, in fact we have a fan pattern (and it is close to being a triangle, with the high-social-support line being almost flat), so we have distinctly nonparallel lines. There are several facts that you should note here.

1. We still have the basic "lower left to upper right" slope to the lines, so the basic stress-to-depression relationship is still relevant and active. If you recheck Table 5.10, you will find that the stress main effect is still statistically significant ($p < .001$) in the last step.
2. The separation between the three lines that we had in Figure 5.6 is reduced, particularly on the left side; is the social support main effect still there? If you recheck the output table (Table 5.10), you will find that it is not still significant ($p = .64$).
3. We have distinctly nonparallel lines, so we should have a statistically significant interaction. We do. Now we have the job of interpreting it.

A word to the wise here: Be careful in interpreting main effects after the interaction term has been added, because these results are conditional upon the interaction term being in the equation. I usually begin with zero-order correlations, then I notice the contributions of the main effects as they are added hierarchically, and then, as before, I notice what the main effects are after the interaction has been added. You will note interesting and illuminating differences along this road.

Simple Slopes of the Three Moderation Lines

One way to interpret an interaction is to notice the steepness of slope of the three lines. In Figure 5.7 you will notice that the low-social-support line is the steepest of the three and the high-social-support line is the flattest of the

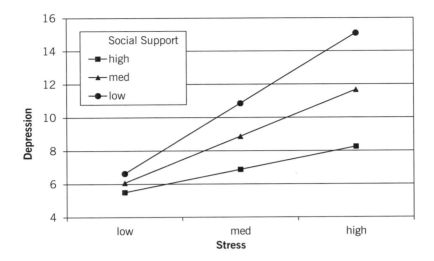

FIGURE 5.7. Graphical depiction of the main effects of stress and social support and the interaction on depression: moderation by social support of the stress-to-depression relationship.

three. This pattern means that the relationship between stress and depression is strongest for individuals who reported the lowest levels of social support, and this relationship is the weakest for those who reported the highest levels of social support. How do we know this?

Examining Simple Slopes of Moderation Lines

Let's do hand computation of these values now. Let us briefly review these equations and computations. Using this equation, we input values of −1 SD (−4.445 + 19.69), the mean (19.69), and +1 SD (4.445 + 19.69) of the variable Z (social support). The B's for the main effect (stress) and the interaction terms were 0.483 and −0.017, respectively. Again, in the general equation I focus on the simple slope and drop the second term of the equation, $(b_2Z + b_0)$.

General equation: $Y = (b_1 + b_3Z)X$

Low SS: $Y = (b_1 + b_3*15.245)X$
$= (.483 + (−.017)(15.245))X$
$= (.483 − .259) = .224$

Medium SS:
$$Y = (b_1 + b_3{}^*19.69)X$$
$$= (.483 + (-.017)(19.69)X$$
$$= (.483 - .335) = .148$$

High SS:
$$Y = (b_1 + b_3{}^*4.445)X$$
$$= (.483 + (-.017)(24.1345))X$$
$$= (.483 - .410) = .073$$

Now let us consider the standard errors of the simple slopes. The equation for that is

$$SE = SQRT\ [s_{11} + 2(Z)(s_{13}) + Z^2\ s_{33}]$$

where s_{11} is the variance for the main effect (0.018), s_{13} is the covariance of the main effect by the interaction (−0.001), and s_{33} is the variance of the interaction (0.000042). The computations are presented in Table 5.17, inserting point values for Z in appropriate places.

   If we divide the simple slopes by the respective standard errors with $(n - k - 1)$ degrees of freedom (137 in this case), we can obtain information about statistical significance (t-values and p-values). I obtained t-values of 4.28, 2.07, and 0.98, respectively, for low to high slopes, and note that the slope for high social support was nonsignificant, whereas the low and medium levels of social support yielded statistical significance. Going back to Figure 5.7, we see that the slope for the high group was flatter than the other two, and this is an indication of a buffer.

TABLE 5.17. Calculation of the Standard Errors for the Simple Slopes of Social Support

	s_{11}	$2(Z)(s_{13})$	$Z^2\ s_{33}$	Sum	SQRT of sum (standard errors)
Low	.018	2(15.245)(−.001) = −.0305	$(15.245)^2(.000042)$ = .00976	−.00274	.0523
Medium	.018	2(19.69)(−.001) = −.0394	$(19.69)^2(.000042)$ = .01628	−.00512	.0716
High	.018	2(24.13)(−.001) = −.0483	$(24.30)^2(.000042)$ = .02480	−.0055	.0742

Conceptual Interpretation: Buffers and Exacerbators

Rose et al. (2004) have noted that moderators can be classified either as buffers or exacerbators. Understanding the distinction between these two types of moderators will further your ability to interpret interactional patterns. Let us begin with *buffers*. We have established that low social support had the steepest slope and that high social support had the flattest slope. What that result means is that social support looks as if it is operating as a *buffer* here. Remember our prediction? We argued that social support would dampen or lessen the effect between stress and depression, and the fact that we found the flattest slope for high social support substantiates that prediction. Conceptually, what it means is that the general relationship between stress and depression is lowest in the case of individuals who report relatively high levels of social support; in fact, the relationship between stress and depression is negligible in this situation. In contrast, those who report the lowest levels of social support manifested the strongest relationship between stress and depression. It seems as though this latter group does not have a defense against the slings and arrows of troubling events, whereas the high-social-support group does.

Exacerbation, on the other hand, refers to a situation in which individuals who report high levels of the moderating variable exhibit a stronger relationship between the IV and the DV. I think we need an example so that you can understand how this result is the opposite of a buffer (see Figure 5.8). In this case, I have data collected from 1,092 adolescents in order to determine whether various coping strategies buffered or exacerbated the basic relationship between stress and negative adjustment (i.e., depression combined with reverse-coded self-esteem). In Figure 5.8 one can see that stress intensity is the IV, externalizing coping (e.g., yelling and screaming at others) is the ModV, and negative adjustment is the DV. What is the basic relationship here? If you focus in on the medium-level ModV line ("medium" refers to a mean of zero for the ModV, and it depicts the average IV-to-DV relationship irrespective of levels of ModV), you will note that it runs from lower left to upper right. This slope tells us that the basic relationship is a positive correlation: Higher stress intensity was associated with higher negative adjustment, and vice versa. It is instructive to notice how the slope of this line changes under conditions of high externalizing coping. If we compare the high ModV line with the medium ModV line, we note that the high ModV line is steeper. This result suggests that for those adolescents who reported higher levels of externalizing coping, the relationship between perceived stress intensity and depression was stronger. The low ModV line is practically flat and suggests that stress intensity is not related to depression under conditions of low externalizing coping. In fact, when I computed the simple slopes, I found that the low ModV line was nonsignificantly different from zero, whereas the other two lines were significantly different from zero. The point of this discussion is to highlight the case in which a ModV worsens or exacerbates the relationship between the IV and the DV, and Figure 5.8 persuasively shows that yelling and screaming at other people seems to do exactly that—that is, those people who yell and scream tend to report a stronger relationship between stress intensity and depression.

Several other issues come up when we are discussing moderational pattern interpretation. First, should we pay attention to the mean levels of the DV for these three lines? This is a difficult question to answer, because I have seen interpretations of moderations that focus on the slopes of the lines (as I did here), and I have also seen seasoned researchers focus on differences in the mean levels of the DV. For example, the first type of interpretation would be something like: "externalizing coping exacerbates the positive stress intensity-to-depression relationship," whereas the second type of interpretation would be something like "the highest level of depression was reported by individuals who reported high stress intensity and high externalizing coping." The latter interpretation notes that the most depressed individuals reported high levels of both the IV and the ModV. My view is that the

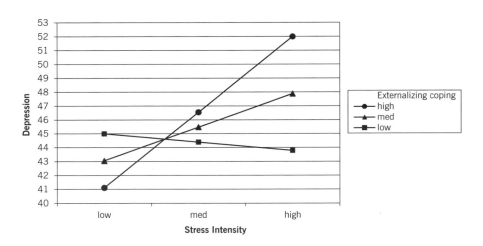

FIGURE 5.8. Example of an exacerbating moderator: Externalizing moderates the stress-to-depression relationship.

best interpretation should probably mention both aspects. In other words, the first interpretation is relatively vague about who is high or low on the DV, whereas the second interpretation is incomplete because focusing on a single mean out of the nine possible means does not capture the entire picture. I would propose that a complete interpretation would be something like this: "externalizing coping functioned as an exacerbator between the IV of perceived stress intensity and the DV of depression in that the highest levels of depression were reported by highly stressed individuals who also reported high levels of externalizing coping." Then the researcher can report the results of the simple slope analyses. The researcher will have then reported all of the important aspects of this interaction.

Can We Use Causal Language?

A second issue concerning the reporting of moderational results is whether causal language should be involved in the explanation. It is very tempting to say something like "externalizing coping, within the context of high stress, *caused* individuals to experience higher depression," but because we have concurrent data in the present case, I would avoid this type of language. My discussion of mediational results from concurrent data is relevant here. In essence, unless we have the advantage of temporal placement of variables, as in an experimental paradigm or longitudinal data, we should avoid using causal language.

KNOWLEDGE BOX. Graphing Moderation Patterns

I use ModGraph in the present discussion because it is what I am most familiar with, but it may be neither the easiest nor the best way to create graphs. Let me suggest a number of other alternatives that you may wish to try.

A freely available applet on the Internet created by Preacher, Curran, and Bauer can be found at **http://www.quantpsy.org/interact/index.html**. It is flexible and produces a number of highly desirable outputs: intercept points, simple slopes, and regions of significance. They have several different applets that handle multiple linear regression, hierarchical linear modeling, and latent curve analysis, and both two- and three-way interactions can be handled.

Jeremy Dawson also has a Web-based set of Excel-based macros that do similar types of graphing tasks, and it is found at **http://www.jeremydawson.co.uk/slopes.htm**. He also offers both two- and three-way graphing capabilities.

Yung-Jui Yang also presents something similar, but in SAS macros: **http://sites.google.com/site/yangyungjui/academic_home/statistics/sas-macros**.

Paul Johnson has created a graphing utility in the R programming language, which is particularly adept at creating figures for regression equations: **http://cran.r-project.org/web/packages/rockchalk/rockchalk.pdf**.

And there are probably other utilities available that perform similar functions, but the ones listed here are the ones I'm aware of at the moment. Please check my list of Web-based programs, macros, and applets at **www.guilford.com/jose-materials** for the most up-to-date URLs and addresses.

The Interpretation of Various Interactional Patterns

There are a finite number of possible interaction patterns, and following is my effort to capture the most distinctive and recognizable ones. I think that there are four basic patterns. In each case, I have suggested a reasonable way to interpret the interaction, so it might be helpful if you read through these and see whether they make sense to you. As you come up with significant results in the future, come back here and model your interpretation on what I have presented as a guide toward creating succinct, clear, and persuasive interpretations.

The Fan Effect

In my experience this is probably the most common pattern that one can obtain. As you can see in Figure 5.9, there is a modest spread, or fan, effect. The fan pattern can occur at either the right or left side, and the general trend of the lines can be either negative or positive in slope.

Let me now present a plausible interpretation for this made-up pattern. Catastrophizing is a tendency to see the worst in a situation, that is, to make a mountain out of a molehill, and I would predict that someone who engaged in more catastrophizing would be someone who would show an amplified relationship between stress and depression. The average stress-to-depression relationship (remember: just look at the medium-level ModV line) is a positive slope. This result tells us that the more stress that a person experiences, the higher his or her reported depression is likely to be. Consequently, my interpretation would be something like: "Catastrophizing functioned as an exacerbator for the positive relationship noted between reported stress

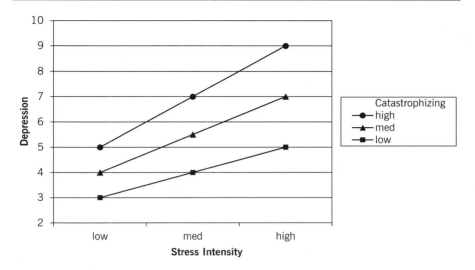

FIGURE 5.9. Example of the fan pattern: Catastrophizing moderates the stress-to-depression relationship.

intensity and reported depression. The highest level of depressive symptoms occurred in individuals who reported high stress intensity and high levels of catastrophizing."

This is a pattern often obtained in large samples. What I find in these cases is a general positive or negative slope that is either buffered or exacerbated to a moderate to modest degree. In smaller samples, one is more likely to obtain one of the following patterns.

The Triangle Pattern

Two aspects are different about this pattern (see Figure 5.10) from the previous one. First, one of the lines yields a flat slope (or something close to a flat slope), and this fact aids in the interpretation of the pattern. Second, at the junction of the three lines, we note that there is little or no separation of the DV means, and this fact also makes it easier to interpret the pattern.

In the current case I am venturing into the world of positive psychology, a subfield of psychology that is interested in identifying what is right in human functioning rather than what is wrong. Most people feel that if they experience positive events (e.g., getting a pay raise at work), then they will consequently feel happy. However, this relationship is not equally strong among all individuals: Some show a great boost from a positive event, and others will show hardly any benefit at all from the same event. Fred Bryant has proposed a possible mechanism for explaining this phenomenon. (For more information on positive psychology and savoring, see *Savoring: A New Model of Positive Experience*, 2006, by Bryant and Veroff.) Perhaps those individuals who savor their positive events—that is, focus on and derive meaning and satisfaction from these events—do a better job of extracting happiness and well-being from these events than do those individuals who do not savor. If I were to obtain data that conformed to the pattern depicted in the previous graph (again, these are made-up data, but you might be interested in some actual results in this vein that I present in Chapter 6, "Special Topics in Moderation"), the following interpretation would be in order:

> "The process of savoring exacerbates the relationship between the experience of positive events and the outcome of happiness. An individual who savors very little does not show any significant relationship between positive events and happiness, but someone who savors a lot shows a strong positive relationship. The greatest happiness is reported by those participants who reported experiencing high levels of positive events and also reported savoring to a high degree."

Notice that the interpretation is easier because one line (it will always be either high or low) yields a flat slope. Thus one can refer to that group and say that no relationship between the IV and DV was noted for that group of individuals. Further, the fact that all three moderation groups yielded almost

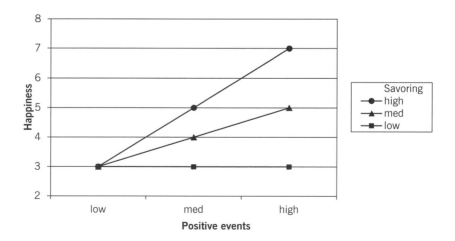

FIGURE 5.10. Example of the triangle pattern: Savoring functions as an enhancer on the positive-events-to-happiness relationship.

identical means for a given point in Figure 5.10 (in this case, low number of positive events) strengthens one's argument that the ModV had its greatest impact on the other end of the continuum, in this case, high number of positive events.

Enhancers and Dampers?

I want to make an explicit comment about the terms *buffering* and *exacerbating* at this juncture. What do we mean by *exacerbating*? The *Collins Compact English Dictionary* (2000) defines *exacerbate* as "to make (pain, emotion, or a situation) worse" (p. 286). Dictionary.com (2011) defines it as "to increase the severity, bitterness, or violence of (disease, ill feeling, etc.); aggravate." Clearly, the most important meaning of the word is to make a bad situation worse. Does that meaning apply to the graph in Figure 5.10? No, it does not. I would like to suggest that we might consider using a term such as *enhancer*, which has the meaning "to increase in value, quality, or power" (*Collins Compact English Dictionary*, 2000), in the present context. I think we need to have a term that describes moderation in the positive sphere; the term *exacerbation* is too narrow in my view.

A similar issue occurs with the word *buffer*. To buffer something is to shield against something bad: "a person or thing that lessens shock or protects from damaging impact, circumstances, etc." (*Collins Compact English Dictionary*, 2000). To use the term *buffer* in the domain of positive things or events is arguably not appropriate, either. For example, Fred Bryant has described a "killjoy" approach to life in which a person discounts or minimizes the impact of positive events. I would hypothesize that the killjoy tendency would yield something similar to Figure 5.11.

The reader will notice that this figure is similar to Figure 5.10, but the high and low ModV lines have been reversed. In this graph we see that a high killjoy tendency yields a nonsignificant relationship between positive events and happiness; that is, in essence, a person who takes a killjoy attitude is one who is not able to derive happiness from positive events. On the other hand, someone who does not employ this approach shows a positive relationship between positive events and happiness. I would be inclined to call this type of moderator a "damper" variable (or "dampener"). To act as a damper is "to have a depressing or inhibiting effect" (*Collins Compact English Dictionary*, 2000, p. 209), and you can see that the killjoy perspective has an inhibiting effect on the IV-to-DV relationship here. In sum, then, I would argue that we should use the terms *buffer* and *exacerbator* with negative variables and the terms *enhancer* and *damper* with positive variables.

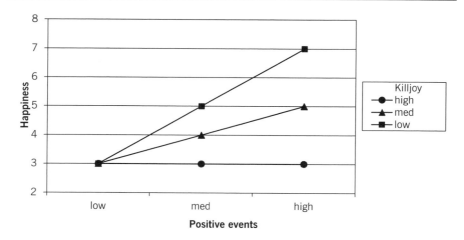

FIGURE 5.11. Example of the triangle pattern: Killjoy attitude functions as a damper on the positive events-to-happiness relationship.

The Funnel Pattern

The funnel pattern is fairly rare, but it does crop up from time to time. It is constituted by a fan effect that is more or less equidistant around a midpoint. You can see in Figure 5.12 that the high level of the ModV and the low level of the ModV yield a more or less mirror image pattern on either side of the medium level of the ModV, which should be relatively flat. The reason that this pattern occurs relatively infrequently is that the high and low levels of the ModV yield slopes that point in opposite directions. It can be situated so that it opens to the right or left, but a true funnel pattern has a medium ModV line that is relatively flat.

Let me attempt to interpret the following (made-up) pattern in Figure 5.12.

Parental warmth does not seem to have a universally positive impact on adolescent academic achievement. In fact, it might very well be the case that adolescents who experience different levels of academic challenge and different levels of parental warmth might produce a figure that looks like Figure 5.12. My interpretation would be something like this:

"Academic achievement by adolescents varies by degree of challenge in the academic environment moderated by the amount of parental warmth. The degree of academic challenge is unrelated to academic achievement under conditions of average parental warmth. In contrast, a

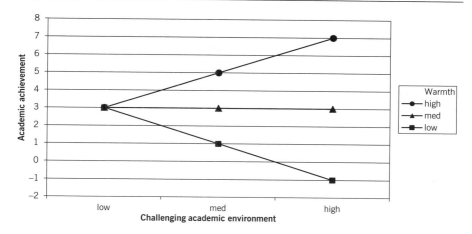

FIGURE 5.12. Example of the funnel pattern: Warmth moderates the academic environment-to-academic achievement relationship.

positive relationship between academic challenge and academic achievement was noted under conditions of high parental warmth, but a negative relationship was noted under conditions of low parental warmth. The highest academic achievement scores were found for adolescents in high challenge environments who had warm parents, whereas the lowest academic achievement scores were obtained for adolescents in high challenge environments who had parents lacking in warmth."

The researcher should also add in results from simple slope analyses at this point.

As you can tell, this interpretation is more complicated than for either the fan or triangle patterns, and the reason for this is that one must explain trends that are opposite from each other. In the present case, I believe the explanation is interpretable—teens thrive in challenging environments when they have adequate support and encouragement, whereas they are likely to perform more poorly in the same environment if they lack this support. As I mentioned earlier, this is a relatively infrequent pattern, and unfortunately it is not always easily interpretable when one does obtain it.

The Crossover Pattern (Butterfly)

The last pattern I present is called the "crossover" or "butterfly" pattern (see Figure 5.13). This pattern of data, again created out of my imagination, has a flat medium ModV line like the funnel pattern. That makes this particular pattern relatively rare. It is more common to obtain butterfly shapes that are somewhat pitched in a general positive or negative direction.

This example comes from the field of social psychology. In this example we create a study in which we wish to manipulate an IV of power. We write vignettes concerning hypothetical people who either wield a high, medium, or low amount of power in a particular situation. The experimenter also manipulates the degree of similarity between the hypothetical person in the vignette and various participants in the study (e.g., by varying gender, age, and ethnicity). We predict that participants' ratings of liking will vary by the interaction of the IV with the ModV, and supposedly we obtain the butterfly pattern shown in Figure 5.13.

The interpretation would be something like:

"No main effect for manipulated power nor a main effect for manipulated similarity were noted on ratings of liking, but a significant interaction was obtained. Under conditions of average manipulated similarity, no relationship was noted between manipulated power and liking. However, under conditions of high manipulated similarity, a positive relationship was found between manipulated power and liking. The opposite trend was seen under conditions of low manipulated similarity."

The researcher would also add in the simple slope analysis results.

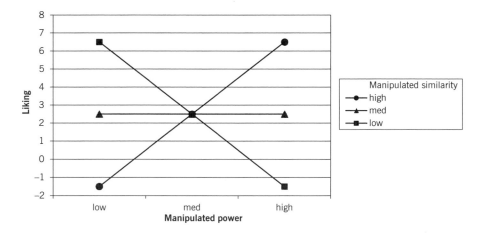

FIGURE 5.13. Example of the crossover pattern: Similarity moderates the power-to-liking relationship.

Main Effects and Interactions

I should probably mention here that most researchers usually report the main effects (if any) before going on to describe the interaction. In the true cross-over pattern, one will usually *not* obtain significant main effects. If you get a pattern that conforms to the lines depicted in Figure 5.13, all main-effect cell means will sit on top of each other, that is, the mean for all cells will be 2.5. If you look back at the funnel pattern (Figure 5.12), you should be able to work out that there would be a significant main effect for the ModV, but not for the IV. And it is likely that significant main effects will be obtained for both the IV and the ModV for the fan and triangle patterns. One typically reports the main effects first, and then says something like this (in the case of the funnel pattern): "the main effect for parental warmth was qualified by the significant interaction." Then you go on to explain the interaction. The interaction qualifies or limits the main effect because it tells the reader the conditions under which the main effect exists. For example, in the case of the funnel pattern, one could note that the significant difference in parental warmth occurs only under conditions of challenging academic environments. In the case of a significant moderation result, one is usually qualifying a main effect (or perhaps both main effects), so considerable attention should be given to being clear about how the interaction adds new and useful information beyond the main effect(s).

Things to Avoid Doing

In this chapter I showed you how to perform a linear regression analysis that would determine whether a significant moderation result is obtained. Unfortunately (as is the case with mediation as well), one cannot (yet) perform a basic moderation analysis on a single statistical software platform and obtain all of the information needed. In the previous cases I performed the regressions in SPSS and then selected certain statistical outputs to put into Mod-Graph in order to visually depict the interaction pattern. Partly because of this division of labor and partly because there is no definitive guide for how to properly conduct a moderational analysis, there are many ways in which a researcher may make a mistake. Let me enumerate the major pitfalls that I have either done myself or seen other people do:

- Failure to properly dummy-code categorical ModVs.
- Confusion about what types of variables are proper ModVs.
- Neglect of the main-effect results.

- Inaccurate graphing of the interaction result (in whatever graphing facility is used).
- Unfamiliarity with simple slope analyses.
- Inexperience with making interpretations of moderational results.
- An inclination to use causal language in interpretation.

I have explained each of these issues herein, so hopefully you will not make these mistakes, or at least make more minor versions of them.

FURTHER READING

The definitive source for understanding moderation (and learning how to graph moderation results) is the following book:

Aiken, L. S., & West, S. G. (1991). *Multiple regression: Testing and interpreting interactions*. Newbury Park, CA: Sage.

Key older readings on this topic are:

Abrahams, N. M., & Alf, E., Jr. (1972). Pratfalls in moderator research. *Journal of Applied Psychology, 56*, 245–251.

Cronbach, L. J. (1987). Statistical tests for moderator variables: Flaws in analyses recently proposed. *Psychological Bulletin, 102*, 414–417.

James, L. R., & Brett, J. M. (1984). Mediators, moderators, and tests for mediation. *Journal of Applied Psychology, 69*, 307–321.

MacCallum, R. C., & Mar, C. M. (1995). Distinguishing between moderator and quadratic effects in multiple regression. *Psychological Bulletin, 118*, 405–421.

McClelland, G. H., & Judd, C. M. (1993). Statistical difficulties of detecting interactions and moderator effects. *Psychological Bulletin, 114*, 376–390.

I would also like to mention these two papers that show how to do moderation in an accessible fashion:

Holmbeck, G. (1989). Masculinity, femininity, and multiple regression: Comment on Zeldow, Daugherty, and Clark's "Masculinity, femininity, and psychosocial adjustment in medical students: A 2-year follow-up." *Journal of Personality Assessment, 53*, 583–599.

Rose, B., Holmbeck, G., Coakley, R., & Franks, E. (2004). Mediator and moderator effects in developmental and behavioral pediatric research. *Journal of Developmental and Behavioral Pediatrics, 25*, 58–67.

A classic paper that clearly describes and tests a moderational hypothesis (i.e., the buffering role of social support in the context of stressful events) is:

Cohen, S., & Wills, T. A. (1985). Stress, social support, and the buffering hypothesis. *Psychological Bulletin, 98*, 310–357.

Of a slightly more technical nature, the following book describes moderation using categorical variables:

Aguinis, H. (2004). *Regression analysis for categorical moderators.* New York: Guilford Press.

IN-CHAPTER EXERCISES

1. *Categorical moderation.* I noted earlier that you can repeat the steps outlined in conducting basic categorical moderation by downloading the dataset named "categorical moderation example.sav" and conducting the analyses detailed herein.

2. *Continuous moderation.* If you would like to try your hand at continuous moderation, then try the dataset cleverly titled "continuous moderation example.sav."

ADDITIONAL EXERCISES

1. You have a dataset in which you want to treat gender as the X variable, disease status (1 = has lupus; 0 = does not have lupus) as the ModV, and optimism as the Y variable. Can you perform moderation on this dataset using linear regression?

2. If you have five levels to the variable "religious affiliation" in your dataset (1 = Catholic; 2 = Protestant; 3 = Jewish; 4 = Muslim; and 5 = Buddhist), how many dummy codes will you use in your moderation analyses? Assuming that your comparison group is Protestant, show how you would compose these dummy codes.

3. You wish to perform a moderation wherein a continuous variable, perspective taking, is your predictor variable, disease status is your moderating variable, and hope is your outcome variable. *Disease status* describes individuals who fall into one of four groups: no disease, tuberculosis, diabetes, and hypertension. How would you set up the predictor terms and be specific about which terms are entered in which order (assume a hierarchical regression)?

4. Explain what is meant in this chapter by the phrase "both main effects and the interaction are represented in the drawn figure."

5. Interpret the following SPSS output of a moderation analysis.

Model	Unstandardized coefficients		Standardized coefficients		
	B	Std. error	Beta	t	Sig.
1. (Constant)	10.188	.359		28.375	.000
stress	.172	.022	.469	7.733	.000
2. (Constant)	10.190	.358		28.440	.000
stress	.177	.023	.483	7.871	.000
probsolv	−.119	.086	−.085	−1.380	.169
3. (Constant)	10.130	.363		27.926	.000
stress	.172	.023	.469	7.460	.000
probsolv	−.126	.086	−.090	−1.458	.146
strxprobsolv	.005	.005	.065	1.048	.296

Note. Dependent variable: anxiety.

6. Perform a moderation analysis on the "stress rumination depression moderation problem#6.sav" dataset, assuming that stress is the predictor variable, rumination is the moderating variable, and depression is the outcome variable. Do you obtain significant moderation? How do you know? If it is significant, draw the moderation graph, and interpret the finding.

7. You submit a manuscript to a journal with the description of the moderation effect as given in the answer to problem 6, and the journal editor comes back with this comment: "The reporting of the moderation effect was incomplete. You need to compute simple slopes for the reported moderation result and interpret." You want to get your paper published, so you go away and do this. Add this information to what you did before.

8. Access the dataset titled "categorical moderation problem#8.sav" and conduct a categorical moderation in which the moderator is composed of more than two groups. In this case, ethnic group is the moderator variable, and it is composed of three groups. Create dummy-coded variables (with European New Zealand as the reference group), create the interaction terms, and run a single moderation analysis. If both interaction terms are significant, run two separate follow-up analyses, and graph any significant interactions. Report any simple slope analyses that you run.

6

Special Topics in Moderation

The previous chapter detailed how to perform basic moderational analyses, and these guidelines will suffice for many beginning users, but of course there are a number of exciting new directions in moderational approaches that many readers will be interested in learning about. I cover in this chapter the following topics:

- Johnson–Neyman regions of significance
- Multiple moderator regression analyses
- Moderation of residualized relationships
- Quadratic moderation
- Basic moderation in path analyses
- Moderation in multilevel modeling
- Moderation with latent variables
- Logistic moderation

My principal goal with this book is to be helpful to beginning users, but I cannot resist devoting some space to some higher level topics that will appeal to more experienced researchers. The novice researcher should scan this chapter to see whether there is material of interest; I daresay that the first two topics will be germane to many beginning users, if not now, then fairly soon in the future. The latter topics require that the reader have knowledge and some expertise with SEM and MLM statistics packages. If you do not know how to perform analyses with these packages, then these sections will likely be opaque and confusing. This chapter is not intended to be read sequentially; the reader should pick and choose what is comprehensible and interesting to him or her.

JOHNSON–NEYMAN REGIONS OF SIGNIFICANCE

The Johnson–Neyman technique, although initially described in the middle of the 20th century (Johnson & Fay, 1950), has increasingly been discussed lately as a useful adjunct to interpreting moderation results. Accounts of the technique have been made by Aiken and West (1991), Cohen and Cohen (1983), and Pedhazur (1997), among others. The question it seeks to answer is where the regions of significance are in the moderation graph, as defined jointly by values of the independent and moderating variables.

If one has a moderation figure (such as in Figure 6.1), one would like to know the values of X where significant differences occur between the two groups (defined by the moderator, Z). In particular, one might suspect that girls report higher levels of the DV for values of 7 and lower and that boys report higher levels of the DV for values of X greater than about 14. The Johnson–Neyman regions computation allows the researcher to identify with precision where the regions of significance and nonsignificance lie.

There are essentially two options at present for individuals who would like to compute the Johnson–Neyman procedure. The first is to hand-compute the Potthoff (1964) equations that will generate values of X for "simultaneous regions of significance." One can find these in Aiken and West (1991) and Pedhazur (1997), and I do not repeat them here, as they are computationally complicated and involved.

The second option is to use an existing statistics program to compute these values for you. Pedhazur (1997) included SPSS and SAS syntax that one could use to do these computations, but there are other options. Scialfa (1987) has written a Basic program to do the same thing. Arguably an easier

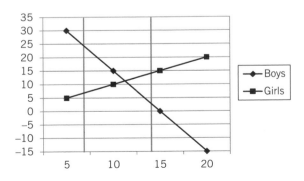

FIGURE 6.1. Example of Johnson–Neyman lines for a categorical moderation.

path to take is to use a macro written by Andrew Hayes called MODPROBE, which can be found at **http://www.afhayes.com/spss-sas-and-mplus-macros-and-code.html**. I am seeing more and more researchers reporting the Johnson–Neyman regions in their published research reports, and I would encourage you to exploit this technique to help explain moderation results.

MULTIPLE MODERATOR REGRESSION ANALYSES

In the previous chapter I gave examples of analyses in which I had a single IV, a single ModV, and a single DV. I did this to keep the presentation simple and to provide examples that could be computed with multiple regression. However, the world is a complicated place, and researchers are often motivated to reflect this compelling fact by including more variables in their analyses. The first way to tackle the complexity issue is to consider analyses in which more than one moderating variable is included. (Incidentally, one can involve more than one IV and more than one DV in analytical schemes, but one must use SEM to tackle path models of this sort. See the section "Quadratic Moderation" later in this chapter for more information on this issue.)

Let us take the following example, in which I consider whether age and/ or tendency to ruminate moderates the stress-to-self-harming relationship. I predicted that adolescents who report high levels of stress would be likely to report a stronger inclination to harm themselves, and this is the basic relationship that I investigate. Further, I wished to see whether age moderates this relationship, *and* I wished to see whether rumination moderates this relationship. And even further, it would be interesting to see whether adolescents of different ages and tendencies to ruminate show differences in the strength of the stress-to-self-harm relationship (i.e., double moderation). My specific (three-way interaction) prediction was that rumination would exacerbate the stress-to-self-harm relationship among older compared with younger adolescents. Instead of performing two separate regressions, I conduct a single regression that involves both ModVs. However, in order to proceed with this plan, I must determine that I have a sample that is sufficiently large to handle the entire analytical procedure. I rely on Jacob Cohen (1988, 1992) to provide guidance on this point, and there are also other sources and Internet applets that can yield useful information on this point. In the present case, I have a sample of 1,774 adolescents ages 9–16 years, and I wish to conduct a regression that will have two ModVs. Do I have sufficient power? The regression involves the following predictors:

1. Stress
2. Age dummy-coded (0 = younger; 1 = older)
3. Rumination
4. Stress × age
5. Stress × rumination
6. Age × rumination
7. Stress × age × rumination

Thus you can see that the regression involves seven predictor terms. In addition, three other sources of information need to be considered in order to come up with an estimate of the sample size. Following from Cohen (1992), these are: (1) the significance criterion (i.e., the alpha level); (2) the power level; and (3) the effect size. In the present case I wish to choose the typical alpha level (.05), the conventional power level of 0.80, and a small effect size, because I think that some of my effects may be fairly subtle. The last remaining variable is sample size, and that is my unknown. By reading Table 2 in Cohen's (1992) article, I see that a sample size of 726 participants is recommended for a regression analysis involving seven independent variables, an alpha level of .05, a power level of 0.80, and a small effect size. Clearly, my present sample size of 1,774 participants far exceeds this recommended minimum sample size, so I judge my sample to be adequate for the present analysis.

Before I go on to present the results, a couple of comments are in order here. First, note that when Cohen (1992) says "independent variables," he means individual and separate predictors. Someone might say that I have only three IVs in the present case (stress, age, and gender) and that the remaining terms are interactions and do not count. Not true. Cohen wishes us to count each predictor as an "independent variable," and I have seven of those in this case. Second, if you are new to the area of power analysis, a bit of reading would be useful so that you can make informed decisions about alpha level and power level. I used the conventional choices in the present case because I am not doing anything out of the ordinary, but researchers may need to vary some or all of these variables to accurately reflect what they are doing in their own special cases.

Helpful Suggestion: The dataset is called "multiple moderators.sav," and you may wish to find it and follow along with these analyses.

A few words about the variables. The age range was dichotomized in the present case in order to simplify analyses and resultant graphs, but one might prefer in some cases to treat it as an ordinal variable with a meaningful range. In this case, I split the range at the age of 13, because this is the age at which self-harming behavior begins to become more common; 60% of the sample was 9–12 years old, and 40% was 13–16 years old. Rumination was composed of the average of four separate items, and stress was composed of the average of four separate items. Self-harm was measured with an average of two frequency items: How many days over the last month did you (1) "think about self-harming" or (2) "perform a self-harming action"? I have not prepared the data (i.e., data recoding and multiplication) in order to give you practice in these basic data preparation skills. You are very welcome.

Let us look at the results. Table 6.1 presents the results of descriptive statistics and the hierarchical regression that I performed. Quite a lot of explanation is in order now. First, why do a hierarchical regression? Some people do a simple simultaneous inclusion regression (i.e., step 3 only in Table 6.1) and take their results from that single step. I like to do the regression hierarchically because I can see how the main effects are qualified (or not) by the interactions. In the present case, one can see that all of the two-way interactions are statistically significant in the second step, but one (stress × rumination) becomes nonsignificant when the three-way interaction is entered in the last step. This result means that although one might wish to examine the stress-by-rumination interaction, it is superseded in this case by the significant three-way interaction. Another reason for doing a hierarchical regression is that SPSS generates an R^2 *change* statistic for steps in a hierarchical regression, and it is useful to report how much variance is accounted for at each step. For example, the three main effects in the first step account for 14%, the two-way interactions account for 4% on the second step, and the three-way interaction accounts for 1.6% on the fourth step. It is not uncommon, as it is here, that the three-way interaction is significant but does not account for much variance. Some journals request this information when one is reporting results about moderation analyses.

Second, how do we interpret the results in Table 6.1? I would like the reader to note that the basic relationship turned out as I expected it to; namely, stress was positively associated with self-harming ($\beta = .24$ on the first step). The interpretation of this is that individuals who reported higher levels of stress also reported higher levels of harming themselves. Then we look to see whether the two ModVs yielded main-effect relationships with the DV: We see on the same step that age was significantly and positively predictive of self-harm ($\beta = .09$) and that rumination was as well ($\beta = .19$).

TABLE 6.1. Descriptive Statistics and Results from the Hierarchical Regression Run to Examine the Effect of Multiple Moderators (Rumination and Age) on the Stress-to-Self-Harm Relationship

Descriptive Statistics

	N	Minimum	Maximum	Mean	Std. deviation
Rumination	1757	1.00	5.00	2.3775	.83640
Stress	1732	1.00	5.00	2.2823	.91857
Valid N (listwise)	1720				

agerecode

		Frequency	Percent	Valid percent	Cumulative percent
Valid	.00 Younger	1071	60.4	60.4	60.4
	1.00 Older	703	39.6	39.6	100.0
	Total	1774	100.0	100.0	

Coefficients

Model	Unstandardized coefficients B	Unstandardized coefficients Std. error	Standardized coefficients Beta	t	Sig.
1. (Constant)	.540	.041		13.100	.000
Rumination	.121	.016	.189	7.598	.000
Stress	.139	.015	.238	9.564	.000
agerecode	.094	.025	.085	3.789	.000
2. (Constant)	1.086	.097		11.215	.000
Rumination	−.077	.039	−.120	−1.968	.049
Stress	−.022	.041	−.038	−.543	.587
agerecode	−.522	.081	−.476	−6.471	.000
rumxage	.187	.031	.445	5.775	.000
rumxstr	.051	.014	.359	3.556	.000
agexstr	.074	.030	.175	2.461	.014
3. (Constant)	.726	.114		6.362	.000
Rumination	.070	.046	.110	1.527	.127
Stress	.138	.049	.237	2.831	.005
agerecode	.506	.193	.462	2.618	.009
rumxage	−.238	.080	−.565	−2.986	.003
rumxstr	−.011	.018	−.082	−.650	.516
agexstr	−.365	.081	−.869	−4.521	.000
agexstrxrum	.171	.029	1.205	5.836	.000

Note. Dependent variable: Self-harm.

These results tell us that older adolescents reported more self-harming than younger adolescents (the older group was coded with 1) and that rumination was positively predictive of self-harming, too. It is important to realize that these relationships are identified while stress is in the regression equation at the same time. Because of shared variance among predictors, these relationships may or may not be similar to zero-order correlations. In fact, rumination was more strongly correlated with self-harming by itself ($r = .29$, $p < .001$), but this zero-order correlation is attenuated by the predictive power of stress and age in this regression. (Incidentally, identifying results such as this may stimulate the researcher to examine mediational relationships among their variables; in this case, stress may explain the rumination-to-self-harming relationship in a mediational analysis.)

Now we move on to the two-way interactions in step 2 (see Table 6.1). We see that all three of these interactions were statistically significant at the conventional $p < .05$ level. What this result suggests is that there may be interesting two-way interactions to probe. Let me emphasize the phrase "may be." I would not run off and graph these results just yet—we have other decisions to make. Most important, did we find a significant three-way interaction?

The answer is yes, we did. If we had *not* found a significant three-way interaction, we could return to the two-ways and begin to probe those. However, because we obtained a three-way interaction, we know that this interaction is the most important one to probe because it qualifies all findings attained in previous steps. How does one probe a three-way interaction? Online graphing facilities exist (e.g., see Kris Preacher's website **http://www. quantpsy.org/interact/index.html**) that can handle this type of graph, and they can produce a single figure to depict this complex three-way interaction. My program, ModGraph, cannot produce a three-way graph because it allows for only a single IV and a single ModV. However, if we split the three-way interaction into two equal parts, then we can graph it with ModGraph. One can dichotomously split either rumination or age, as these are our two moderating variables. Age has already been dichotomously split into younger (9–12 years) and older (13–16 years) adolescents, so I would be inclined to do the division this way; but one could also do a median split on rumination and divide the sample into high versus low ruminators.

In SPSS, I would go to DATA, and then choose SPLIT FILE, and then select "organize output by groups" and insert age (dummy-coded) as this organizing variable. Then you go back to ANALYZE, choose REGRESSION, and then move on to reconstitute your hierarchical regression. Essentially remove all reference to age; remove age as a main effect and all interactions involving the age variable. Run the analysis, and you will get one of two outcomes: (1) one group will have a significant interaction and the other will not; or (2) both groups will yield a significant interaction, but they will be different in direction and pattern. Let us see what we obtained in the present case.

Table 6.2 contains the output for the younger adolescent group, and Table 6.3 contains the output for the older adolescent group. If you look at the bottom line in each table, you will see that we obtained the first alternative: The younger adolescents did not yield a significant interaction ($p = .473$), but the older adolescents did ($p = .000$). Everything else between the two groups is similar, by the way.

TABLE 6.2. Statistical Outputs of Regression for Younger Group

| Model | Unstandardized coefficients | | Standardized coefficients | | |
	B	Std. error	Beta	t	Sig.
1. (Constant)	.792	.045		17.483	.000
Stress	.109	.016	.226	6.890	.000
Rumination	.043	.018	.081	2.464	.014
2. (Constant)	.726	.103		7.026	.000
Stress	.138	.044	.287	3.127	.002
Rumination	.070	.042	.132	1.686	.092
strxrum	−.011	.016	−.096	−.718	.473

Note. agerecode = .00 (younger). Dependent variable: Self-harm.

TABLE 6.3. Statistical Outputs of Regression for Older Group

| Model | Unstandardized coefficients | | Standardized coefficients | | |
	B	Std. error	Beta	t	Sig.
1. (Constant)	.254	.072		3.550	.000
Stress	.180	.028	.250	6.543	.000
Rumination	.240	.029	.311	8.142	.000
2. (Constant)	1.232	.176		7.009	.000
Stress	−.227	.072	−.314	−3.134	.002
Rumination	−.167	.073	−.217	−2.291	.022
strxrum	.159	.026	.963	6.062	.000

Note. agerecode = 1.00 (older). Dependent variable: Self-harm.

So what do we do next? Typically we would not graph the younger group because no significant moderation was obtained, but we would graph the older group because a significant interaction was found there. However, just to remind you what a nonsignificant moderation looks like, I have graphed the former result (younger adolescents) in Figure 6.2.

Let me first note that there is a slight positive slope to the lines, which reflects the significant main effect for stress on self-harm. Also, there is slight separation of the lines, which signifies the main effect for rumination on self-harm. But, as I expected, the lines are essentially parallel, which indicates a nonsignificant interaction ($p = .47$). The important point to take from this graph is that *nothing interesting is happening here*, at least with regard to an interaction. I do not include graphs such as this in my research reports, because everyone already knows what a nonsignificant interaction looks like, and I would suggest that you adopt this practice. In the present case of decomposing a three-way interaction, just tell the reader that the younger adolescent group did not yield a significant interaction and display the graph of the significant interaction for the older adolescent group.

When I graphed this latter result, I obtained the pattern in Figure 6.3. This figure shows a dynamic in which older adolescents who ruminate at high levels manifest a stronger relationship between stress and self-harm than do

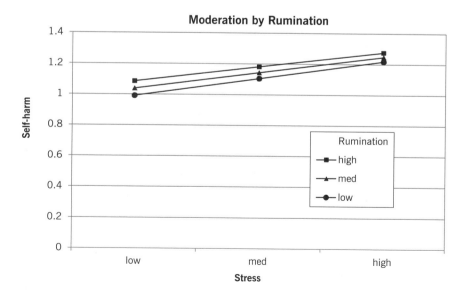

FIGURE 6.2. Depiction of the nonsignificant moderation result for the younger group.

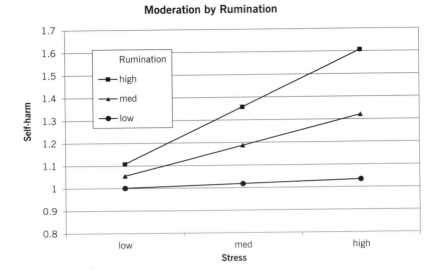

FIGURE 6.3. Depiction of the significant moderation result for the older group: Rumination moderated the stress-to-self-harm relationship.

those who ruminate less. (This is a classic triangle pattern, by the way, for those of you who have read Chapter 5.) The simple slope analyses would probably indicate that the slopes for the medium- and high-rumination groups were statistically different from zero, but the low-rumination group seems to manifest a nonsignificant slope. It seems that rumination is an exacerbator in the sense that it seems to amplify the relationship of stress on self-harm; however, because we have conducted this analysis on concurrent data, I am not sure what causal relationships may be lurking behind this very intriguing moderation result. I have longitudinal data on these variables (three times of measurement separated by 1 year each), so I can examine more specifically and powerfully how these variables affect each other causally. In the meantime, however, I have obtained a result that is worth reporting.

Other Considerations

Nonsignificant Three-Way Interaction

What happens when we run one of these multiple moderator regressions and the three-way interaction *does not* turn out to be significant? If we get this type of result, it means that we did not get double moderation, and that just happens sometimes. We may still have single moderation (two-way interactions), and, if we do, then these should be probed. However, there is a minor wrinkle here: We may have obtained a "significant" two-way interaction because of the inclusion of other two-way terms. Another way to say this is: A particular two-way interaction term may be significant only in conjunction with this particular set of two-way interactions. I take a conservative approach in that I report two-way interactions only if they "stand on their own," that is, if they show up in a focused regression. Let us say that the preceding three-way interaction did not turn out to be significant and that I obtained the three significant two-ways noted before. I would run three more regressions, and each would be focused on a single two-way interaction. If an interaction term proved to be significant in any of these focused analyses, then I would graph and report it or them. If one or several turn out to be nonsignificant, then I would ignore it or them because I would then have adequate basis to be concerned about robustness. Other advisors may urge you to graph all of the significant interactions, but I like to err on the side of caution.

More Than Two ModVs

The preceding example I gave involved two moderating variables; what about three or more? Let me first state that proposing a basic (i.e., IV by ModV) moderational prediction is not easy. Refer to Chapter 5 of this book about the four particular patterns obtainable from regression analyses and the associated section on buffers, exacerbators, enhancers, and dampers (pp. 185, 191). In my experience, it is difficult to anticipate correctly how two variables will interact with each other to predict a third from all of these possibilities. Many researchers make claims about "z variable will moderate the relationship between x variable on y variable" or some other rather vague thing, and they often are not more specific because they actually do not know how this moderation will be evidenced. It is rare for a researcher to go further and say that the ModV will buffer or exacerbate a particular relationship in a particular way. All of this is to say that to consider two, three, or even four moderators is indeed a very brave thing to do. My recommendation: Be clear about whether what you are doing is exploratory or deductive. I sometimes will include three or four ModVs just to see what types of interactions may be lurking in the data, and I try to be very clear that this is exploratory. However, sometimes I strike out in the direction of trying to confirm a specific hypothesis with such a regression.

One such example is illustrated in a recent article of mine in *Journal of Youth and Adolescence* (Jose & Brown, 2008). From my reading of Susan Nolen-Hoeksema's proposed theory of the onset of rumination in early adolescence (Nolen-Hoeksema, 1994), I surmised that a four-way interaction would be an appropriate test. In short, I interpreted her theory to say that females in early adolescence would evidence an exacerbating effect of rumination on the stress-to-depression relationship. Let me spell it out: An exacerbating effect of rumination (first ModV) on the relationship of stress (IV) to depression (DV) should be found only among early adolescent girls (age as a second ModV and gender as a third ModV). How did it turn out? Despite a marginally significant four-way interaction appearing in the regression analysis, the obtained pattern did not conform to the prediction. This is an example of an attempt on my part to deductively evaluate a theoretical hypothesis with a complicated moderation analysis, and the interested reader may wish to examine the details of how I did this in the actual article (Jose & Brown, 2008). But as one can see with the significant three-way interaction that I found previously that predicted self-harming thoughts and behavior, I hypothesized and then subsequently found a perfectly sensible and interpretable three-way interaction. I could add another moderator on top of this analysis—for example, maybe predicting that I would find this relationship in New Zealand but not in Taiwan—and come up with a perfectly reasonable four-way interaction prediction. They are hard to generate, but not impossible.

Examining two or more moderators at the same time is a good thing to do because undoubtedly these analyses will approximate the real world better than focused one-moderator-at-a-time types of analyses, but the researcher should be prepared for the complexities involved. First of all, the sample size must be adequate to support a regression with a greater number of terms (be sure to read Cohen [1992] on power analyses on this point). Second, construct your regression to deductively test a hypothesis. And third, be sure to emphasize that the highest level interaction is the most illuminating, and point out that it qualifies any lower level main and interaction effects.

MODERATION OF RESIDUALIZED RELATIONSHIPS

The title of this section may be a bit vague, so let me hasten to explain. Not many researchers or statisticians have worked out how to use moderation with longitudinal data, but one application that seems to be accepted in the literature is moderation of residualized relationships. In this situation we begin with four variables: (1) IV at Time 1; (2) ModV at T1; (3) DV at T1; and (4) DV at T2. The researcher residualizes the DV (DV at T1 predicts

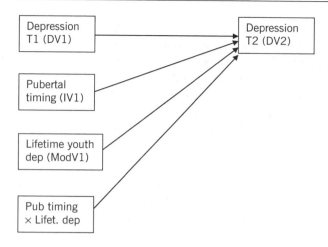

FIGURE 6.4. Path model of the residualized moderation example.

DV at T2) and then proceeds with a typical moderation analysis. The point of doing this type of analysis is that one can see whether the IV and ModV separately and together predict *change in a DV*. And from Chapter 4 in this book, you will know that using residualized regressions is an important tool in the researcher's toolbox for studying developmental change. Using these variables, Figure 6.4 depicts how this analysis would look for a regression or SEM analysis.

Let me give an example of such an analysis published in 2010 by my colleague Karen Rudolph, at the University of Illinois, Urbana–Champaign, and her colleague Wendy Troop-Gordon, at North Dakota State University. Their dataset and a .pdf copy of the paper are located at **www.guilford.com/jose-materials**. Read the paper and try out this analysis with their dataset to get a sense of how to do this type of analysis. They were interested in determining whether a variety of potential risk factors (such as family stress and children's responses to stress) would moderate the relationship between pubertal timing and subsequent depression. They examined a large number of moderators and found a large number of intriguing and interpretable relationships, but I focus on only one: moderation by lifetime youth depression.

> **Helpful Suggestion:** The authors have kindly made a portion of their dataset available, so if you download "residualized moderation example. sav," you can follow along and repeat the following analyses.

If you look at Rudolph and Troop-Gordon's Table 3 (2010, p. 442), you will see a list of these moderation analyses. Focus on the second regression: They covaried out Wave 1 depression scores (to do the residualization), then entered the IV (pubertal timing) and the ModV (lifetime youth depression), and on the last step they entered the pubertal timing × lifetime youth depression interaction, which proved to be statistically significant.

If you perform the same analysis, you will obtain the regression output reported in Table 6.4.

A brief note to those of you actually performing these analyses and comparing the results with the published paper: You will notice that the obtained results in Table 6.4 are close to those reported in the published paper, but are not exactly the same. The reason for this is that Rudolph and Troop-Gordon used multiple imputation of their data to cope with missing values, and rather than asking you to do the same—which can be tedious and complicated—I provide only one of the multiple datasets used. The resulting figure is very similar to the one presented in the published paper, and the statistical outputs are similar enough so that you can use this as an example. Another point of information: All variables, other than the interaction, were standardized. This means that all variables (except for the interaction term) yielded a mean of 0 and a standard deviation of 1. It is not necessary to standardize predictors for moderation analyses, but some researchers prefer to use standardized rather than centered variables to assist interpretation when they graph the results. However, as noted in Chapter 5, one does not need to center or standardize.

So now we have the regression results. I used ModGraph to create the graph (you can use whatever program you want), and I obtained Figure 6.5. If you are following along with this discussion by actually doing the

TABLE 6.4. Statistical Outputs of Residualized Moderation Analysis

Model	Unstandardized coefficients		Standardized coefficients		
	B	Std. error	Beta	t	Sig.
1. (Constant)	−.019	.052		−.364	.716
Wave1 depression	.687	.067	.687	10.244	.000
Pubertal timing	.216	.052	.216	4.173	.000
Lifetime youth depression	−.004	.068	−.004	−.060	.952
Pubertal timing × Lifetime youth depression	.220	.049	.234	4.485	.000

Note. Dependent variable: Wave2 depression.

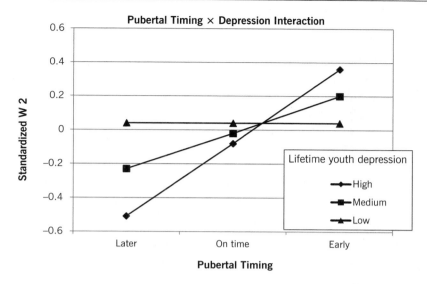

FIGURE 6.5. Graphical depiction of the residualized moderation example.

analysis and graphing, one other critical bit of information is in order. ModGraph automatically uses "low," "medium," and "high" as the labels for the IV and ModV in the figure, and the graph generated with these statistical outputs will have these usual labels along the x-axis for pubertal timing. Rudolph and Troop-Gordon (2010) constructed this variable differently because they had information about *timing* of puberty, not *amount* of puberty: Low numerical values on this variable were indicative of later puberty, medium values with "on time" puberty, and high values with early puberty. I have relabeled these x-axis labels in ModGraph to conform to Rudolph and Troop-Gordon's labels.

Once we have the figure generated, then we propose a succinct and descriptive interpretation. Here is what Rudolph and Troop-Gordon (2010) said:

> For W1 depression, earlier maturation predicted heightened subsequent depression in youths experiencing high, $b = 0.35$, $t(60) = 4.38$, $p < .001$, and moderate, $b = 0.21$, $t(482) = 3.64$, $p < .001$, but not low, $b = 0.07$, $t(65) = 0.78$, ns, levels of depression (see Figure 1a). Likewise, for lifetime history of depression, earlier maturation predicted heightened subsequent depression in youths experiencing high, $b = 0.46$, $t(34) = 5.33$, $p < .001$, and moderate, $b = 0.23$, $t(207) = 4.01$, $p < .001$, but not low, $b = 0.00$, $t(2,717) = 20.04$, ns, levels of lifetime depression (see Figure 1b).

Further on in the paper they say, "In sum, results supported the idea that prior depression, personality traits, and maladaptive responses to stress accentuated the depressogenic effect of earlier maturation" (p. 444).

There are two points to be made here: (1) Rudolph and Troop-Gordon (2010) cited simple slope analyses to help them explain their moderation finding, and (2) they referred to the moderation as "accentuation" (which is a synonym for *exacerbation* or *enhancing*).

In the Discussion section, Rudolph and Troop-Gordon (2010) say:

> Earlier maturation was also associated with subsequent depression in youths with a lifetime history of depression but not those without such a history. That a history of depression accentuated the effects of earlier maturation even after adjusting for recent depression suggests that youths with a history of depression suffer some core, lasting deficits that contribute to their emotional vulnerability in the face of earlier maturation. (p. 445)

Notice that the authors made use of the simple slopes results here by citing the group without a history of depression as manifesting "no relationship." They go on to link the finding with other literature and theory. I think that this is a compelling example of how moderation can be used with longitudinal data, and I would encourage other researchers to think about using moderation with residualized DVs, as was done here.

QUADRATIC MODERATION

As noted in Chapter 2, Baron and Kenny in 1986 suggested that researchers may wish to investigate whether quadratic moderation occurs in their datasets. This suggestion has largely not been taken up for several reasons. First, most researchers do not typically think in terms of quadratic hypotheses; it does not occur to them that they might obtain curvilinear relationships. And this is a shame, because many curvilinear relationships exist in data, and I would urge you to think along these lines. Second, most researchers do not really know how to conduct a quadratic analysis in SPSS or any other statistics package. I am about to correct that lack of knowledge in the present section of this book, so just keep reading. And third, there does not seem to be a widely available graphing program that would allow a user to quickly and readily create a figure of a quadratic moderation. ModGraph, as currently constructed, does not do this. I am currently working on a program to do this, and I include a screen shot from its output later to illustrate a quadratic moderation result (see Figure 6.7).

Some foundational knowledge would be helpful here first. When one computes a garden-variety multiple regression, one almost always conducts a *linear* regression in that the predictors are expected to predict the DV in a linear fashion, that is, the slope of the coefficient line is straight. A basic Pearson correlation would yield a straight line, for example. However, it is possible to discover and describe curvilinear relationships between variables, and that is where quadratic regression comes in. Quadratic relationships are depicted with a curved line that has a single bow, cubic relationships have two bows (they look like the letter s), and so forth, ad infinitum. We keep it simple and focus on quadratic relationships here.

Now let us step back in time to the Baron and Kenny (1986) article and reread what they had to say about this:

> The quadratic moderation effect can be tested by dichotomizing the moderator at the point at which the function is presumed to accelerate. If the function is quadratic . . . the effect of the independent variable should be greatest for those who are high on the moderator. Alternatively, quadratic moderation can be tested by hierarchical regression procedures described by Cohen and Cohen (1983). Using the same notation as in the previous paragraph, Y is regressed on X, Z, XZ, Z^2, and XZ^2. The test of quadratic moderation is given by the test of XZ^2. The interpretation of this complicated regression equation can be aided by graphing or tabling the predicted values for various values of X and Z. (p. 1176)

There are a number of notable points to amplify here. First, Cohen and Cohen (1983), Cohen et al. (2003), and Aiken and West (1991) discuss polynomial terms and curvilinear relationships well, and for further information and deep background, see these valuable sources.

Second, the equation that one must set up is a bit "complicated," as Baron and Kenny say in the preceding quote. The equation is

$$Y = b_1X + b_2Z + b_3XZ + b_4Z^2 + b_5XZ^2 \qquad (6.1)$$

where Y is the dependent variable, the coefficients b_1 through b_5 are slopes associated with the five predictors, X refers to the main effect, and Z refers to the moderator. As many authors opt for centering to assist in the graphing, I carry that strategy forward here, but please remember that centering is not necessary for the statistical computations. So, first of all, if we choose this alternative, both X and Z variables will need to be centered. Second, three interaction terms need to be created: (1) the usual XZ interaction term; (2) the quadratic term, Z^2, which is created by squaring the moderator; and (3) the quadratic moderation term, XZ^2, which is created by multiplying the quadratic term by the IV (X).

Two more important points need to be made before we move to an empirical example. First, the main effects and the basic moderation term need to be entered into the equation with the quadratic terms in order to accurately test whether quadratic moderation occurred or not. In other words, one *must* enter all five of these terms. Second, I like to enter the terms hierarchically in order to see how and to what extent the quadratic terms qualify the main effects and the basic moderation term, as you will see.

In this empirical example, I was interested in seeing whether avoidance would moderate the relationship between stressful life events and amount of sleep. In our sample of 1,774 adolescents, we asked how many problems (stressful events) they had experienced in the areas of school, friends, family, and body over the last month, and we summed these across these four domains to constitute our independent variable. For our dependent variable, we asked how many nights over the preceding week they had obtained at least 8 hours of sleep, and this was intended to be an assessment of the degree of adequate sleep that they had obtained in the previous week. We anticipated that greater stress would be predictive of less sleep. Further, we sought to determine whether avoidance coping would moderate this basic relationship, that is, would individuals who avoided their problems sleep better under conditions of high stress? And finally we thought that there was a possibility that the moderating relationship might exhibit a quadratic shape, that is, that avoidance might evidence a curvilinear relationship with stress to predict sleep behavior.

> **Helpful Suggestion:** The name of the present dataset is "quadratic moderation example.sav," and I invite you to prepare the data and run the following regression. You are entirely welcome to graph the quadratic moderation result as well.

How to Do Quadratic Moderation

First, I centered the IV (stressc) and ModV (avoidc). Second, I created the three interaction terms: stressc × avoidc (XZ); avoidc × avoidc (Z^2); and avoidc × avoidc × stressc (XZ^2). Third, I ran a hierarchical regression with five steps, entering each term in a separate step. When I performed this analysis on the entire sample, I obtained a weak but significant quadratic moderator ($p = .03$), which was heartening but a little bit disappointing. I wanted to find a strong effect to present here, so I considered the possibility that I might have another moderator operating, namely gender. The stress and coping literature frequently finds that males avoid problems more than females do, so I thought that I might find this effect here as well. I ran the regression stipulated for the two genders separately (using splitfile in SPSS), and I found that females yielded a distinctly nonsignificant quadratic moderation result ($p = .40$) but that males ($N = 819$) yielded a distinctly significant quadratic moderation result (see Table 6.5).

TABLE 6.5. Statistical Outputs of the Quadratic Moderation Analysis

Model	Unstandardized coefficients		Standardized coefficients		
	B	Std. error	Beta	t	Sig.
1. (Constant)	5.258	.064		82.375	.000
stressc	−.052	.018	−.103	−2.966	.003
2. (Constant)	5.266	.064		82.587	.000
stressc	−.042	.018	−.083	−2.316	.021
avoidc	−.168	.074	−.082	−2.276	.023
3. (Constant)	5.248	.066		80.088	.000
stressc	−.047	.019	−.093	−2.522	.012
avoidc	−.163	.074	−.079	−2.203	.028
stress×avoid	.021	.017	.042	1.177	.240
4. (Constant)	5.223	.078		66.577	.000
stressc	−.046	.019	−.091	−2.469	.014
avoidc	−.180	.079	−.087	−2.267	.024
stress×avoid	.018	.018	.036	.985	.325
avoidsq	.036	.061	.022	.587	.557
5. (Constant)	5.214	.078		66.662	.000
stressc	−.014	.022	−.028	−.650	.516
avoidc	−.133	.081	−.065	−1.647	.100
stress×avoid	.049	.021	.100	2.279	.023
avoidsq	.029	.061	.018	.481	.631
stress×avoidsq	−.037	.014	−.139	−2.674	.008

Note. Y1Gender = male. Dependent variable: Y1 How many nights in last week got 8 hours sleep.

As expected, stress was a significant negative predictor of sleep behavior ($\beta = -.10$), and avoidance on the second step was a weak negative predictor of sleep behavior ($\beta = -.08$) as well. The basic moderational term proved to be a nonsignificant predictor on the third step, and the quadratic term was nonsignificant as well. However, the quadratic moderation term (XZ^2) proved to be statistically significant. It is important to note that the two main effects are qualified by this interaction; in fact, they both "disappear" when the last term is entered. Let me now return to Baron and Kenny's (1986) comments about quadratic moderation. I find it amusing that they say "The interpretation of this complicated regression equation can be aided by graphing or tabling the predicted values for various values of X and Z" (p. 1176). I find this comment droll because the process of graphing a quadratic moderation result is not for the faint of heart (or a person short on time). I sat down to graph this result, and it took me more than an hour. I made a minor error in algebraic computation, which took a little more time to straighten out, and at the end of it, I had Figure 6.6.

Let me first describe how I created the graph in case any of you decide to hand-compute the means and draw the figure. The first decision to be made, and it is not trivial, is to determine the number of set points for the IV and ModV. You can probably see that I chose five for each variable: 2 SDs below the mean (Vlow); 1 SD below the mean (Low); the mean (Med); one SD above the mean (High); and two SDs above the mean (Vhigh). The first thing to be acknowledged here is that three points (as Aiken and West, 1991, suggest and as ModGraph uses) is not sufficient. We will have a difficult time ascertain-

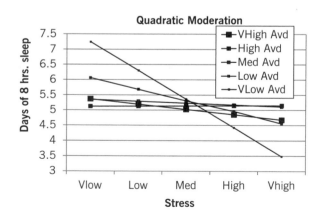

FIGURE 6.6. Graphical depiction of the hand-computed quadratic moderation result.

ing a curvilinear relationship with nine means (3 × 3). Actually, the better way to say it is that one will *not* be able to identify a curvilinear relationship with three points. So how many points should one solve for: four, five, six, or more? I decided that five might be adequate in the present case, but more is better. The implication of five points for each of the IV and the ModV is that one will have to hand-compute 25 complicated algebraic equations to obtain 25 means. Five values of the IV times five values of the ModV equals 25 means. If you choose 7 × 7, for example, you will do 49 equations, and it will take even more time.

The first equation, for Vhigh Avoidance by Vhigh Stress, looked like this:

[B for Stressc(mean + 2sd)] + [B for Avoidc(mean + 2sd)] + [B for Avoidc^2(mean + 2sd) ^{2}] + [B for 1st interaction term * [(mean + 2sd of Avoidc)] * [(mean + 2sd of Stressc)]] + [B for 2nd interaction term * [(mean + 2sd of Avoidc)]^2 * [(mean + 2sd of Stressc)]] + constant

And so forth. I won't take you through the whole process, but it is long and arduous.

It is now time to look at Figure 6.6 and try to understand what it has to say. I think that you will probably have the same reaction that I did, which was: This figure is as clear as mud. In short, graphing 5 × 5 was probably not sufficient for this quadratic moderation result. At the time I was writing this book, I was also developing a computer program named M&M (for Mediation and Moderation) that will compute these types of equations, and in the program I have chosen nine points for the moderating variable and a virtually infinite number for the IV in order to maximize the ability to capture the quadratic pattern. Figure 6.7 (on page 220) is a screenshot of this output.

The figure is not "publication ready" because it does not allow for the insertion of legends and labels, so let me tell you what should be in the figure. The IV along the bottom is stress, and those values represent the entire range of available data on that variable, no more and no less. The y-axis is "number of days per week of 8-hr sleep," and it represents the range of available data for that variable as well, no more and no less. The shaded lines represent nine levels of the moderator, avoidance. A dark line means high avoidance, and a light line means low avoidance.

Interpretation of Quadratic Moderation

If you examine this pattern, you will doubtless be puzzled because there are no curves. The "curvilinear" relationship is evident in the slopes of the lines

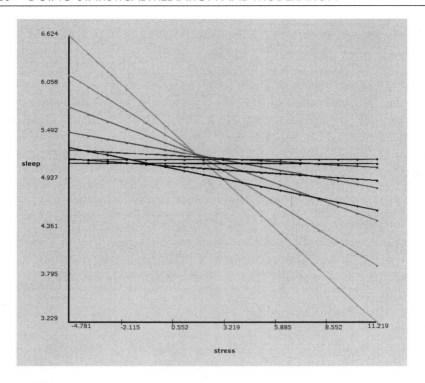

FIGURE 6.7. Screenshot of M&M's graphical depiction of the quadratic moderation result: Avoidance quadratically moderated the stress-to-sleep relationship. (Note: Dark lines represent high levels of the moderator, and light lines represent low levels of the moderator.)

along the range of the moderator. The lines for low levels of the moderator are the steepest, the flattest lines are for medium and medium-high avoidance, and the slope begins to tilt again in a negative direction for the very-high-avoidance group. If we took the time to generate simple slopes for these lines (see Aiken & West, 1991), we would find that the low-avoidance groups are statistically different from zero and that some of the intermediate groups evidence a flatter slope, and I think that it is likely that the highest avoidance group would manifest a steeper slope than the medium-avoidance groups. That is where the quadratic moderation is evident: The basic negative slope is not symmetrical across the nine levels of the moderator. If it were, the highest avoidance group should show virtually a flat slope.

Now let me show you something else. Figure 6.7 is the preferred way to depict moderation, but it is not the only way. If we reverse the IV and the ModV, we get a different pattern (see Figure 6.8), and I think that this latter approach has merit in terms of facilitating interpretation. The first point to make is that the means are identical to those in Figure 6.7. The second point is that some reviewers and researchers will *not* prefer this method because levels of the IV are depicted by lines on the graph, not by points on the *x*-axis. This presentation, in my view, is not wrong; it is just atypical.

In Figure 6.8 the curvilinear relationship is obvious. Let us see whether the same interpretation that we derived before applies here. We noted that the steepest slopes occurred for the individuals with Vlow and Low avoidance and that the next steepest slope occurred for the individuals with Vhigh avoidance. In this altered depiction of the same data, that is where we are finding the largest dispersion of means across different levels of stress.

I would be inclined to interpret this graph in this fashion: No differences in sleep patterns are noted for individuals who report intermediate to high levels of avoidance (Med and High) regardless of whether they experience different levels of stress. A person who avoids his or her problems to a medium to high degree will report sleeping 8 hours for 5 days out of 7, regardless of whether he or she experiences very low stress, medium-level stress, or very

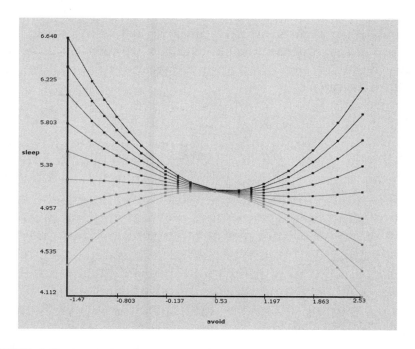

FIGURE 6.8. Screenshot from M&M of an alternative way to graph a quadratic moderation. (Note: The moderating variable is arrayed on the x-axis, and lines represent different levels of the independent variable, stress.)

high stress. On the other hand, levels of stress make a large difference for those individuals who rarely avoid: In that case, more sleep is obtained under conditions of low stress, and less sleep is obtained under conditions of high stress. And finally we see a trend for those individuals who are very high avoiders; levels of stress seem to make some difference in levels of obtained sleep. If we extended the range for the IV and ModV to 3 SDs, I would expect that the very, very high avoiders (+3 SD) would evidence a spread of sleeping scores similar to those obtained for the low avoiders.

Hopefully you noticed that the same interpretation applies to both Figures 6.7 and 6.8, although the interpretations differ slightly in how they are worded. Which figure is visually clearer? I would vote for Figure 6.8, despite the fact that it is an atypical presentation of a moderation result. Not only do we see curved lines, but also I think that the areas of difference and similarity are more apparent in this presentation. However, most reviewers and editors expect to see the former of these two styles, so if you choose the latter style, be sure to explain why you have chosen to do so.

Other Quadratic Variations

So, are we done? There is one more tantalizing tidbit that I would like to present to those researchers who like to explore the boundary between the traditional and the cutting edge. Let us reexamine the equation that I gave you before (Equation 6.1):

$$Y = b_1X + b_2Z + b_3XZ + b_4Z^2 + b_5XZ^2$$

I hope that this equation is more interpretable now and that you know what it is saying. Can we push the envelope to some degree and add more terms? What about this equation?

$$Y = b_1X + b_2Z + b_3XZ + b_4Z^2 + b_5X^2 + b_6XZ^2 + b_7X^2Z + b_8X^2Z^2 \quad (6.2)$$

What I have done is suggest that one can square the IV and then involve this quadratic term with the linear moderator, as well as the quadratic version of the moderator. So what do these terms refer to? They all refer to various combinations of linear and quadratic effects of the two predictor variables in question (IV and ModV). They are all legitimate in the statistical sense, but they may or may not make sense with regard to your particular variables. My advice: Make quadratic predictions where you can and test them using the first equation. If you are unsure about what you will find (which is probably true in most cases with quadratic terms), be honest about the fact that you are exploring possibilities, and if you find useful and interesting findings, report them as exploratory. In my experience, researchers rarely make quadratic predictions, and they tend to stay with basic quadratic terms when they do. The preceding suggestions may help you to stray off the beaten path a little, and hopefully you will find some curvilinear relationships worthy of note.

BASIC MODERATION IN PATH ANALYSES

Chapter 5 is devoted to a thorough and complete delineation of how to perform basic moderation with multiple regression. It may not be evident to everyone that the same analysis can be performed with path analyses in SEM or, further, that it will yield the identical result. I feel that it is necessary to mention this important fact here for two main reasons:

1. As you become more familiar and facile with SEM programs, and with path analyses in particular, you will find that it may be easier to compute moderation in SEM rather than going back to SPSS, SYS-TAT, SAS, or some other program to do the moderation in regression. Or you may wish to do basic moderation in SEM to obtain findings on the same platform in order to be consistent with some other analyses that you have performed.
2. The other chief reason that researchers do moderation in SEM is to embed it within other, more complicated path models.

On the second point, I have devoted the next chapter to the topic of hybrid models (i.e., cases in which researchers wish to combine mediation with moderation in some fashion). If you are interested in the prospect of embedding a moderational analysis in a larger path model, then you should read this chapter. One must have the understanding, however, that moderation in multiple regression yields identical estimated parameters as moderation in SEM in order to go on to appreciate mediated moderation and some other variants conducted in SEM.

Just to be utterly clear on this point, let me present findings for a basic moderational result in both formats, and you will see what I mean. The dataset is "continuous moderation example.sav," which we used before. The regression result is presented (again) in Table 6.6. And the Amos printout of

TABLE 6.6. Statistical Output for the Continuous Moderation Example in Linear Regression

	Unstandardized coefficients		Standardized coefficients		
Model	B	Std. error	Beta	t	Sig.
1. (Constant)	1.811	4.774		.379	.705
stress	.483	.133	1.328	3.626	.000
social support	.111	.232	.072	.476	.635
strxss	−.017	.006	−1.040	−2.677	.008

Note. Dependent variable: depression.

the same analysis is presented in Table 6.7. One can see that the output values are virtually identical (taking into account rounding error). However, the last remaining issue is how one specifies this model in SEM. The Amos model is presented in Figure 6.9.

As you can see, it is relatively simple to set it up, but one issue needs further comment. Note that covariances are specified between the three predictors (i.e., the double-headed arrows between the exogenous variables)—these need to be included because the model needs to take into account the shared variance among the predictors. Multiple regression deals with this through

TABLE 6.7. Statistical Output for the Continuous Moderation Example in Amos

	Regression weights (Group number 1 – Default model)				
	Estimate	S.E.	C.R.	P	Label
dep ← stress	.483	.132	3.666	***	
dep ← socsup	.111	.230	.481	.630	
dep ← strxss	−.017	.006	−2.706	.007	

	Standardized regression weights (Group number 1 – Default model)
	Estimate
dep ← stress	1.328
dep ← socsup	.072
dep ← strxss	−1.040

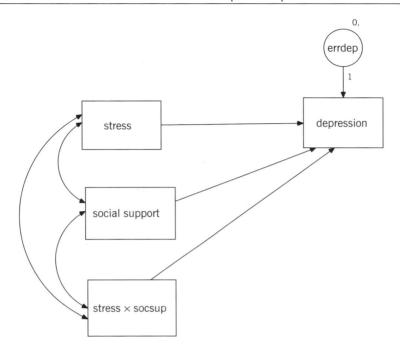

FIGURE 6.9. Amos model assessing the effect of a continuous moderating variable (social support) on the stress-to-depression relationship.

semipartial correlations. I make this observation here because some beginning students fail to include the covariances. In addition, the DV needs to have a residual term specified.

MODERATION IN MULTILEVEL MODELING (MLM)

In multilevel modeling (MLM), moderation can occur at Level 1, at Level 2, and/or between these two levels (see diagram of the two basic levels usually examined in multilevel data in Chapter 4). I do not repeat the orientation to MLM datasets that I gave in Chapter 4, so if you are unfamiliar with the basic structure of these datasets, you may want to review that material now before you proceed with this section.

In the present example, I examine repeated-measures data. You may know that there are two types of nesting that MLM can elucidate: (1) variables nested within individuals over time and (2) individuals nested within groupings, such as hospitals, schools, and community organizations. Although I use the first case as an example, much of what I talk about here would apply to the second type of nesting, as well.

The example I use in the present case concerns the dynamic of savoring pleasant events over time. A recent focus of my research is what people do to derive happiness from experiences in their lives. I am interested in savoring's role in this respect (see Bryant & Veroff, 2006) because it seems that it might operate as a moderator. Think of it this way: People naturally vary with regard to their willingness and ability to make the most of positive events (i.e., savoring). If the same positive event happened to a range of individuals, would some of these individuals be happier because they have the capacity to enjoy this event and some less happy because they don't have the capacity? That is what I investigate in the present context.

I conducted a diary study in which I texted university students at a random time each day for 30 consecutive days and asked them to write down any positive events that had happened in the previous hour. Further, I asked them how much they enjoyed these events, which was my measure of savoring, and, last, I asked them how happy they felt. The basic relationship here is the association between the number of positive events (IV) and happiness (DV). I assumed that a person who reported more positive events would also report that he or she was happier. I sought to determine whether my measure of savoring would moderate this basic relationship; in particular, I hypothesized that those individuals who reported more savoring would evidence a stronger positive relationship between the IV and the DV. A note in passing: In the old parlance, this hypothesis would be an example of exacerbation, that is, a moderator that amplifies the relationship between the IV and the DV; but you might agree with me that *exacerbation* is a poor word to describe this pattern. Instead, I would suggest that we should use the word *enhancer*.

I ended up with 58 participants (about equal numbers of males and females), who gave me reasonably complete data. This is a technical term, or at least it is when I use it in this context. *Reasonably complete data* refers to individuals who gave me data at 90% of the times of measurement; that is, they missed 3 or fewer days out of 30. MLM is quite robust for missing data, and I could probably have been more lenient than this, but I wanted to compose a fairly complete dataset.

> ***Helpful Suggestion:*** If you would like to repeat these analyses, download "Level 1 HLM moderation example.sav" and "Level 2 HLM moderation example.sav" and follow along.

As I noted in Chapter 4, one has multiple choices for an MLM analytical program. I have used HLM, Mplus, and SPSS, and there are other options, too. I demonstrate the use of HLM in the present case as it is arguably the most common program used for MLM, but similar or identical results are obtainable with the other programs. And, as you probably know—that is, if you have had some experience with HLM—one must prepare two datasets in order to get the program to compute the estimates. (For those of you who dislike generating two datasets, know that other MLM programs, e.g., Mplus, do not require this preparatory step.) The first dataset is termed the "Level 1 dataset," and in my case it had 30 lines for each participant, one line for each day's data. The second dataset is termed the "Level 2 dataset," and it has one line for each participant; it contained information such as gender, ethnicity, and age. In MLM parlance, one would say that data for all 30 days at Level 1 are nested within the individual's data at Level 2.

I should probably echo the warning that I voiced in Chapter 4 with mediation analyses in multilevel modeling again: What I am describing here is meant to acquaint you with the procedures, not teach you all of the details. I do not have room to explicate every nuance of these techniques, so it must suffice that I give you an overview and motivate you to go out and obtain high-quality instruction and guidance on how to do multilevel modeling (MLM). I gloss over certain issues, such as whether to do group-mean or grand-mean centering, which the informed reader will know makes a significant difference in computing and graphing the results.

Moderation with a Level 1 Variable (Using a 1–1–1 Model with Random Slopes)

I consider the first case, in which we wish to examine moderation by a Level 1 variable on a basic relationship that occurs at Level 1. In order to examine moderation within Level 1, we must create the interaction in the Level 1 dataset before we upload it into HLM. So in my case I multiplied my IV (number of pleasant events) by my ModV (enjoyment). Having learned about this issue in the preceding chapter, I am sure that you are now keen to ask the question as to whether one should center the variables before the multiplication. The answer is that it matters chiefly with regard to the statistical outputs of the intercept. I performed the HLM analyses on centered and uncentered variables, and the only difference it yielded was a difference in the intercept. The coefficients, standard errors, t-ratios, and p-values did not change. The intercept matters when we graph the result, so it is good practice to center variables before subjecting them to MLM analyses in order that the figures will be more comparable across studies. So in this case I centered the key variables in question here.

After this preparatory task, I uploaded the two datasets into HLM, and then I was ready to begin analyses. Let me review. All four variables in question exist at Level 1: pleasant events, enjoyment, pleasant × enjoyment, and happiness. If I want to do a regression to determine whether the interaction term is a significant predictor of happiness, this is what I do. First, under Level 1, I click on "happiness" and indicate that I want it to be the "outcome variable." Then I click on "pleasant events" and indicate that I want to "add variable uncentered." I do the same for "enjoyment" and the interaction term. (Remember, the variables were already centered before uploading into HLM.) I also double-click the residual terms for each of the four Level 2 equations to highlight them (indicating that this is a random slopes model). The resulting model will look like the syntax presented in Table 6.8.

The first term is the fixed intercept, the second is the slope of pleasant events, the third is the slope for enjoying (savoring), the fourth is the slope of the interaction term, and the fifth is the error term. We are going to ignore the Level 2 models right now because they are not relevant yet. Then I clicked on "run analysis," and HLM cogitated for a few seconds and then generated the output presented in Table 6.9.

The first line refers to the fixed intercept, and the p-value is statistically significant, but that only tells me that there was significant variation in the happiness means among my 58 individuals around the overall group mean of 1.95. The next three lines are more informative. The second line tells me that the slope for pleasant events was positive and statistically significant (coeff = 0.30); in other words, across the 30 days, the variable of number of pleasant events was positively related to reports of happiness. The third line tells me that the slope for enjoying was positive and statistically significant (coeff = 0.56); in other words, if a person reported more enjoying (savoring) efforts,

TABLE 6.8. HLM Model Syntax for Level 1 Moderation

Level-1 Model

$HOWHAPPY_{ti} = \pi_{0i} + \pi_{1i}*(PLEASC_{ti}) + \pi_{2i}*(ENJOYC_{ti}) + \pi_{3i}*(PLEASC×ENJOYC_{ti}) + e_{ti}$

Level-2 Model

$\pi_{0i} = \beta_{00} + r_{0i}$
$\pi_{1i} = \beta_{10} + r_{1i}$
$\pi_{2i} = \beta_{20} + r_{2i}$
$\pi_{3i} = \beta_{30} + r_{3i}$

TABLE 6.9. HLM Statistical Output for the Level 1 Moderation Analysis

Final estimation of fixed effects (with robust standard errors)

Fixed effect	Coefficient	Standard error	t-ratio	Approx. df	p-value
For INTRCPT1, π_0					
INTRCPT2, β_{00}	1.952705	0.049135	39.741	58	<.001
For PLEASC slope, π_1					
INTRCPT2, β_{10}	0.304476	0.037914	8.031	58	<.001
For ENJOYC slope, π_2					
INTRCPT2, β_{20}	0.558818	0.033161	16.852	58	<.001
For PLEASCxENJOYC slope, π_3					
INTRCPT2, β_{30}	0.034481	0.015838	2.177	58	.033

Note. The outcome variable is HOWHAPPY.

they also reported greater happiness. And the fourth line tells me that the interaction term was a significant predictor of happiness, too.

As with output from a basic regression, we need to graph this result before we can interpret its pattern. I typically graph these results in Mod-Graph, so let us discuss that option first. HLM generates means and standard deviations of the key variables when one creates the .mdm file earlier in the process of uploading the data, and these values are needed here. The "coefficients" in the HLM output are B's (unstandardized regression coefficients), so just transfer them, and it should be obvious that the intercept is the intercept. In the present case, when I graphed this result, I obtained Figure 6.10.

I expected something like this pattern, fortunately, so I am pleased that I obtained this result (I think that I will count this as a pleasant event in my day, as I tend to be a high savorer). First of all, the general upward tilt to the right reflects the main effect of number of positive events, that is, a positive slope. The more positive events one reports, the higher his or her happiness. Second, the separation between the lines tells us about the main effect of enjoying. Individuals who enjoy events more also report higher levels of happiness. And third, the diverging lines reflect the interaction. The slope of the low-enjoyment group is relatively flat compared with the slopes of the other two groups. The steepest slope is manifested by the high-enjoyment group, and this result tells us that number of pleasant events is most strongly associated with happiness for this group. Further, this result tells me that the main effect for pleasant events and the main effect of enjoying are qualified by levels of enjoying. Individuals who do not enjoy events very much

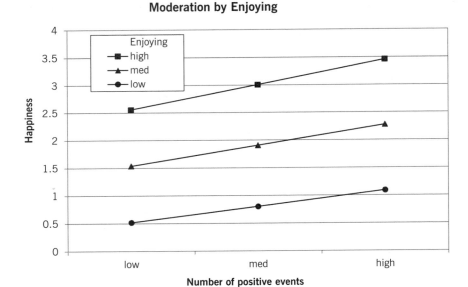

FIGURE 6.10. Graphical depiction of the effect of a Level 1 moderator (enjoying) on a Level 1 relationship between number of positive events and happiness.

exhibit a weaker relationship between number of positive events and happiness compared with individuals who enjoy (savor) these events. This result is a classic amplification pattern, and I would prefer to call enjoying (savoring) an "enhancer" rather than an "exacerbator"; I gave my reasons for this usage earlier.

Another way to graph the results of a 1–1–1 multilevel moderation model can be found on Kris Preacher's website: **http://www.vanderbilt.edu/psychological_sciences/bio/Kristopher-preacher.Methods**. In fact, his utility is more flexible than ModGraph in that it can graph a variety of different types of MLM models (not just 1–1–1 models), and his utility also computes simple slopes and Johnson–Neyman bands of significance, which are very useful. ModGraph was not designed for MLM moderation, so I would recommend Preacher's utility over ModGraph because it was specifically designed for this type of analysis.

Moderation with a Level 2 Variable

Level 2 variables are variables that are classic moderators in that they tend to be demographic variables, such as gender, age, and ethnicity, or relatively stable variables, such as trait anxiety. In the present case, I would like to see whether gender moderates the relationship of pleasant events to happiness and the relationship of savoring to happiness. And I can determine whether gender moderates the 1–1–1 moderation that we just identified. It is hard to hypothesize about these relationships, as there has been very little research to date on savoring, but I thought that females would show stronger relationships across the board for these three relationships.

Let us return to HLM and explore Level 2 variables. In this case I have gender, ethnicity, age, and a number of continuous variables that I think are fairly stable. I wish to include gender in the analysis that I performed earlier. Click on "Level-2" in the upper left-hand corner of the HLM program. It lists your Level 2 variables. Left click on "Gender" in this case, and, because entering this variable in a centered form makes no sense (because it is a dichotomous categorical variable), I choose to "add variable uncentered." If I had a continuous variable, then it would make sense to add it centered. You will notice that the first Level 2 model has now included gender as a second term in the equation. The first equation refers to the intercept and will tell you whether there is a significant mean group difference in happiness between males and females. Now, in turn, click on each of the following Level 2 equations and add gender as an uncentered variable. When you are done, you should have four equations that look like Table 6.10.

What these equations do is set up gender as a moderator for all four terms specified in the Level 1 equation (i.e., the intercept, main effect for pleasant events, main effect for savoring, and the interaction term). So, the next step is to run the analysis and check the output. I obtained the output in Table 6.11.

Some clarification is needed. First of all, the first two lines tell us about the intercepts. The B_{00} line merely says that there is significant variation among the 58 participants with regard to their mean values of happiness. The B_{01} line tells us that there was not a significant mean group difference between males and females on happiness; they were about equally happy, on average, over this 30-day period.

TABLE 6.10. HLM Syntax to Specify Gender as a Moderator of Level 1 Relationships

Level-2 Model

$$\pi_0 = \beta_{00} + \beta_{01}(\text{GENDER}) + r_0$$
$$\pi_1 = \beta_{10} + \beta_{11}(\text{GENDER}) + r_1$$
$$\pi_2 = \beta_{20} + \beta_{21}(\text{GENDER}) + r_2$$
$$\pi_3 = \beta_{30} + \beta_{31}(\text{GENDER}) + r_3$$

TABLE 6.11. HLM Output of the Analysis to Examine Whether Gender Functioned as a Moderator of Level 1 Relationships

Final estimation of fixed effects (with robust standard errors)

Fixed effect	Coefficient	Standard error	t-ratio	Approx. df	p-value
For INTRCPT1, π_0					
INTRCPT2, β_{00}	1.880345	0.097577	19.270	57	<.001
GENDER, β_{01}	0.113265	0.111308	1.018	57	.314
For PLEASC slope, π_1					
INTRCPT2, β_{10}	0.298389	0.069156	4.315	57	<.001
GENDER, β_{11}	0.015645	0.082006	0.191	57	.850
For ENJOYC slope, π_2					
INTRCPT2, β_{20}	0.562985	0.055281	10.184	57	<.001
GENDER, β_{21}	0.002887	0.068511	0.042	57	.967
For PLEASC×ENJOYC slope, π_3					
INTRCPT2, β_{30}	0.003533	0.027459	0.129	57	.898
GENDER, β_{31}	0.045329	0.033466	1.354	57	.181

Note. The outcome variable is HOWHAPPY.

Now we move to the next pair of findings. B_{10} tells us (again) that we obtained a significant main effect for number of pleasant events on happiness. The B is 0.30, signifying that there was a positive relationship between number of events and happiness, but we already knew this from the earlier analysis. We see something similar for the B_{20} line, namely, that there was a positive relationship between enjoying and happiness, which we also already knew. And when I look at the interaction term, line B_{30}, it shows up this time as nonsignificant, whereas it was significant in our previous analysis. This nonsignificant result occurred because we involved gender as a moderator and the variance was divided up differently this time.

The critical question we asked was whether gender significantly moderated any of these four relationships, and if we look at B_{01}, B_{11}, B_{21}, and B_{31}, we see that none of them turned out to be statistically significant. This result means that the mean group difference in happiness by gender was nonsignificant (B_{01}), and, further, neither of the two main effects (B_{11} and B_{21}) nor the interaction (B_{31}) was moderated by gender. Let us now take a closer look at one of these results to more fully understand these nonsignificant differences.

I want to focus on the enjoyment-by-gender interaction. We could graph it with one of Preacher's utilities, or we could get HLM to do this. It is actually reasonably well set up within HLM to do this. After you perform your analysis, click on "File," then on "Graph Equations," and then on "Model

Graphs." The specification of variables is fairly nonintuitive, but here is how you do it. Under X focus, Level-1, click on the down arrow and choose the variable that is associated with the outcome, in this case "enjoying." Under Z focus, Level-2, bring up "gender." Then click on "OK." You will see a graph that looks like Figure 6.11.

As I expected, the slopes for the female (gender = 1) and male (gender = 0) groups are virtually identical. We suspected that they would look fairly parallel because we obtained a nonsignificant result for this moderation, but here we see what that means. The females' line is slightly higher than the males' line because there was a nonsignificant mean group difference in favor of the female group.

I did the same for the pleasant-events-by-gender interaction, and it yielded a similar figure. A graph for the interaction term (see Figure 6.12) showed a divergence between the two lines representing males and females.

Despite the lines being apparently nonparallel, the HLM output indicated that the Level 2 moderation of the Level 1 moderation was *not* statistically significant, $p = .18$. The HLM output is not easy to read because the font is very small; the nearly flat line refers to males and the positive slope refers to females. I predicted that females would benefit from enjoying positive events more than males, so I can say that the trend is in the predicted direction, but it failed to yield statistical significance.

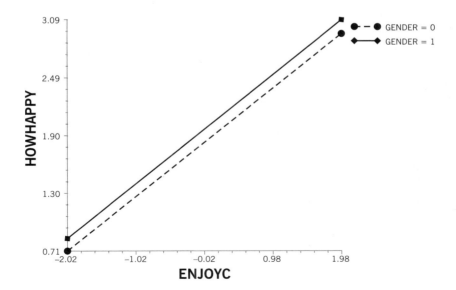

FIGURE 6.11. An HLM-generated graph of the effect of a Level 2 moderating variable (gender) on the Level 1 enjoying-to-happiness relationship.

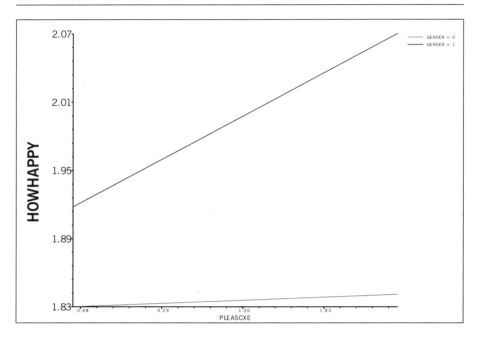

FIGURE 6.12. An HLM-generated graph of the effect of a Level 2 moderating variable (gender) on the Level 1 positive-events-to-happiness relationship.

These results taken together suggest that males and females evidenced similar patterns for the association between pleasant events and happiness and for the Level 1 interaction between pleasant events and enjoyment. To amplify this latter point, the Level 1 moderation showed us that high enjoyers evidenced the strongest positive relationship between frequency of pleasant events and happiness, and the nonsignificant Level 2 finding tells us that this enjoying (savoring) phenomenon occurs at about the same rates among females and among males. If we had obtained a significant Level 2 moderation for the Level 1 moderation, that would have resulted in a significant three-way interaction (two variables at Level 1 and one variable at Level 2). Graphing a result like this is challenging but possible; we could create two graphs, the Level 1 moderation separately by the two gender groups.

I think that is probably enough now on this very interesting topic. However, I have only covered the basics. There is much more that can be done with moderation in MLM. MLM is a powerful tool that increasing numbers of researchers are employing to examine relationships between variables across levels. And as I have demonstrated, one can explore moderation within a level, across the levels, or both within and across levels. These approaches provide some very potent analytical tools for researchers to exploit, and I wish you well in your efforts to obtain interpretable results with HLM or other multilevel modeling programs.

MODERATION WITH LATENT VARIABLES

Just as it is preferable to conduct latent variable path modeling over observed variable path modeling because of the ability to identify and set aside error variance, it has been something of a search for the holy grail to come up with a method for conducting moderation with latent variables. Am I exaggerating? Only slightly. A number of statisticians over the last two decades have had a go at trying to come up with a method that would work well (e.g., Bollen & Paxton, 1998; Jaccard & Wan, 1996; Joreskog & Yang, 1996; Kenny & Judd, 1984; Lin, Wen, Marsh, & Lin, 2010; Moosbrugger, Schermelleh-Engel, & Klein, 1997; Ping, 1996), but I would say that not one of these approaches has been embraced by a majority of the people in the statistics and research communities. It is not my goal to compare and contrast these various methods; it is quite possible that I have not yet appreciated the strengths of a particular method. However, I present two methods that I have tried and that I believe have significant merit. Other researchers will need to test them against the other approaches, and hopefully soon we will come up with a consensus about the best way to tackle this problem.

Todd Little and colleagues (2006) laid out an interesting possible solution to this problem. What they proposed was *complete orthogonalization*. One of the issues in creating the interaction term is that it might have an excessive degree of multicollinearity among the three predictors in the subsequent regression; in particular, we are interested in reducing the correlation between the interaction term and its two constituent parts, the IV and the DV. Ordinarily the product term is moderately to highly correlated with these two main effects because it is created from the multiplication of these two terms. Extending this issue to the SEM world, this fact makes it very difficult to create a latent interaction variable that captures the interaction between the IV and the ModV without also being highly correlated with the IV and ModV latent variables. The problem that everyone has wrestled with is how to construct a latent variable interaction term that functions well within SEM. If we could significantly reduce the degree of correlation between the indicators of the interaction term and the indicators of the IV and ModV, then it might be possible to model this equation. That is where complete orthogonalization comes in. Little et al. (2006) ask the question: What if we made the interaction term *completely* orthogonal to its component parts? If they were completely orthogonal, then they would be totally uncorrelated, and this set of relationships might make it easier to run the model in SEM—that is, the models might be more likely to converge and yield interpretable estimates.

How does one create indicators that are completely orthogonal? Here is a short example of how to do this technique. The data, taken from 575 early adolescents, were self-reported levels of stress, rumination, and depression, collected by one of my master's program students. Little et al. (2006) recommend that measures composed of many items be parceled into exactly three clusters of items for each construct. Accordingly, the 50 stress items were randomly assorted into three parcels, the 18 rumination items were randomly assorted into three parcels, and the 27 depression items were randomly assorted into three parcels. Simply add the selected items, divide by their number, and label each variable with a distinctive name (e.g., "strparl" refers to "stress parcel #1" in my dataset). After we have created three parcels for each of the three variables—that is, each triad acts as the set of indicators for the latent construct—then we are ready to create the interaction term indicators. Now create nine indicators for the latent interaction term by systematically multiplying each of the three indicators of the IV by each of the three indicators of the ModV. In the present case, multiply the first parcel of stress by the first parcel of rumination ($s1 \times r1$); the first parcel of stress by the second parcel of rumination ($s1 \times r2$); and so forth.

Next we do the orthogonalization. The way we do this is by performing nine separate regressions. In order to create a completely orthogonalized indicator, we must create a new variable that is the residual of the regression of the constituent parts regressed on the individual product terms. To be specific, the first regression is one in which all IV parcels are the predictors and $s1 \times r1$ is the dependent variable. Go into SAVE and click on "unstandardized residuals." Run the analysis, and you will find that the program has saved a new variable, creatively titled RES_1, and stuck it to the immediate right of your previous variables. This new variable is your first completely orthogonalized residual interaction term indicator. Now go ahead and conduct all nine regressions, relabel these variables to something more sensible, such as $s1 \times r1$res, and then you are ready to conduct your SEM analysis. By the way, you can check whether the indicators are totally orthogonalized by running a correlation and determining that you have obtained new variables that are explicitly uncorrelated with their constituent parts.

I originally ran this analysis in LISREL, and Figure 6.13 is the graphical depiction of the obtained model. The graphical output of LISREL is not aesthetically pleasing nor very clear, but I think that several key points can be appreciated here. First, one can see the nine interaction terms that are

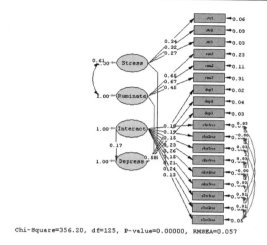

Chi-Square=356.20, df=125, P-value=0.00000, RMSEA=0.057

FIGURE 6.13. A LISREL-generated figure of the statistical output of a latent variable moderation analysis: Rumination moderated the stress-to-depression relationship.

generated by the multiplication of the three IV parcels by the three ModV parcels. Second, these nine indicators are allowed to covary with each other in a specific way. And last, the model succeeded in converging (no small feat for such a model) and yielded a sensible and good fitting model.

As I said earlier, this approach, espoused by Little et al. (2006), is not the only possible way to compute latent moderation, and I would like to mention a second method. Mplus has a facility for doing this type of analysis as well, named the "Xwith command" (see Klein & Moosbrugger, 2000, and Muthen & Asparouhov, 2003). I have succeeded in running an analysis with this command, which I present here; but the difficulty with this approach, as well as other latent moderation programs, is that it is not easy to know how to graph the results. I show you my way through this, but there may be better ways to do this.

The dataset is "stress_socanx_dep_example.dat," and it contains three variables. We are going to consider stress (three parcels) as the independent variable, social anxiety (three parcels) as the moderator, and depression as the single indicator DV. For stress, fifty items were randomly sorted into three parcels, and then averaged within parcels, so two parcels had 17 items each and one parcel had 16 items. When you do this sort of preparation be sure to average the appropriate number of items in each parcel. The social anxiety measure randomly sorted 22 items among three parcels yielding 7, 7, and 8 items for the three parcels. The depression score remains a single value.

It is not necessary to center each of the six parcels, but users may wish to do so in order to expedite graphing of the results.

I expected that social anxiety would function as an exacerbator on the stress-to-depression relationship—in other words, individuals who suffer from social anxiety are likelier to manifest a stronger stress-to-depression relationship.

The Mplus syntax is presented in Table 6.12.

After reporting descriptive statistics (means, covariances, and correlations), it generates the model results presented in Table 6.13. (Note that the shaded numerical values are those needed for input into ModGraph.)

TABLE 6.12. Mplus Syntax to Use the Xwith Function to Test for Latent Variable Moderation

```
DATA: FILE IS e:\stress_socanx_dep_example.dat;
 FORMAT IS 7F8.2;
 VARIABLE: NAMES ARE
 stressa
 stressb
 stressc
 socanxa
 socanxb
 socanxc
 depress;

 USEVARIABLES ARE
 stressa
 stressb
 stressc
 socanxa
 socanxb
 socanxc
 depress;

 ANALYSIS:
 type = random;
 algorithm = integration;

 MODEL:
 socanx by socanxa  socanxb  socanxc;
 stress by stressa  stressb  stressc;
 strxsocanx | socanx xwith stress;
 depress on stress socanx strxsocanx;

 OUTPUT: SAMPSTAT tech1 tech8;
```

TABLE 6.13. Mplus Outputs for the Latent Variable Moderation Analysis

SAMPLE STATISTICS

Means

STRESSA	STRESSB	STRESSC	SOCANXA	SOCANXB
0.461	0.428	0.359	2.453	2.197

Means

SOCANXC	DEPRESS
2.351	1.386

Covariances

	STRESSA	STRESSB	STRESSC	SOCANXA	SOCANXB
STRESSA	0.144				
STRESSB	0.102	0.122			
STRESSC	0.092	0.087	0.109		
SOCANXA	0.056	0.046	0.043	0.514	
SOCANXB	0.066	0.063	0.056	0.343	0.422
SOCANXC	0.059	0.053	0.045	0.360	0.354
DEPRESS	0.032	0.031	0.027	0.055	0.066

Covariances

	SOCANXC	DEPRESS
SOCANXC	0.459	
DEPRESS	0.059	0.066

Correlations

	STRESSA	STRESSB	STRESSC	SOCANXA	SOCANXB
STRESSA	1.000				
STRESSB	0.771	1.000			
STRESSC	0.735	0.753	1.000		
SOCANXA	0.207	0.183	0.183	1.000	
SOCANXB	0.267	0.278	0.263	0.737	1.000
SOCANXC	0.231	0.225	0.203	0.741	0.804
DEPRESS	0.326	0.346	0.314	0.300	0.397

Correlations

	SOCANXC	DEPRESS
SOCANXC	1.000	
DEPRESS	0.339	1.000

cont.

TABLE 6.13. *(cont.)*

MODEL RESULTS

	Estimate	S.E.	Est./S.E.	Two-Tailed P-Value
SOCANX BY				
SOCANXA	1.000	0.000	999.000	999.000
SOCANXB	1.000	0.039	25.845	0.000
SOCANXC	1.027	0.041	25.237	0.000
STRESS BY				
STRESSA	1.000	0.000	999.000	999.000
STRESSB	0.942	0.045	21.143	0.000
STRESSC	0.850	0.040	21.433	0.000
DEPRESS ON				
STRESS	0.196	0.032	6.195	0.000
SOCANX	0.129	0.020	6.419	0.000
STRXSOCANX	0.165	0.056	2.952	0.003
STRESS WITH				
SOCANX	0.059	0.010	6.127	0.000
Intercepts				
STRESSA	0.461	0.016	28.880	0.000
STRESSB	0.428	0.015	29.090	0.000
STRESSC	0.359	0.014	25.799	0.000
SOCANXA	2.452	0.030	81.277	0.000
SOCANXB	2.197	0.027	80.386	0.000
SOCANXC	2.351	0.029	82.409	0.000
DEPRESS	1.376	0.011	125.955	0.000
Variances				
SOCANX	0.345	0.029	12.080	0.000
STRESS	0.108	0.011	10.203	0.000

The critical value that we care most about is the "STRXSOCANX" line: estimate = .165, *SE* = .06, *p* = .003. This result tells us that we obtained significant moderation. To determine what it means, we, of course, need to graph it. Although the values needed for input into ModGraph (shaded above) are difficult to identify in some cases, I have sorted them out, and they are reported in Table 6.14.

TABLE 6.14. Summary of Statistical Outputs Gleaned from the Mplus Output That Are Necessary for Graphing the Moderation Result

	B	Mean	SD
Stress	.196	.416	.329
Social anxiety	.129	2.334	.587
Stress × Socanx	.165		
Intercept	1.376		

I will identify here where you find these values in the Mplus output. The Bs for the main effects are found just above the B for the interaction term. The intercept (or constant) is the intercept for the DV: depression. The two means are derived by averaging the three parcel means for each variable separately. And the standard deviations are obtained by taking the square root of the relevant variances. If you graph these results, it should look like Figure 6.14.

The upward tilt reflects the positive slope of the main effect of stress,

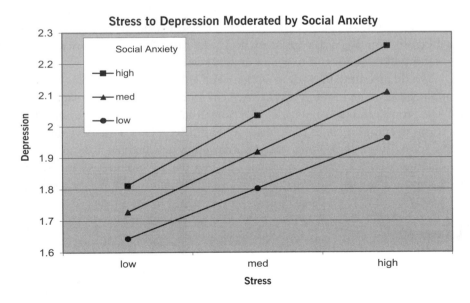

FIGURE 6.14. Graphical depiction of the latent variable moderation result obtained by the Mplus analysis: The stress-to-depression relationship moderated by social anxiety.

that is, that individuals who report more stress are more depressed; and the separation between the lines indicates the main effect for social anxiety, that is, that individuals who are more socially anxious are more depressed. The fan effect at the right side is evidence of the interaction, and the steepest slope of the three lines describes the group of highly socially anxious individuals. This pattern, as predicted, tells us that social anxiety exacerbated the stress-to-depression relationship. In other words, individuals who are socially anxious manifest a stronger relationship between stress and depression.

LOGISTIC MODERATION?

This approach refers to determining whether an interaction predicts a categorical (typically dichotomous) DV. Many researchers, particularly in the worlds of health (e.g., asthmatic vs. not asthmatic) and consumer research (e.g., purchased vs. didn't purchase), do not always study continuous DVs, so a logistic moderation approach would be very useful. The wrinkle in using logistic regression to perform moderation is that "this method subjects the dependent variable to a nonlinear transformation, [and] the resulting interaction coefficients do not properly reflect moderation effects in the original probabilities" (Hess, Hu, & Blair, 2010, p. 2). So one cannot take B's and standard errors from logistic regression and then plug them automatically into something like ModGraph to get a graphed result.

I would recommend reading Gelman and Hill's (2007) book *Data Analysis Using Regression and Multilevel/Hierarchical Models* for their approach. They use the programming language R to perform their analyses, and because this platform is enjoying more popularity among researchers, I suspect that this approach will see increasing use. Another approach has been described by Hayes and Matthes (2009) in which one can use SPSS and SAS macros to perform the analyses.

SUMMARY

I noted at the outset of this chapter that I suspect that most readers will want to cherry-pick their favorite topics from this chapter. However, if you persevered through all of the entries, then congratulations—you have learned to conduct multiple moderator regression analyses, quadratic moderation, basic moderation in SEM, moderation in HLM, and latent variable moderation. And perhaps I have tickled your curiosity concerning logistic moderation.

These variants of basic moderation enable the skillful researcher to examine interactions in a variety of different contexts, and, as wide-reaching as they are, I have to admit that these six topics do not exhaust all of the possibilities. Keep an eye out for other moderation techniques.

FURTHER READING

On the topic of quadratic moderation, one should read the original Baron and Kenny article, of course, as well as:

Cohen, J., & Cohen, P. (1983). *Applied multiple regression/correlation analysis for the behavioral sciences* (2nd ed.). Hillsdale, NJ: Erlbaum.

Cohen, J., Cohen, P., West, S. G., & Aiken, L. S. (2003). *Applied multiple regression/correlation analysis for the behavioral sciences* (3rd ed.). Mahwah, NJ: Erlbaum.

Another couple of helpful readings are:

MacCallum, R. C., & Mar, C. M. (1995). Distinguishing between moderator and quadratic effects in multiple regression. *Psychological Bulletin, 118,* 405–421.

Ping, R. A. (1996). Latent variable interaction and quadratic effect estimation: A two-step technique using structural equation analysis. *Psychological Bulletin, 119,* 166–175.

Moderation in multilevel modeling has received a fair amount of attention, and the following papers and books will prove useful to someone who wants to perform this type of analysis:

Bauer, D. J., Preacher, K. J., & Gil, K. M. (2006). Conceptualizing and testing random indirect effects and moderated mediation in multilevel models: New procedures and recommendations. *Psychological Methods, 11,* 142–163.

Bickel, R. (2007). *Multilevel analysis for applied research: It's just regression.* New York: Guilford Press.

Gelman, A., & Hill, J. (2007). *Data analysis using regression and multilevel/hierarchical models.* Cambridge, UK: Cambridge University Press.

Kenny, D. A., Korchmaros, J. D., & Bolger, N. (2003). Lower level mediation in multilevel models. *Psychological Methods, 8,* 115–128.

Latent variable moderation is a topic that has attracted quite a number of people, who have proposed various approaches to solve this problem. Some of the key articles (although this list is not exhaustive) are:

Algina, J., & Moulder, B. C. (2001). A note on estimating the Joreskog–Yang model for latent variable interaction using LISREL 8.3. *Structural Equation Modeling, 8,* 40–52.

Bollen, K. A., & Paxton, P. (1998). Interactions of latent variables in structural equation models. *Structural Equation Modeling, 5,* 266–293.

Jaccard, J., & Wan, C. K. (1996). *LISREL approaches to interaction effects in multiple regression* (Sage University Paper Series: Quantitative applications in the social sciences, series no. 07-114). Thousand Oaks, CA: Sage.

Joreskog, K. G., & Yang, F. (1996). Nonlinear structural equation models: The Kenny–Judd model with interaction effects. In G. Marcoulides & R. Schumacker (Eds.), *Advanced structural equation modeling* (pp. 57–87). Mahwah, NJ: Erlbaum.

Kenny, D. A., & Judd, C. M. (1984). Estimating the nonlinear and interactive effects of latent variables. *Psychological Bulletin, 96,* 201–210.

Little, T. D., Bovaird, J. A., & Widaman, K. F. (2006). On the merits of orthogonalizing powered and product terms: Implications for modeling interactions among latent variables. *Structural Equation Modeling, 13*(4), 497–519.

McClelland, G. H., & Judd, C. M. (1993). Statistical difficulties of detecting interactions and moderator effects. *Psychological Bulletin, 114,* 376–390.

Moosbrugger, H., Schermelleh-Engel, K., & Klein, A. (1997). Methodological problems of estimating latent interaction effects. *Methods of Psychological Research Online, 2,* 95–111.

Moulder, B. C., & Algina, J. (2002). Comparison of methods for estimating and testing latent variable interactions. *Structural Equation Modeling, 9,* 1–19.

Ping. R. A. (1996). Latent variable interaction and quadratic effect estimation: A two-step technique using structural equation analysis. *Psychological Bulletin, 119,* 166–175.

Logistic moderation is another cutting-edge area in mediation and moderation, but in this case few articles have been written on it thus far, and few proposals have been made concerning how to do it. The key resources that I've found are:

Gelman, A., & Hill, J. (2007). *Data analysis using regression and multilevel/hierarchical models.* Cambridge, UK: Cambridge University Press.

Hayes, A. F., & Matthes, J. (2009). Computational procedures for probing interactions in OLS and logistic regression: SPSS and SAS implementations. *Behavior Research Methods, 41,* 924–936.

Hess, J., Hu, Y., & Blair, E. (2010). On testing moderation effects in experiments using logistic regression. Unpublished paper. Retrieved September 24, 2010, from **http://www.cba.uh.edu/jhess/documents/OnTestingModerationEffectsin-ExperimentsUsingLogisticRegressionAug172009.doc.**

IN-CHAPTER EXERCISES

1. *Multiple moderators*. I hope that you ran the regressions noted herein to see whether you were successful in preparing the data correctly and running the analyses correctly. You may also wish to graph the results to see whether you obtained the same patterns as I did.

2. *Moderation of residualized relationships*. The dataset provided by Rudolph and Troop-Gordon (2010) is named "residualized moderation example. sav," and you can see whether you can duplicate the results detailed in this chapter. Remember that slight differences from the published results will be obtained because these authors used multiple imputation (beyond the scope of this book) and because the present dataset is merely one of the datasets that they used. The .pdf of the article is also found at the website, so you can scan it for more information about how to explain significant moderation results.

3. *Quadratic moderation*. Although the construction of the interaction and powered terms is somewhat tedious, we are occasionally rewarded with a significant quadratic moderation result (as here for males). However, then we have the arduous task of hand-computing the many algebraic equations required for the graphing of such a result. Unless you can find a program to do the graphing for you. . . .

4. *Moderation in multilevel modeling*. I have provided both datasets: "Level 1 HLM moderation example.sav" and "Level 2 HLM moderation example.sav" so that you can try out these analyses. (I haven't exhausted all of the possibilities in these datasets, so if you find something interesting, write me.)

ADDITIONAL EXERCISES

1. Using a slightly different dataset than used above for multiple moderators, you are going to determine whether age (dichotomized) and gender jointly moderate the stress-to-self-harm relationship studied before. Pull up "multiple moderators problem#1.sav." Prepare the data, and run a regression in which you determine whether you obtain double moderation. Interpret the result(s) with graphs as needed.

2. Let us try a residualized moderation analysis now. Pull up "residualized moderation problem#2.sav" and see whether you can perform this analysis. Well-being scores are measured at two points in time (1 year apart), and well-being T2 is the DV in this case. We seek to know whether the main effect of social support T1 predicts the residualized well-being scores

over time and whether age moderates this relationship. Prepare the data, construct the regression, and determine whether a significant moderation is obtained. If a moderation result is obtained, compute simple slopes to determine whether older adolescents would evidence a positive slope and younger adolescents would evidence a flat slope.

3. Solve a quadratic moderation problem (find "quadratic moderation problem#3.sav"). I want to see whether confidence (IV) leads to greater number of nights of good sleep (DV) and whether social support (ModV) quadratically moderates this basic relationship. Prepare the dataset, run the hierarchical regression, and determine which terms are statistically significant. Interpret as you can.

4. Perform a basic moderation analysis in SEM and graph the result (without resorting to linear regression or descriptive statistics). The dataset is called "SEM moderation problem#4.sav," and stress is the IV, distraction is the ModV, and depression is the DV.

5. Access the two HLM datasets titled "Level 1 HLM moderation problem#5. sav" and "Level 2 HLM moderation problem#5.sav." First, run a Level 1 model in which PTOT1 (positive events total on day 1) predicts HAPTOT1 (happiness total on day1) to see whether general positive event frequency predicts general happiness. If this is a significant relationship, then see whether it is moderated by *either* depression (BDITOT) or gender (SHSTOT). In other words, run two more models, one with depression as a Level 2 moderator of the Level 1 equation and the other with gender at Level 2 of the same Level 1 equation.

6. If you have access to Mplus, you might want to practice performing a latent variable moderation analysis. Pull up the dataset "latent var moderation problem#6.sav." This dataset is similar to the one described earlier, except that the moderator is composed of three parcels for the construct of "corumination." Corumination is construed as an interpersonal form of rumination. People typically ruminate with their own thoughts, but corumination occurs when a person excessively discusses his or her own or his or her friend's problems. In this case I thought that corumination might exacerbate the relationship of rumination (IV) to depression (DV). If you obtain a significant moderation, graph it and interpret the pattern. (I have centered the six predictor parcels, but of course this is not necessary.)

Mediated Moderation and Moderated Mediation

Lately a great deal of interest has been expressed in figuring out how to combine the two approaches of mediation and moderation. Baron and Kenny (1986) expressly included in their article an example of mediated moderation (see my description of it in Chapter 2). However, judging from my students' and colleagues' comments, I daresay that few people understand how to perform such an analysis and how innovative this approach is. When I attempt to explain how these hybrids are computed and what they mean, my listener's eyes often glaze over, and I am met with comments such as "Tell me that part again." I think that many people find these issues confusing because they did not clearly understand basic mediation and basic moderation to begin with. You should not have that excuse if you have read and mastered the previous chapters on how to perform these basic techniques. I hold out more hope for you.

I would consider the literature on how to perform and interpret these hybrid analyses to be in its infancy, and I say this principally because of the diversity of methods proposed by various articles that I have read on this topic. I have found that authors have proposed a number of different ways to tackle this issue. In other words, there is a lack of consensus about how to do these analyses. But this state of affairs provides an opportunity for the enterprising researcher to read about these techniques, try them out, and learn for him- or herself. I do my best to present some of these basic methods clearly, and by so doing I trust that by the end of the chapter you will acquire some basic techniques for conducting these analyses and be stimulated to read the innovative articles and books that will undoubtedly be published in the near future.

In this chapter I present:

- Basic mediated moderation in the context of SEM (modeled after the example presented in Baron & Kenny, 1986).
- Basic moderated mediation in the context of SEM.
- Hayes and Preacher's SPSS macro for performing moderated mediation through bootstrapping.
- More complicated versions such as "moderated mediated moderation."

THE LITERATURE

I begin by noting that even terminology in this area is not consistent and resolved. Although most people refer to these techniques as "moderated mediation" and "mediated moderation," some would prefer to be more precise in their language. Fairchild and MacKinnon (2009) argue that "mediation of a moderated effect" and "moderation of a mediated effect" are better labels for these two approaches. I think this perspective has merit, but in principle, for efficiency's sake, most people probably use the terms *moderated mediation* and *mediated moderation* because they are shorter.

I am not certain of the earliest mentions of moderated mediation and mediated moderation, but it seems that usage of these terms was filtering into the field of psychology in the early 1980s. James and Brett (1984) presented an extended example of moderated mediation; however, they did not explore the obverse face of the coin, mediated moderation. Baron and Kenny (1986) did exactly this 2 years later in their seminal article, but they spent more space on the issue of mediated moderation than on moderated mediation. In 1986 it would have been extremely difficult for a researcher to have implemented either of these techniques due to a lack of understanding of the statistical mechanisms and also because statistical software was ill equipped to deal with these complicated models.

In the past few years, a spate of articles specifically delineating both of these methods in relation to each other have been published: Muller, Judd, and Yzerbyt (2005); Edwards and Lambert (2007); Hayes (2009); Little, Card, Bovaird, Preacher, and Crandall (2007); MacKinnon (2008); Preacher et al. (2007); Wirtz (2007); and others. Not everyone agrees on exactly how these techniques should be done, and there are many subtleties that still remain to be worked out. But the other good news is that these techniques are easier to compute with software today compared with the past; specifically, most analyses are performed with SEM software. In this chapter I give several basic examples set within the world of SEM as a way to introduce readers to this complex set of developments. (I do not take on the issues of MLM, as I have already touched on these topics in Chapters 4 and 6. If you are interested in MLM applications, see useful papers by Krull & MacKinnon, 1999, and Bauer et al., 2006.)

MEDIATED MODERATION: A BARON AND KENNY-TYPE EXAMPLE

In essence, a mediated moderation analysis involves including an interaction term in a path model. Perhaps this does not sound difficult on the surface of it, but there are some important considerations in doing this type of model that Baron and Kenny (1986) glossed over. Let's get into an example with real data, and I make these points as I go through it.

> *Helpful Suggestion:* You may wish to download "mediated modera-tion example.sav" and follow along with the analyses.

In this case, I use my dataset of 926 adolescents (ages 11–16 years) who were asked to self-report a variety of different psychological tendencies: rumi-nation, perceived control, anxious symptoms, and depressive symptoms. I wished to know whether perceived control would moderate the relationship of rumination to both anxiety and depression, so I created the Amos model presented in Figure 7.1.

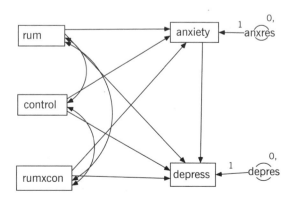

FIGURE 7.1. Amos model for the Baron and Kenny-type mediated moderation analysis.

You might recognize that this mediated moderation model is identical in structure to Baron and Kenny's model (1986), except that the variables are somewhat different; but I think that it is a good place to begin because of its relative simplicity. I multiplied rumination by control in SPSS before importing the variables into Amos. Anxiety and depression are continuous outcome variables. The model suggests that: (1) rumination and perceived control might be main-effect predictors of both anxiety and depression; (2) perceived control might moderate the association between rumination and anxiety and between rumination and depression; and (3) anxiety might be a mediator between the two main effects and the interaction on the final outcome variable, depression. When I ran this model (in Amos), I obtained the output presented in Figure 7.2.

It turned out that all of the estimated parameters were statistically significant, and some of these relationships are immediately interpretable: (1) as predicted, rumination was a positive predictor of both anxiety and depression; (2) as predicted, perceived control was a negative predictor of both anxiety and depression; and (3) as predicted, anxiety was a positive predictor of depression.

But what cannot be immediately apprehended are the two significant parameters between the interaction term and the two outcome variables. As we have seen in other contexts, a significant relationship with an interaction term requires graphing, and this situation is no different.

Figure 7.3 confirms what I suspected about these data, namely, that under conditions of perceived low control, adolescents reported a stronger positive relationship between rumination and anxiety. Simple slopes analy-

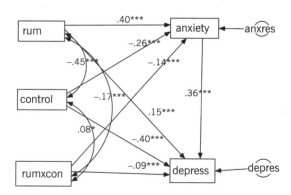

FIGURE 7.2. Amos statistical output for the Baron and Kenny-type mediated moderation analysis.

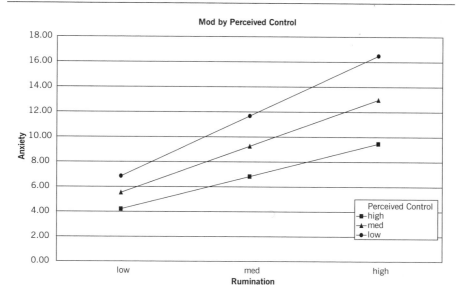

FIGURE 7.3. Graphical depiction of the first moderation in the mediated moderation analysis: Perceived control moderated the rumination-to-anxiety relationship.

ses showed that all three slopes were statistically significant, but you can see that the slope is steepest for low perceived control and flattest for high perceived control. In essence, for individuals who perceive that they possess relatively little control over their environment, the process of rumination is more strongly related to anxiety than for individuals who believe that they exert more control over their environment. Perceived control acted as a buffer.

When I graphed the second interaction result, I obtained Figure 7.4. Note that it is similar to the previous graph. This result should not be too surprising, because anxiety and depression are often moderately and positively correlated with each other (as in the case here). Again we can say that perceived control functioned as a buffer for the relationship between rumination and depression.

The last issue to examine was the prediction that anxiety would mediate between the three exogenous terms (rumination, perceived control, and their interaction term) and the final outcome variable, depression. Amos output produces total, direct, and indirect effects (if you ask it to), and these estimates proved illuminating when I looked at them. The standardized *indirect* effects of the three exogenous variables on depression were: 0.14 (rumination); −0.09 (perceived control); and −0.05 (interaction). Amos,

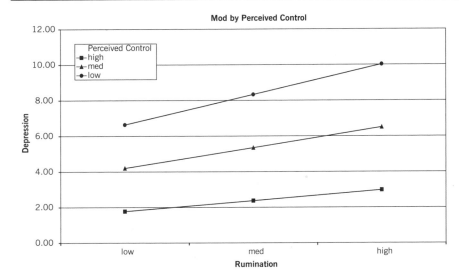

FIGURE 7.4. Graphical depiction of the second moderation in the mediated moderation analysis: Perceived control moderated the rumination-to-depression relationship.

if you ask it to bootstrap the mediated effects, produces significance tests for these indirect effects. When I asked for these estimates, I found that all three indirect effects proved to be statistically significant: for rumination, 95% CI = 0.12 to 0.17, p = .002; for perceived control, 95% CI = −0.07 to −0.12, p = .01; and for the interaction, 95% CI = −0.03 to −0.07, p = .02. The standardized *direct* effects were: 0.15 (rumination); −0.40 (perceived control); and −0.09 (interaction). And when I computed the standardized regression ratio index (indirect/total), I obtained (respectively): 0.48, 0.18, and 0.35. These final numbers are useful in that they tell the user the size of the indirect effects that went through the mediating variable of anxiety. As one would expect (well, I expected it, anyway), anxiety mediated more of the effect of rumination on depression than the other two exogenous variables. The reason for this is that rumination and anxiety are similar psychological dynamics; one typically ruminates about a stressful situation because one is anxious about how it will turn out.

What is interesting and different about this mediational model is that *the effect of a moderation term is mediated.* In essence, the interaction term explains variance in depression through its direct path, but it also explains variance in depression indirectly through anxiety. The patterns of the inter-

action term on anxiety and depression are extremely similar, so we are justi-
fied in claiming that the interaction term explains a significant amount of the
variance in depression *through anxiety*—namely, that individuals who possess low levels of perceived control evidence a stronger relationship between
rumination and depression partly because individuals who possess low levels of perceived control evidence a stronger relationship between rumination
and anxiety. You may find that you will need to read this last sentence a few
times to get the gist of this finding. At present, there seems to be no consensus about a way to unpack this complicated relationship (i.e., to conduct post-
hoc analyses), but Muller et al. (2005) and Edwards and Lambert (2007) have
proposed promising techniques for doing so. It will be necessary for someone
to invent a method of explaining this exceedingly complex type of finding in
a way that leads to greater understanding, not more confusion.

MODERATED MEDIATION

As I noted in Chapter 2, Baron and Kenny (1986) did a better job explaining mediated moderation than they did the case we take up next: moderated
mediation. In some ways, I think that this method is easier to understand,
perform, and interpret than mediated moderation, but I leave it up to you
to see what you think about this. In this case, we ask the question "Does a
particular mediational pattern function similarly or differently for various
groups of individuals?"

> **Helpful Suggestion:** The dataset in question here is called "moder-
> ated mediation example.sav."

I use my large adolescent dataset to ask whether resilience-type coping
efforts (e.g., "I don't let problems bother me") mediate between total problem
intensity and negative adjustment differentially for younger versus older adolescents. The sample includes 691 10- to 11-year-olds and 517 14- to 15-year-
olds, and I use concurrent data in this case (all Year 1). My hypothesis was
that older adolescents would be more likely to effectively use whatever resilience resources they have to cope with their problems than younger adolescents, and this is a classic moderated mediation question. The mediation
triangle is presented in Figure 7.5. In the past researchers would run the
mediational analysis on both groups *separately* and then compare the results.
So I present the results of these analyses in Figure 7.6.

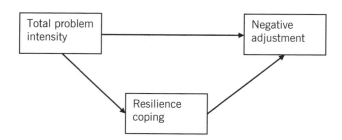

FIGURE 7.5. Hypothesized mediation pattern in the moderated mediation example.

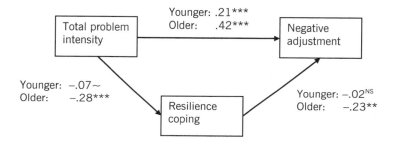

FIGURE 7.6. Obtained zero-order correlations among variables in the moderated mediation example.

Two apparent facts emerge from this set of results: (1) younger adolescents do not evidence a significant relationship between resilience and negative adjustment, and (2) differences in size of relationships between the two groups seem to emerge in all three relationships. There are ways to test the size of each of these relationships between two groups in multiple regression (Cohen et al., 2003), but this approach does not adequately evaluate the question of whether the mediation functions differently between the two groups.

The more elegant way to perform these comparisons is to conduct equality constraints in SEM. For those unfamiliar with this technique, Byrne (2009) is an accessible book on this issue. I follow her guidance using Amos in this case.

We must set up our dataset so that the moderator (age in this case) has two discrete values. I arbitrarily identified 10- to 11-year-olds as 0 and 14- to 15-year-olds as 1 under a variable called "agedichot" (age dichotomized). I open Amos and attach the dataset. I then "manage groups" and set up two groups: younger and older. These are then identified in the "select datafile" menu in Amos and connected with the two values.

Then I draw my mediational hypothesis (seen earlier) and run the analysis. This analysis yields separate estimates for the two groups and will yield a chi-square value of zero because it is a just-identified model. This run is called the "base model." I am now prepared to run an omnibus test on the three estimated parameters taken together comparing the two groups. I specify the parameter from problems to adjustment to be p_1, the parameter from problems to resilience to be p_2, and the parameter from resilience to adjustment to be p_3. What this accomplishes is that it constrains all three estimated parameters to be equal between the two groups (and that is how we get the phrase "equality constraint"). I run this analysis, and it frees up 3 degrees of freedom because these three parameters are set to be equal rather than estimated, and it yields a $\chi^2 = 10.59$. I go to the back of any good statistics book, find the chi-square table, and determine that a value of 10.6 with 3 degrees of freedom is significant at $p = .014$ (or one could find an Internet applet to do this computation). This result tells me that I obtained a significant difference across these three parameters for these two groups; however, because it is an omnibus test, I cannot tell where these differences specifically lie.

The next step is to remove these three equality constraints and then do each of the three constraints one step at a time. When I did this, I obtained the results presented in Table 7.1. These results are much more illuminating than those obtained from the previously described "separate analyses" approach. Now we know that significance differences occurred for all three links: Older adolescents yielded stronger positive relationships for all three links.

What does this mean? I can argue that these results supported my hypothesis that older adolescents would employ resilience-type coping efforts to deal with problems better than younger adolescents. This latter

TABLE 7.1. Summary of Equality Constraints for the Age Groups for the Moderated Mediation Example

Parameter	Chi-square change	df	p-value
Problems to Negative adjustment	11.10	1	.001
Problems to Resilience	12.60	1	.001
Resilience to Negative adjustment	4.70	1	.03

result suggests that resilience might be age dependent in certain respects, but this result is more illuminating than performing an ANOVA and noting that older adolescents use higher levels of resilience coping than younger ones. This result tells us *how* older adolescents use resilience.

Note that I would not obtain "significant mediation" (in the strict Baron and Kenny sense) with the younger sample because two links were non-significant and the third was marginally significant. One might, if one was interested, try to bootstrap this mediation separately for the two age groups to determine whether significant mediation was obtained for the older group and nonsignificant mediation was obtained for the younger group. One might, for example, try problem 2 at the end of the chapter.

What about Continuous Moderators?

At this time, it seems that the only way to incorporate continuous moderators using equality constraints is to dichotomize (or trichotomize) the distribution. So, for example, if I had a continuous moderator such as SES of the families in which these youths were raised, I would find the median and create two groups: low SES and high SES. (However, read the next section about bootstrapped moderated mediation; this approach can handle continuous moderators.) It is also important to note that when one uses a program that allows for the creation of additional parameters (for example, LISREL or Mplus), then performing and interpreting moderated mediation with continuous moderators is functionally easier. We can compute simple slopes for the interaction, use them as parameters in a model, and then use these simple slopes to compute indirect effects at these conditional values. Preacher et al. (2007) describe their macros, which can be used to conduct moderated mediation in SAS and Mplus. I recommend that you examine Andrew Hayes's website, which describes PROCESS, MODMED, and other helpful tools to examine mediation, moderation, and combinations of mediation and moderation: **http://www.afhayes.com/spss-sas-and-mplus-macros-and-code.html#modmed**.

More Than Two Groups?

If you have a trichotomous moderator (e.g., high, medium, and low SES) or if you have more than two levels of a categorical variable (e.g., four ethnic groups), then you would be interested in making all pairwise comparisons among the various groups. To do so is time-consuming and awkward, but at present it seems to be the preferred way to make these comparisons.

WHERE TO FROM HERE?:
BOOTSTRAPPING FOR MODERATED MEDIATION

What I have shown you here is very basic. This SEM-based moderated mediation method will probably suffice in many cases, but there are a number of promising developments on the horizon that you will wish to investigate. For example, Kris Preacher and Andrew Hayes have ventured into the area of computing moderated mediation with bootstrapping methods (Preacher & Hayes, 2004, 2005; Preacher et al., 2007). The logic of doing bootstrapping has been covered previously in this book (see Chapter 4), but I repeat briefly here that it is a powerful method of estimating the key relationships in mediation for small samples or variables that display non-normal distributions. And a case could certainly be made that handling continuous moderators is better than doing moderated mediation in SEM using dichotomous or trichotomous moderators.

I briefly note that Preacher and Hayes's SPSS macro allows one to examine moderated mediation in a variety of ways. I just mention in passing that the macro can examine moderation of the three parameters noted earlier (namely IV to MedV, IV to DV, and MedV to DV), but it can also handle moderation of the MedV-to-DV relationship by the IV, double moderators (IV to MedV moderated by Z and MedV to DV moderated by Y), and double moderation (both IV to MedV and MedV to DV moderated by Z). Thus it is very flexible, and one can use this macro to examine seemingly all important aspects of the mediational triangle. The chief drawback to this approach, in my view, is that one must master the SPSS macro system, which at times is awkward and balky. Nevertheless, this is the best way to do bootstrapping for simple mediation and for moderated mediation at present. I recommend that you examine these possibilities.

MORE COMPLICATED VARIANTS:
MODERATED MEDIATED MODERATION

Believe it or not, it is possible to pile one variant on top of another, as in "moderated mediated moderation." Baron and Kenny (1986) did not discuss this possibility, and few souls have been ambitious (or brave) enough to go down this road, but let me lay out one example that will give you a flavor for this possibility. This example comes from a study that I performed over two decades ago, so this should indicate that there is nothing inherently new about doing such a study.

I published a paper in *Developmental Psychology* with my advisor, Bill Brewer, in 1984 with the title "Development of Story Liking: Character Identification, Suspense, and Outcome Resolution." In it I tested a path model that involved an interaction term. Let me briefly explain the reason for the study. We felt that character valence (good vs. bad story characters) would predict story character liking. In simple language, children in our study were expected to like characters who behaved morally (good) and dislike characters who behaved immorally (bad). In addition, we expected that readers would like stories that had a positive outcome (i.e., a happy ending) more than those with a negative ending. Last, we predicted that the interaction term (created by multiplying character valence with outcome valence) would be liked by older children (12 years old) more than younger children (8 years old). The interaction term was created to operationalize what is termed "a belief in the just world" (Lerner, 1980), and it works like this: People tend to like narratives in which good characters obtain positive outcomes and bad characters obtain negative outcomes, and they dislike narratives in which good characters obtain negative outcomes and bad characters obtain positive outcomes. Our study focused on the possibility that older children would be more likely to manifest the prevalent adult belief in the just world compared with younger children; in essence, the interaction term should be a significant predictor of outcome liking in older children but not for younger children. The relevant portion of the larger path model for younger children (second graders) looked like the path model contained in Figure 7.7.

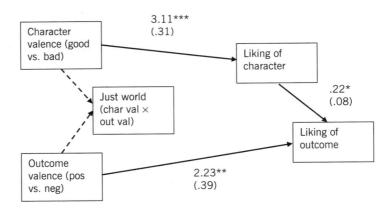

FIGURE 7.7. Obtained statistical outputs for younger children's (second graders) path model from Jose and Brewer (1984). (*Note.* Nonparenthetical numerical values are unstandardized regression coefficients and parenthetical values are standard errors. ***$p < .001$; **$p < .01$; *$p < .05$.)

In short, what we found was that the just-world variable (the interaction) did *not* predict outcome liking for younger children, but these children liked good characters and they liked positive outcomes. (By the way, the solid lines with arrows reflected significant positive relationships, and the dotted lines indicated that the "just world" variable was created by multiplying the two constituent variables. Also, I have reported B's and standard errors here rather than beta weights.)

And moving on, what did the older children evidence? The fourth graders yielded a model intermediate between the second graders and the sixth graders, but I do not show it here for the sake of brevity. The oldest group (sixth graders) yielded the path model in Figure 7.8.

I hope that you can see the point I was trying to make: The interaction term succinctly captured a meaningful psychological phenomenon, and its ability to predict an outcome varied across different groups. So, to recap, why is this called "moderated mediated moderation"? Let's break it down: (1) the first term, *moderated*, refers to age of children; (2) the second term, *mediated*, refers to the fact that we are examining how variables might mediate within a path model; and (3) the third term, *moderation*, refers to the just-world-belief interaction term that is embedded within the path model.

There are some shortcomings in this example. The disadvantage in showing you this old research result is that it does not reflect current up-to-date techniques. What I did statistically back in the early 1980s is considered to be inadequate today. In particular, I constructed these path models by

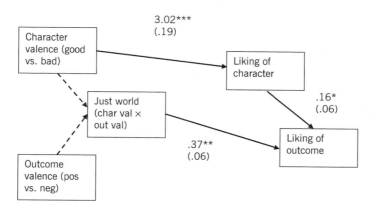

FIGURE 7.8. Obtained statistical outputs for oldest children's (sixth graders) path model from Jose and Brewer (1984). (*Note.* Nonparenthetical numerical values are unstandardized regression coefficients, and parenthetical values are standard errors. ***$p < .001$; **$p < .01$; *$p < .05$.)

performing a series of multiple regression analyses. Although LISREL existed back then, I had not yet learned it, so I relied on this standard method. I do not recommend doing path models in this fashion, and it is probably a lost art at this point anyway. Another key drawback is that at that time I did not know how to do explicit post hoc comparisons on the strength of various estimated parameters between groups. Today in any SEM program, one can perform an equality constraint in a two-group run to compare the strength of a particular parameter, and on the data in question, I would have liked (going back in time with a time machine) to have done so for the parameter between the interaction term and outcome liking across the three age groups. What I did back in 1984 was to say, essentially: "See, I got a significant link for the sixth graders but not for the second graders: this supports my hypothesis." By today's standards, that is not good enough. Bottom line: Do the equality constraints.

So are these all of the possible variations? Well, no, probably not. It is possible to combine these two building blocks in various ways. Let us consider some other possibilities.

Other Variants

Mediated Mediation

You will occasionally have the opportunity to examine whether two or more mediating variables can be usefully interposed between exogenous (x variables) and end-point outcome variable(s) (see Figure 7.9). This example can be called "mediated mediation" because a particular mediational relationship is further mediated by a second mediating variable. In practice, most researchers do not think in terms of this label; they just examine these types of possibilities. I include it here in order to be thorough and complete.

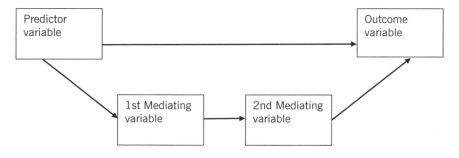

FIGURE 7.9. Graphical depiction of a mediated mediation path model.

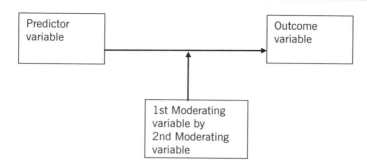

FIGURE 7.10. Graphical depiction of a moderated moderation path model.

Moderated Moderation

I covered the possibility depicted in Figure 7.10 in Chapter 6; namely, if one includes more than one moderating variable in the equation at the same time, then one can obtain "moderated moderation."

We have covered the cases of moderated mediation, mediated moderation, and moderated mediated moderation already. But what about mediated moderated mediation? I have not seen anyone do this, and frankly, I am not sure how this particular model would be constructed and run. What about "moderated mediated mediation"? Well, this one makes sense to me in that one could do equality constraints on a mediated mediation path model. But I am not sure that "mediated moderated moderation" is a useful method.

SUMMARY

What have we learned here? As I said at the outset of this chapter, I am intrigued by the possibilities of combining basic mediation and basic moderation, but it should also be clear that there are daunting challenges ahead for us to figure out how to perform and interpret these hybrid models. Computer programs lag behind in their capability to perform these analyses (as is usually the case) and to generate clear output, but on a positive note, SEM programs that conduct multiple variable path models with equality constraints can conduct the most important variants noted here. I am confident that much more will be developed over the near term to allow researchers to push the envelope with regard to these combinations. There also seem to be unusual hybrid models that no one has explicitly examined that may be explored in the future.

FURTHER READING

The set of readings on these hybrid approaches are published chiefly in the high-end statistical journals, but they should be read and digested before attempting these analyses. I recommend the following papers:

Baron, R. M., & Kenny, D. A. (1986). The moderator–mediator variable distinction in social psychological research: Conceptual, strategic, and statistical considerations. *Journal of Personality and Social Psychology, 51,* 1173–1182.

Edwards, J. R., & Lambert, L. S. (2007). Methods for integrating moderation and mediation: A general analytical framework using moderated path analysis. *Psychological Methods, 12,* 1–22.

Muller, D., Judd, C. M., & Yzerbyt, V. Y. (2005). When moderation is mediated and mediation is moderated. *Journal of Personality and Social Psychology, 89,* 852–863.

Preacher, K. J., Rucker, D. D., & Hayes, A. F. (2007). Assessing moderated mediation hypotheses: Theory, method, and prescriptions. *Multivariate Behavioral Research, 42,* 185–227.

An accessible book that teaches the use of equality constraints in SEM is:

Byrne, B. (2009). *Structural equation modeling with Amos: Basic concepts, applications, and programming.* New York: Taylor & Francis.

A couple of papers that give good examples of moderated mediation and mediated moderation are:

Rose, B., Holmbeck, G. N., Coakley, R. M., & Franks, L. (2004). Mediator and moderator effects in developmental and behavioral pediatric research. *Journal of Developmental and Behavioral Pediatrics, 25,* 58–67.

Wirtz, P. W. (2007). Advances in causal chain development and testing in alcohol research: Mediation, suppression, moderation, mediated moderation, and moderated mediation. *Alcoholism: Clinical and Experimental Research, 31,* 57–63.

Here is the citation for my developmental study that used moderated mediated moderation:

Jose, P. E., & Brewer, W. F. (1984). Development of story liking: Character identification, suspense, and outcome resolution. *Developmental Psychology, 20,* 911–924.

And finally, if you want to pursue this topic in multilevel modeling, this is an excellent paper:

Bauer, D. J., Preacher, K. J., & Gil, K. M. (2006). Conceptualizing and testing random indirect effects and moderated mediation in multilevel models: New procedures and recommendations. *Psychological Methods, 11,* 142–163.

IN-CHAPTER EXERCISES

1. Try your hand with a mediated moderation dataset, "mediated moderation problem#1.sav," which has four variables: negative life events (NLE), grit, life satisfaction, and hope. My prediction was that grit would moderate the effect of negative life events in predicting life satisfaction in the first instance and predicting hope in the second instance. In other words, the effects of NLE, grit, and NLE × grit on hope would be mediated by life satisfaction. Conceptually, this model suggests that individuals who are high in grit (perseverance and tough-mindedness) are likely not to experience negative effects of NLEs on life satisfaction and hope.

2. As hinted before in the section on moderated mediation (Figure 7.5), I would like you to conduct a bootstrapped moderated mediation analysis in SEM to determine whether the mediation for younger adolescents is truly nonsignificant and the mediation for older adolescents is truly significant.

Suggested Answers to Exercises

CHAPTER 3

Additional Exercises

1. Because gender is a categorical variable, it can function only in the role of the IV in the mediation triangle. If one chooses three variables for which significant relationships are noted, then intelligence is left out entirely. The following table details all of the 10 possible combinations of variables.

IV	MedV	DV
Gender	Extraversion	Happiness
Gender	Extraversion	Stress
Gender	Stress	Extraversion
Gender	Stress	Happiness
Extraversion	Happiness	Stress
Extraversion	Stress	Happiness
Stress	Happiness	Extraversion
Stress	Extraversion	Happiness
Happiness	Extraversion	Stress
Happiness	Stress	Extraversion

Bonus point: Yes, two more mediations are possible, and they would be:

IV	MedV	DV
Gender	Extraversion	Happiness
Gender	Stress	Happiness

2. This is an example of a mediating variable that is a suppressor variable because its inclusion in the mediation model led to an increase in the predictor-to-outcome relationship (.29 to .34) instead of a decrease. Probably one or two variables here are heterogeneous, that is, not composed of a single construct—and hence relationships with each other manifest unusual relationships due to shared variance.

3.

	Value
Direct effect	0.370
Indirect effect	0.274
Total effect	0.644
Ratio	0.425

4.

	Value
Direct effect	0.401
Indirect effect	0.121
Total effect	0.522
Ratio	0.232
IV to MedV	0.313

5. The two sets of numbers, although they have different means, have exactly the same variances (and standard deviations).

	x_i	$(x_i - \bar{x})^2$	y_i	$(y_i - \bar{y})^2$
Subj. 1	1.00	9	17.00	9
Subj. 2	6.00	4	14.00	0
Subj. 3	7.00	9	11.00	9
Subj. 4	2.00	4	12.00	4
Subj. 5	4.00	0	16.00	4
Mean	4.00	Var = $\Sigma/(n-1)$ = 26/4 = 6.50	14.00	Var = $\Sigma/(n-1)$ = 26/4 = 6.50
Standard deviation		SQRT(6.5) = 2.54951		SQRT(6.5) = 2.54951

6. Total effect ($a + b$); direct effect (a); indirect effect (b). Bonus point: Area d refers to the residual variance, that is, variance not explained by either the IV or the MedV.

7.

Areas	Part correlations	Variances	
$a + b$	−.205	0.042	Total effect
a	−.090	0.008	Direct effect
c	.556	0.309	
b		0.034	Indirect effect

3.4% of the variance in happiness was jointly explained by negative life events and hope.

8.

	B	SE
a	0.260	0.033
b	0.245	0.041

$$z\text{-value} = \frac{a*b}{\text{SQRT}(b^2*s_a^2 + a^2*s_b^2)}$$

$$= \frac{(.260)*(.245)}{\text{SQRT}(.245^2*.033^2 + .260^2*.041^2)} = \frac{.0637}{\text{SQRT}(.060*.001 + .0676*.0017)}$$

$$= \frac{.0637}{\text{SQRT}(.0000654 + .000113636)}$$

$$= \frac{.0637}{\text{SQRT}(.000179)} = \frac{.0637}{.013379} = 4.76, p < .000001$$

	Estimate of indirect effect	±	(Asym. 95% CI coefficient	×	Standard error)
Lower limit	0.0637	−	(1.62	×	0.013379)
	0.0637	−		0.02167	
	0.0420				
Upper limit	0.0637	+	(2.25	×	0.013379)
	0.0637	+		0.03010	
	0.0938				

The answer is that significant mediation was obtained in the present case. Not only was Sobel's z-test significant, but also the 95% CI yielded a range (0.04–0.09) that did not include the value of zero. Thus one can conclude that rumination mediated between stressful life events and anxiety in this dataset.

9. Sobel's z-score was 1.59, $p = .111$, and the two CIs were computed as:

	Estimate of indirect effect	±	(Sym. 95% CI coefficient	×	Standard error)
Lower limit	0.4955	–	(1.96	×	0.31082)
	0.4955	–		0.60921	
	−0.1137				
Upper limit	0.4955	+	(1.96	×	0.31082)
	0.4955	+		0.60921	
	1.1047				

	Estimate of indirect effect	±	(Asym. 95% CI coefficient	×	Standard error)
Lower limit	0.4955	–	(1.62	×	0.31082)
	0.4955	–		0.50352	
	−0.0080				
Upper limit	0.4955	+	(2.25	×	0.31082)
	0.4955	+		0.699345	
	1.1948				

This is an example of narrowly missing establishing statistically significant mediation. The right interpretation here is to say "significant mediation was not identified for life satisfaction between the treatment and gratitude," but of course it was close to making the $p < .05$ cutoff. I had you generate three significance tests so that you can appreciate that the asymmetric CI, although it is less conservative than the symmetrical CI, still did not return a decision of "statistically significant" and that all three offer slightly different estimates of the significance of the indirect effect. Still, the consensus among all three is "nonsignificant."

Conceptually this is an interesting result, because the experimental mediation example given earlier in the chapter found that gratitude significantly mediated between the treatment and subsequent life satisfaction; however, this reversal of the MedV and DV did not yield significance. One can argue, therefore, that gratitude passed on more of the effect of the treatment to life satisfaction than life satisfaction passed on to subsequent gratitude. Thus one could argue that gratitude was a better mediator of the effect of the treatment than life satisfaction. However, this observation needs to be qualified with the knowledge that the former mediation was just barely statistically significant and the latter mediation was just barely nonsignificant. A test of the relative sizes of the indirect effects would probably indicate that they were of a similar size.

CHAPTER 4

In-Chapter Exercises

1. It is not specified, so one cannot tell. This model posits two "full mediations" from stress to depression: one through control and one through rumination. One would need to insert an arrow from stress to depression in conjunction with these paths in order to derive a direct effect.

2. Indirect effects through vocabulary = 0.14; through math skills = 0.18; and through impulsivity = 0.01. According to the CIs, the first two paths are significant, and the last one is not.

3. The 95% CI did not include the value of zero, so one can conclude that the mediational pattern yielded statistical significance.

4. No, this dataset does not yield statistically significant longitudinal mediation.

$$z\text{-value} = \frac{.027^* - .073}{\text{SQRT}(.027^2{*}.0505^2 + .073^2{*}.0147^2)} = \frac{.001971}{.00173513} = 1.136$$

5.

	Unstandardized coefficients	Standard errors	Standardized coefficients
a_1	0.157	0.038	0.096
b_1	0.089	0.016	0.123
c'_1	0.019	0.030	0.016
Direct effect			0.016
Indirect effect			0.012
Total effect			0.028
Ratio (indirect/total)			43%

$$z = \frac{.157^*.089}{\text{SQRT}(.089^2{*}.038^2 + .157^2{*}.016^2)} = \frac{.013973}{.0042128} = 3.3170, p = .0009$$

	Estimate of indirect effect	±	(Asym. 95% CI coefficient	×	Standard error)
Lower limit	0.014	–	(1.62	×	0.0042)
	0.014	–		0.0068	
	0.0072				
Upper limit	0.014	+	(2.25	×	0.0042)
	0.014	+		0.0095	
	0.0235				

Both Sobel's test and the CI support the view that longitudinal mediation was obtained in the present case.

6.

	Unstandardized coefficients
a	0.076
b	−0.124
c	−0.035
c'	−0.033
Direct effect	.0256
Indirect effect	.0094
Total effect	.0350
Ratio (indirect/total)	27%

CHAPTER 5

Additional Exercises

1. Yes, you can, but it would be easier (and mathematically equivalent) to perform the analysis in ANOVA.

2.

Religious affiliation	Dum1	Dum2	Dum3	Dum4
Protestant	0	0	0	0
Catholic	1	0	0	0
Jewish	0	1	0	0
Muslim	0	0	1	0
Buddhist	0	0	0	1

3. You will first create three dummy codes (Dum1 = normal vs. TB; Dum 2 = normal vs. diabetes; and Dum3 = normal vs. hypertension). The next step is to multiply the perspective-taking (PT) variable by each of the three dummy codes. The list of terms in steps is as follows:

	Enter
Step 1	PT
Step 2	Dum1, Dum2, Dum3
Step 3	PT*Dum1, PT*Dum2, PT*Dum3

4. When one graphs the result of a moderation analysis, one includes statistical information for all three terms: main effect for the IV, main effect for the ModV, and the interaction term. Mathematical information for all three components are incorporated into the single graph.

5. The IV, stress, was a significant predictor of anxiety, so the basic relationship was established as robust. However, the moderating variable, problem solving, was not a main-effect predictor of anxiety (after stress was entered into the equation). Most important, the interaction term, entered on the third step, yielded a p-value greater than .05, so one can conclude that problem solving did not significantly moderate the effect of stress on anxiety in this dataset.

6.

	N	Minimum	Maximum	Mean	Std. deviation
Stress	364	.0000	3.4286	1.134223	.7103263
Rumination	364	6.0000	42.0000	23.601648	9.8804478
Depression	364	.0000	48.0000	12.884615	10.9854843
Valid N (listwise)	364				

Model	Unstandardized coefficients		Standardized coefficients	t	Sig.
	B	Std. error	Beta		
1. (Constant)	5.450	.985		5.534	.000
stress	6.554	.736	.424	8.903	.000
2. (Constant)	−4.626	1.210		−3.822	.000
stress	3.742	.675	.242	5.547	.000
Rumination	.562	.048	.506	11.591	.000
3. (Constant)	1.339	2.062		.650	.516
stress	−1.940	1.735	−.125	−1.118	.264
Rumination	.302	.087	.272	3.459	.001
strxrum	.226	.064	.521	3.545	.000

Note. Dependent variable: depression.

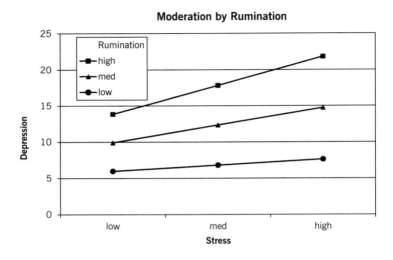

Moderation by Rumination

The regression analysis indicated that both stress and rumination manifested significant main effects on depression on entry; both were positive when entered, suggesting that both higher stress and higher rumination were associated with higher depression. However, when the interaction term was entered, the main effect of stress became nonsignificant, suggesting that it was absorbed into the interaction effect. The significant interaction term, after it was graphed, qualified these main effects by revealing a classic exacerbating moderation effect. Individuals who reported high levels of rumination revealed the steepest slope between stress and depression of the three groups. In addition, the greatest differences among the three groups were noted under conditions of high stress; in other words, levels of rumination made the most difference in depression scores under conditions of high stress.

7. Using values taken from the covariance matrix, compute the simple slopes either by hand or through a program such as ModGraph. Here is the matrix:

Model	str	rum	strxrum
Covariances			
str	3.010	.106	−.102
rum	.106	.008	−.005
strxrum	−.102	−.005	.004

One needs three values from this matrix plus the N of the sample:

Variance of stress	3.010
Variance of interaction term (strxrum)	.004
Covariance of stress by interaction	−.102
N of sample	364

Hand-computing the simple slopes yields the following results:

General equation: $Y = (b_1 + b_3Z)X$

Low SS: $Y = (b_1 + b_3*13.72)X = (-1.94 + (.226)(13.72))X = (-1.94 + .226)$
$= 1.161$

Medium SS: $Y = (b_1 + b_3*23.60)X = (-1.94 + (.226)(23.60)X =$
$(-1.94 + 5.3336) = 3.394$

High SS: $Y = (b_1 + b_3*33.48)X = (-1.94 + (.226)(33.48))X =$
$(-1.94 + 7.5665) = 5.626$

$$SE = SQRT\ [s_{11} + 2(Z)(s_{13}) + Z^2\ s_{33}]$$

where s_{11} is the variance for the main effect (3.010), s_{13} is the covariance of the main effect by the interaction (−.102), and s_{33} is the variance of the interaction (.004). The computations are presented in the following table, inserting point values for Z in appropriate places.

	s_{11}	$2(Z)(s_{13})$	$Z^2\ s_{33}$	Sum	SQRT of sum (standard errors)
Low	3.010	2(13.72)(−.102) = −2.799	$(13.72)^2(.004)$ = .75295	.9641	.9819
Medium	3.010	2(23.60)(−.102) = −4.8144	$(23.60)^2(.004)$ = 2.22784	.4234	.6507
High	3.010	2(33.48)(−.102) = −6.82992	$(33.48)^2(.004)$ = 4.4864	.6637	.8147

	Low rum	Medium rum	High rum
Simple slope	1.161	3.394	5.626
Standard error	.982	.651	.815
t-value	1.18	5.21	6.90
p-value	.25	.0000001	0

Hopefully, your hand-computed results agree with these (within rounding errors). What these simple slopes tell us is that individuals reporting medium (average) or high levels of rumination yield a positive association between stress and depression, whereas individuals reporting low levels of rumination yield a nonsignificant association between the predictor and the outcome variables. These results help us interpret the result because they show which individuals manifest a positive and significant relationship between stress and depression (i.e., medium and high ruminators).

8. The dummy codes will be composed like this:

Ethnic group	Dum1	Dum2
European NZ	0	0
Maori	1	0
Pacific Islander	0	1

The SPSS output will look like this:

	Unstandardized coefficients		Standardized coefficients		
Model	B	Std. error	Beta	t	Sig.
1. (Constant)	−.516	.054		−9.619	.000
stress	.029	.002	.456	13.750	.000
2. (Constant)	−.493	.057		−8.697	.000
stress	.029	.002	.463	13.787	.000
dum1	−.077	.083	−.031	−.919	.358
dum2	−.104	.092	−.039	−1.137	.256
3. (Constant)	−.608	.070		−8.651	.000
stress	.036	.003	.561	11.474	.000
dum1	.182	.131	.075	1.395	.163
dum2	.109	.158	.041	.688	.491
strxdum1	−.012	.005	−.164	−2.615	.009
strxdum2	−.010	.006	−.116	−1.790	.074

Note. Dependent variable: depression.

Because both interaction terms were significant or marginally significant, I decided to run separate analyses for both dummy codes. The comparison of European NZers with Pacific Islanders (Dum2) proved to be nonsignificant by itself, but the other comparison (Dum1) yielded statistical significance:

	Unstandardized coefficients		Standardized coefficients		
Model	B	Std. error	Beta	t	Sig.
1. (Constant)	−.516	.054		−9.619	.000
stress	.029	.002	.456	13.750	.000
2. (Constant)	−.507	.055		−9.205	.000
stress	.029	.002	.458	13.751	.000
dum1	−.055	.081	−.022	−.675	.500

3. (Constant)	−.567	.062		−9.079	.000
stress	.032	.003	.506	12.387	.000
dum1	.141	.127	.058	1.110	.267
strxdum1	−.009	.004	−.117	−2.006	.045

Note. Dependent variable: depression.

Graphing this result yielded this figure:

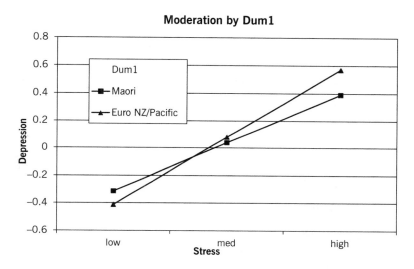

The simple slopes analysis yielded slopes that were fairly similar to each other:

	ENZ/Pacific	Maori
Simple slope	.032	.023
Standard error	.0026	.0036
T-value	12.36	6.35
p-value	0	0

Taken all together, these results suggest that European New Zealanders and Pacific Islanders evidenced a stronger association between stress and depression than did Maori youths. Although the two slopes were fairly similar, the interaction (albeit a weak one at $p = .045$) tells us that with this sample of 757 individuals, the slopes did manifest a significant difference. In contrast, the slopes for the Euro NZ/Maori and Pacific Island youths did not differ significantly. (As a point of information, this analysis cannot illuminate whether Maori and Pacific Islanders differed or not; one would need to reconstitute the dummy codes to test this possibility.)

CHAPTER 6

Additional Exercises

1. The regression result is this:

Model	Unstandardized coefficients		Standardized coefficients		
	B	Std. error	Beta	t	Sig.
1. (Constant)	.714	.036		19.669	.000
stress	.184	.013	.316	13.832	.000
agedichot	.089	.025	.081	3.549	.000
Gender	.021	.024	.019	.849	.396
2. (Constant)	.889	.054		16.484	.000
stress	.100	.022	.171	4.615	.000
agedichot	−.237	.073	−.217	−3.270	.001
Gender	−.055	.067	−.051	−.825	.409
strxage	.160	.027	.383	5.894	.000
strxgend	.048	.026	.117	1.814	.070
agexgend	−.085	.049	−.064	−1.714	.087
3. (Constant)	.922	.059		15.622	.000
stress	.085	.024	.145	3.521	.000
agedichot	−.328	.097	−.300	−3.374	.001
Gender	−.119	.081	−.111	−1.473	.141
strxage	.199	.039	.476	5.122	.000
strxgend	.076	.033	.187	2.293	.022
agexgend	.091	.135	.069	.676	.499
threeway	−.076	.054	−.147	−1.402	.161

Note. Dependent variable: selfharm.

Thus one can conclude that a nonsignificant three-way result was obtained. The next step is to run three separate regressions, one for each of the two-way interactions (even the marginally significant ones). The three interactions yielded the following outputs:

Model	Unstandardized coefficients		Standardized coefficients		
	B	Std. error	Beta	t	Sig.
1. (Constant)	.726	.034		21.481	.000
stress	.184	.013	.316	13.817	.000
agedichot	.089	.025	.081	3.557	.000
2. (Constant)	.861	.041		21.238	.000
stress	.124	.017	.212	7.421	.000
agedichot	−.282	.068	−.258	−4.176	.000
strxage	.161	.027	.384	5.903	.000

Note. Dependent variable: selfharm.

| | Unstandardized coefficients | | Standardized coefficients | | |
Model	B	Std. error	Beta	t	Sig.
1. (Constant)	1.144	.021		53.556	.000
agedichot	.102	.026	.091	3.839	.000
gender	−2.875~	.026	.000	−.001	.999
2. (Constant)	1.130	.024		47.176	.000
agedichot	.139	.038	.125	3.646	.000
gender	.029	.033	.026	.858	.391
agexgender	−.072	.053	−.054	−1.362	.173

Note. Dependent variable: selfharm. ~, this value is presented in scientific notation and signifies this value: .00002875.

| | Unstandardized coefficients | | Standardized coefficients | | |
Model	B	Std. error	Beta	t	Sig.
1. (Constant)	.744	.035		20.962	.000
gender	.021	.025	.020	.874	.382
stress	.187	.013	.321	13.999	.000
2. (Constant)	.796	.048		16.723	.000
gender	−.078	.066	−.073	−1.194	.233
stress	.164	.019	.282	8.569	.000
strxgend	.044	.027	.107	1.640	.101

Note. Dependent variable: selfharm.

I would graph the single significant interaction, and it should look like this:

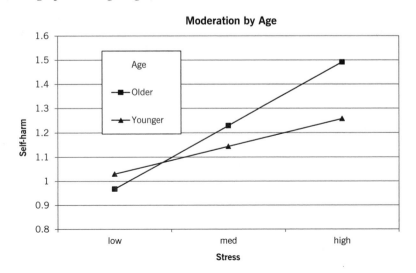

Moderation by Age

In sum, no double moderation was obtained, and this means that gender did not interact with age to affect differential associations between stress and self-harm. Instead, only a single two-way interaction was obtained, which revealed that older adolescents evidenced a stronger relationship between stress and self-harm than did younger adolescents.

2. The regression output should look like this:

Model	Unstandardized coefficients		Standardized coefficients		
	B	Std. error	Beta	t	Sig.
1. (Constant)	1.679	.091		18.553	.000
well-being T1	.581	.022	.539	26.796	.000
2. (Constant)	1.641	.108		15.224	.000
well-being T1	.567	.028	.526	20.120	.000
age dichotomized	−.050	.023	−.044	−2.202	.028
social support T1	.026	.030	.023	.870	.384
3. (Constant)	1.780	.132		13.460	.000
well-being T1	.566	.028	.525	20.111	.000
age dichotomized	−.436	.214	−.384	−2.037	.042
social support T1	−.005	.035	−.004	−.139	.890
agexss	.088	.048	.343	1.813	.070

Note. Dependent variable: well-being T2.

This output tells us that well-being was reasonably stable over 1 year's time ($\beta = .54$, $p < .001$), but the anticipated main effect for social support was not found ($\beta = .02$, $p = .38$). On the other hand, the age main effect tells us that older adolescents reported a significant decrease in well-being from T1 to T2 compared with younger adolescents. The predicted moderation was found to be marginally significant. Because I predicted that older individuals would evidence a positive slope and younger individuals would evidence a flat slope, I decided to probe this interaction. Here is the graph:

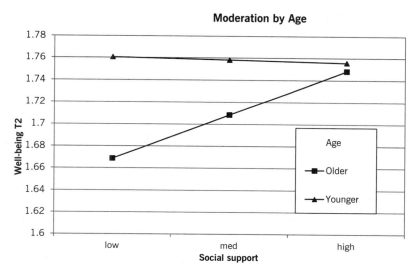

Moderation by Age

As expected, older adolescents evidenced a positive slope, and the younger adolescents seemed to manifest a flat slope. If you performed the simple slopes, then you should find the result that the older group manifested a significant simple slope (.083, $t = 2.62$, $p = .009$), but the younger group manifested a nonsignificant slope (−.005, $t = −.158$, $p = .87$). Given the marginally significant interaction, one might be reluctant to report this result, but the pattern was predicted and sensible, and I might include this interaction in a paper.

3. The SPSS output should look like this:

Model	Unstandardized coefficients		Standardized coefficients		
	B	Std. error	Beta	t	Sig.
1. (Constant)	3.420	.295		11.608	.000
confidence	.442	.070	.150	6.327	.000
2. (Constant)	2.880	.410		7.022	.000
confidence	.349	.085	.119	4.096	.000
social support	.211	.112	.055	1.893	.059
3. (Constant)	5.103	1.472		3.467	.001
confidence	−.241	.385	−.082	−.626	.531
social support	−.323	.357	−.084	−.903	.367
ssxconfid	.140	.089	.305	1.572	.116
4. (Constant)	5.268	1.687		3.122	.002
confidence	−.143	.621	−.049	−.231	.818
social support	−.499	.952	−.130	−.525	.600
ssxconfid	.117	.145	.255	.808	.419
ssquad	.032	.160	.069	.200	.841
5. (Constant)	14.963	4.047		3.698	.000
confidence	−3.480	1.410	−1.183	−2.468	.014
social support	−6.072	2.319	−1.577	−2.619	.009
ssxconfid	1.926	.701	4.199	2.745	.006
ssquad	.789	.329	1.692	2.400	.017
ssquadxconfid	−.236	.089	−3.110	−2.635	.008

Note. Dependent variable: how many nights in last week got 8 hours sleep.

The basic relationship was supported: Individuals who were more confident got more good nights of sleep. However, social support did not manifest a significant main effect on sleep (with confidence already in the equation). The basic moderation term did not yield significance, either; nor did the squared moderation term (social support squared). However, the quadratic moderation term did yield significance. Without the ability to graph this relationship quickly, most researchers will ignore a finding like this. I do not necessarily expect you to compute all of the algebraic equations necessary in order to graph this, but if you can find an applet or macro that can do this, you should do so. My program yielded the following graph:

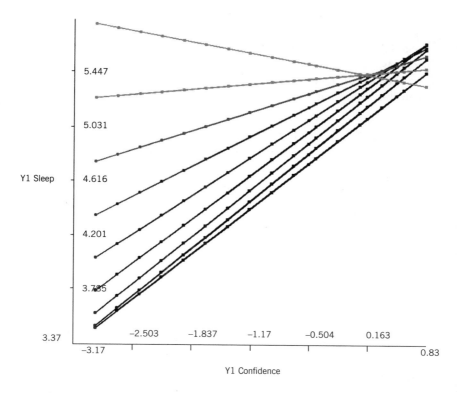

The graph is depicting a complicated result, so the interpretation will be somewhat complicated as well. Dark lines depict high levels of social support, and light gray lines depict low levels of social support. The highest level of social support (very, very, very high social support) is the black line, and it is the bottom line in this group (i.e., these individuals reported getting the least sleep of any group). Individuals who reported slightly less social support (very high social support) evidenced a slightly steeper line than the highest social support group, and, obviously, individuals who reported very little to no social support evidenced essentially a flat line. What this means is that the basic positive relationship between confidence and good sleep is moderated differentially by social support over the range of social support. The strongest association between confidence and sleep was not found at the highest level of social support; it was 1 or 2 *SD*s below the highest level. And then at the low end of social support, we see that the positive association noted for the overall group does not apply at all.

Aiken and West (1991) describe how to generate simple slopes for different moderation groups, and that would be very helpful in the present case, because you would see that the slopes do not rise or fall in a linear fashion as a function of the moderator (as in usual moderation). Instead, the slopes rise and then fall over this range, which is the definition of a quadratic relationship.

4. All SEM programs (as far as I know) will give you means, SDs, B's, and the intercept, if you know where to look for them or perform a few perfunctory conversions. I'll explain how Amos does it, and this should generalize to other SEM packages.

    First of all, request "covariances of estimates" and "estimate means and intercepts" in the output. Draw your model so that it looks like this:

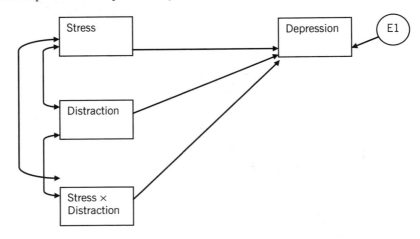

When you open up the output, you should look for these particular outputs that are necessary for graphing:

	B (unstandardized reg coeff)	Mean	SD
stress	.787	33.988	19.336
distraction	.186	33.292	4.529
interaction term	–.019		
intercept	–2.949		

The intercept is not found under "regression weights"; instead, it is referred to as "Intercepts," and it will be identified with the DV (depression). The means come from the box titled "Means" (yes, I know, it is very tricky), but the SDs are nowhere to be found. However, if you call up the covariances, you can take the square roots of the variances for stress and distraction. If you do that, you should obtain the values given here.

With this information you should be able to produce this graph:

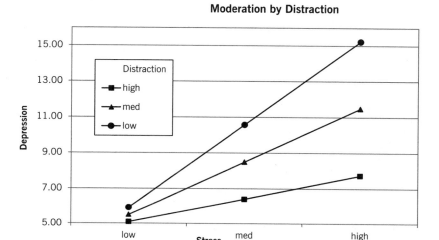

Moderation by Distraction

By now you should recognize this result as a classic buffer moderation result: Individuals who engaged in high distraction evidenced the weakest relationship between stress and depression. Nolen-Hoeksema (1994) has theorized that distraction operates as a buffer for this relationship, but I do not know whether she has ever examined it precisely like this.

5. I would enter PTOT1 as grand mean centered. Be sure to double-click on the residual for the second Level 2 equation. This is the syntax for the problem, and the Level 1 equation is significant:

Level 1 Model

$$Y = \pi_0 + \pi_1*(PTOT1) + E$$

Level 2 Model

$$\pi_0 = \beta_{00} + R_0$$
$$\pi_1 = \beta_{10} + R_1$$

Final estimation of fixed effects (with robust standard errors)

Fixed effect	Coefficient	Standard error	t-ratio	Approx. df	p-value
For INTRCPT1, π_0					
INTRCPT2, β_{00}	9.794792	0.202671	48.328	97	<.001
For PTOT1 slope, π_1					
INTRCPT2, β_{10}	2.212613	0.096031	23.041	97	<.001

This output says that happiness scores significantly varied around the intercept (β_{00}) and, as predicted, that frequencies of positive events significantly and positively predicted total happiness at Level 1 (β_{10}).

Depression was not a significant moderator of this Level 1 equation:

Final estimation of fixed effects (with robust standard errors)

Fixed effect	Coefficient	Standard error	t-ratio	Approx. df	p-value
For INTRCPT1, π_0					
INTRCPT2, β_{00}	9.787275	0.190936	51.259	96	<.001
BDI_TOT, β_{01}	−0.113450	0.029458	−3.851	96	<.001
For PTOT1 slope, π_1					
INTRCPT2, β_{10}	2.207753	0.095900	23.021	96	<.001
BDI_TOT, β_{11}	−0.006813	0.014000	−0.487	96	.628

We see here that depressed people reported lower mean levels (−.11) of Level 1 happiness (β_{01}), but, contrary to prediction, depressed people did not report a differential association between positive events and happiness compared with nondepressed people (β_{11}).

And, last, gender was found to be a marginally significant predictor of the Level 1 equation:

Final estimation of fixed effects (with robust standard errors)

Fixed effect	Coefficient	Standard error	t-ratio	Approx. df	p-value
For INTRCPT1, π_0					
INTRCPT2, β_{00}	8.748717	0.655892	13.339	96	<.001
SEX, β_{01}	0.615056	0.395107	1.557	96	.123
For PTOT1 slope, π_1					
INTRCPT2, β_{10}	2.794976	0.313618	8.912	96	<.001
SEX, β_{11}	−0.342110	0.188101	−1.819	96	.072

Gender did not predict intercept values of Level 1 happiness (β_{01}), but it marginally moderated the Level 1 equation (β_{11}). Because I know that gender was coded 2 = females and 1 = males, I can see in the following graph that males evidenced a marginally steeper slope for the relationship between positive events and happiness than did females.

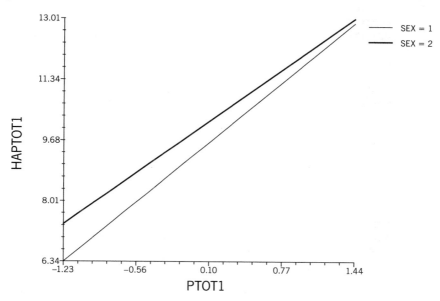

6. The Mplus output is this:

Means

RUMINAC	RUMINBC	RUMINCC	CORUMAC	CORUMBC
-0.001	-0.004	-0.003	0.000	0.000

Means

CORUMCC	DEP
0.001	2.692

```
MODEL RESULTS
```

	Estimate	S.E.	Est./S.E.	Two-Tailed P-Value
RUM BY				
RUMINAC	1.000	0.000	999.000	999.000
RUMINBC	1.363	0.070	19.395	0.000
RUMINCC	1.304	0.072	18.116	0.000
CORUM BY				
CORUMAC	1.000	0.000	999.000	999.000
CORUMBC	1.005	0.030	33.373	0.000
CORUMCC	0.996	0.029	34.105	0.000
DEP ON				
RUMXCOR	0.364	0.148	2.461	0.014
CORUM WITH				
RUM	0.205	0.026	7.932	0.000
Intercepts				
RUMINAC	-0.018	0.028	-0.637	0.524
RUMINBC	-0.026	0.033	-0.794	0.427
RUMINCC	-0.024	0.033	-0.729	0.466
CORUMAC	-0.048	0.046	-1.059	0.290
CORUMBC	-0.049	0.045	-1.092	0.275
CORUMCC	-0.047	0.044	-1.079	0.281
DEP	2.617	0.066	39.583	0.000
Variances				
RUM	0.256	0.026	9.952	0.000
CORUM	0.773	0.053	14.648	0.000

	B	Mean	SD
Rumination	1.334	−0.003	.506
Co-rumination	1.000	0.000	.879
Rum X Corum	.364		
Intercept	2.617		

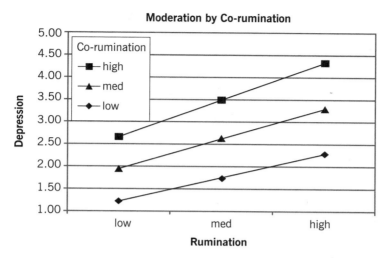

The result, as predicted, is an exacerbating influence of corumination on the rumination-to-depression relationship, $p = .014$. The resulting pattern is very similar to that obtained for social anxiety, although the corumination interaction is not as statistically strong as the social anxiety moderation.

CHAPTER 7

In-Chapter Exercises

1. The Amos model would look like this:

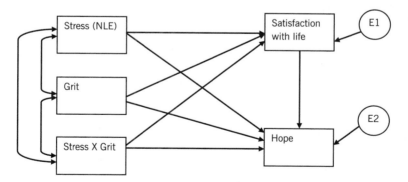

The resulting beta weights are the following:

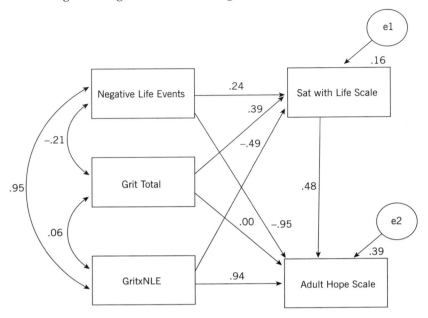

All relationships are significant except for the link between NLE and life satisfaction (0.24) and the link between grit and hope (0.00). The link between NLE × grit and life satisfaction was only marginally significant (−0.49). Because the NLE × Grit interaction was a significant predictor of hope, this should be graphed, and here is the resulting figure:

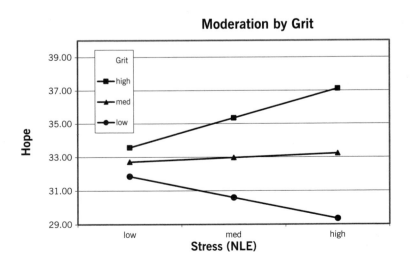

The last issue is whether significant mediation was identified from the three exogenous variables through life satisfaction to hope. Bootstrapped results yielded this:

Standardized Indirect Effects
(Group number 1 – Default model)

Standardized Indirect Effects—Lower Bounds (BC)
(Group number 1 – Default model)

	NegLifeEvts	NLE × grit	Grit	LifeSat
LifeSat	.000	.000	.000	.000
Hope	−.104	−.466	.110	.000

Standardized Indirect Effects—Upper Bounds (BC)
(Group number 1 – Default model)

	NegLifeEvts	NLE × grit	Grit	LifeSat
LifeSat	.000	.000	.000	.000
Hope	.366	.004	.265	.000

Standardized Indirect Effects—Two-Tailed Significance (BC)
(Group number 1 – Default model)

	NegLifeEvts	NLE × grit	Grit	LifeSat
LifeSat	. . .	. . .	. . .	. . .
Hope	.435	.106	.006	. . .

These bootstrapped results say that neither the NLE × Grit interaction nor negative events (stress) yielded a significant mediation, but grit separately did.

Taken together the key results here are:

1. Negative life events (negatively) predicted levels of hope, but this variable was not related to life satisfaction.
2. Grit predicted life satisfaction positively, as one would expect, but it did not predict hope.
3. The interaction of NLE × grit did not predict life satisfaction, but it did predict hope.
   a. A classic funnel pattern was obtained
   b. Individuals who reported high grit showed a positive relationship between NLE and hope, whereas
   c. Individuals who reported low grit showed a negative relationship between NLE and hope.

4. The bootstrapped results showed that
   a. Grit yielded a positive indirect effect through life satisfaction to hope, whereas
   b. Neither NLE nor the interaction term yielded a significant indirect effect through life satisfaction to hope.

It seems that grit functioned to negate the negative effects of NLE, and in fact it seemed that grit, in the context of high NLE, actually led to a higher positive outcome, namely higher hope.

2. Simply use the Amos graphics model generated before and tick the boostrapping options. Once it has run, check the output for the bootstrapped estimates. Note that you can toggle back and forth between the two age groups by clicking on "younger" and "older" at the lower left of the output screen. When you do this, you should obtain these results for the younger group:

Standardized Indirect Effects
(Younger – Default model)

	problems	resilience
resilience	.0000	.0000
negadjust	−.0001	.0000

Standardized Indirect Effects—Lower Bounds (BC)
(Younger – Default model)

	problems	resilience
resilience	.0000	.0000
negadjust	−.0061	.0000

Standardized Indirect Effects—Upper Bounds (BC)
(Younger – Default model)

	problems	resilience
resilience	.0000	.0000
negadjust	.0044	.0000

Standardized Indirect Effects— Two-Tailed Significance (BC)
(Younger – Default model)

	problems	resilience
resilience	. . .	. . .
negadjust	.8916	. . .

And here are the results for the older group:

Standardized Indirect Effects
(Older – Default model)

	problems	resilience
resilience	.0000	.0000
negadjust	.0325	.0000

Standardized Indirect Effects—Lower Bounds (BC)
(Older – Default model)

	problems	resilience
resilience	.0000	.0000
negadjust	.0139	.0000

Standardized Indirect Effects—Upper Bounds (BC)
(Older – Default model)

	problems	resilience
resilience	.0000	.0000
negadjust	.0545	.0000

Standardized Indirect Effects— Two-Tailed Significance (BC)
(Older – Default model)

	problems	resilience
resilience	. . .	. . .
negadjust	.0055	. . .

These results supported what we suspected, namely, that the indirect effect for the younger age group, −0.0001, was statistically nonsignificant, whereas the indirect effect for the older age group was statistically significant, 0.033, SE = 0.01, 95% CI = 0.014 to 0.055. These results support the equality constraint results obtained earlier.

SPSS, Amos, and Mplus Models

In this appendix, I present SPSS syntax for both basic mediation and moderation, and I also show how to perform mediation and moderation in Amos and Mplus as well. I have described in previous chapters how to perform mediation and moderation in HLM and do not repeat those analyses here.

SPSS SYNTAX TO PERFORM BASIC REGRESSION-BASED MEDIATION

In this example, these three variables are defined in the following way (read the description in Chapter 3):

IV:	positive life events (PLE)
MedV:	gratitude (grat)
DV:	happiness (Subjective Happiness Scale or SHS)

I usually run a simple correlation matrix first to determine that all of the variables are related in the way that I think they should be (and also to assess significance of relationships). Use this syntax:

```
CORRELATIONS
  /VARIABLES=ple grat shs
  /PRINT=TWOTAIL NOSIG
  /MISSING=PAIRWISE.
```

Run the following syntax, inserting the appropriate variables in the appropriate places. When you use this syntax for your own analyses, substitute your variable names for the lower-case variable names in this syntax. This syntax describes the regression in which gratitude (the mediating variable) is the outcome and positive life events (the IV) is the predictor.

```
REGRESSION
  /MISSING LISTWISE
  /STATISTICS COEFF OUTS R ANOVA
  /CRITERIA=PIN(.05) POUT(.10)
  /NOORIGIN
  /DEPENDENT grat
  /METHOD=ENTER ple.
```

The second regression involves the IV (PLE) and the MedV (grat) as the predictors for the outcome (SHS) using this syntax:

```
REGRESSION
  /MISSING LISTWISE
  /STATISTICS COEFF OUTS R ANOVA ZPP
  /CRITERIA=PIN(.05) POUT(.10)
  /NOORIGIN
  /DEPENDENT SHS
  /METHOD=ENTER PLE Grat.
```

This should yield the second regression. Follow the directions in Chapter 2 to identify the appropriate B's and SEs that are required to compute Sobel's test in Preacher's website. This regression also outputs the part correlations (semipartials) needed for computing R^2 estimates of effect sizes. If you want to use MedGraph, then you will need to also take two Pearson correlations from the correlation matrix run earlier. And the correlation matrix will also tell you what your sample size is (listwise), in case you don't know this from some other source.

SPSS SYNTAX TO PERFORM BASIC REGRESSION-BASED CATEGORICAL MODERATION

In this example, these three variables are defined in the following way (read the description in Chapter 5):

IV:	Social support (ss)
ModV:	Gender (gender)
DV:	Depression (depression)

I make certain that my categorical variable is properly dummy-coded: In the present case, all individuals should have either a 0 or a 1 value. (Because my categorical variable has two levels, I have a single dummy variable. If I had a categorical variable with four levels—e.g., ethnic group—such as in the dummy coding tutorial in Chapter 6, then I would have three separate dummy variables.)

```
DESCRIPTIVES VARIABLES=ssc
  /STATISTICS=MEAN STDDEV MIN MAX.

FREQUENCIES VARIABLES=gender
  /ORDER=ANALYSIS.
```

Now we're ready to create the interaction term:

```
COMPUTE ssxgend=ss * gender.
EXECUTE.
```

(In the case of multiple dummy variables—let's continue with our example of four ethnic groups and three dummy variables—one would multiply the IV [SS] by each of the three dummy variables.)

Now we construct the hierarchical regression. I usually insert each of the three predictors in individual steps in order to learn more about how each of the three terms explains the DV, but some people just enter all three predictors in a single step. The first option is enacted in the following syntax. I request the R^2 change statistic to assist in this task, and I also ask for the variance–covariance matrix so that I can compute the simple slopes.

```
REGRESSION
  /MISSING LISTWISE
  /STATISTICS COEFF OUTS BCOV R ANOVA CHANGE
  /CRITERIA=PIN(.05) POUT(.10)
  /NOORIGIN
  /DEPENDENT depression
  /METHOD=ENTER ss
  /METHOD=ENTER gender
  /METHOD=ENTER ssxgend.
```

(In the case of multiple dummy variables, one would enter all three dummy variables in the second step and would enter all three interaction terms on the third step.)

This regression analysis will yield all of the relevant statistical outputs that you will need to graph the interaction (if you find one that is significant). The variance–covariance matrix will supply the two variances and the covariance needed for that computation. The sample size can be obtained from a frequencies or descriptives analysis.

SPSS SYNTAX TO PERFORM BASIC REGRESSION-BASED CONTINUOUS MODERATION

In this example, these three variables are defined in the following way (read the description in Chapter 5):

IV:	Stress (stress)
ModV:	Social support (socsup)
DV:	Depression (dep)

Now we're ready to create the interaction term:

```
COMPUTE strxss=stress * ss.
EXECUTE.
```

Now we construct the hierarchical regression. I usually insert each of the three predictors in individual steps in order to learn more about how each of the three terms explains the DV, but some people just enter all three predictors in a single step. The first option is enacted in the following syntax. I request the R^2 change statistic to assist in this task, and I also ask for the variance–covariance matrix so that I can compute the simple slopes.

```
REGRESSION
  /MISSING LISTWISE
  /STATISTICS COEFF OUTS BCOV R ANOVA CHANGE
  /CRITERIA=PIN(.05) POUT(.10)
  /NOORIGIN
  /DEPENDENT depression
  /METHOD=ENTER stress
  /METHOD=ENTER ss
  /METHOD=ENTER strxss.
```

This regression analysis will yield all of the relevant statistical outputs that you'll need to graph the interaction (if you find one that is significant). The variance–covariance matrix will supply the two variances and the covariance needed for that computation. The sample size can be obtained from a frequencies or descriptives analysis.

AMOS GRAPHICS MODEL TO PERFORM BASIC MEDIATION

Mediation in SEM poses an interesting problem: Must one demonstrate a significant IV-to-DV relationship before a MedV is interposed between them? If you wish to do this, then you would do two models; the first one is the simple IV-to-DV relationship:

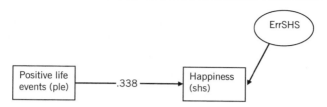

You can see from the analyses in Chapter 3 that this relationship (referred to as c in the book) was significant, $\beta = 0.338$, $p < .001$. Then you would run the full mediational triangle in Amos to see whether the basic relationship decreased (c becomes c'):

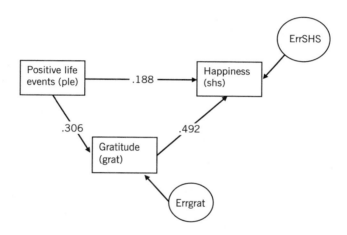

This model tells us that the basic relationship decreased to $\beta = 0.188$, $p < .001$. So how does one get the Sobel z-score from this? Amos does not compute this value, so here are two suggestions. First, obtain the B's and SEs from the Amos output just as with the regression outputs, and then go to Preacher's website or use MedGraph to obtain the Sobel z-score. A second useful tack is to examine the size of the indirect effect that Amos identifies. Before you run the preceding model, go to VIEW, click on ANALYSIS PROPERTIES, and then choose the OUTPUT tab. Tick "Indirect, direct, & total effects" and "standardized estimates," and then when you check the output after the run, you will find under ESTIMATES a series of outputs describing the sizes of the direct, indirect, and total effects in both unstandardized and standardized forms (not too surprisingly). Amos told me in the present case that the size of the standardized indirect effect was 0.15. The 0.15 is identical to the ratio computed by MedGraph (either $c - c'$ or ab). Unfortunately, Amos doesn't tell the user whether this reduction is statistically significant or not. In contrast, LISREL computes the same estimates but also includes information concerning whether the indirect effect is significant or not. Or one could do bootstrapping in Amos (see next section), which does generate statistical significance indicators.

Bootstrapping

It is possible to perform bootstrapping in Amos for mediations such as this. If you are interested in learning how, Dave Kenny has a very useful Web-based tutorial at **http://amosdevelopment.com/video/indirect/flash/indirect.html**. I repeat the basics here:

1. Choose "Indirect, direct, & total effects" and "standardized effects" in the OUTPUT page.
2. Go to the BOOTSTRAP tab and tick two boxes: "perform bootstrap" and "bias-corrected confidence intervals," and, for the "number of bootstrap samples," put a value greater than 1,000.
3. Run the analysis on your model.
4. Pull up the output. Click on "Estimates" and then tick on "Matrices." Under this heading you will find estimates of all three types of effects, and in this case, my output told me that the size of the standardized indirect effect was 0.15. It is good that the bootstrapping method obtained a result similar to what the regression-based analysis told me.
5. Now to check whether this is a statistically significant result, I go to the box in the middle on the left, which is about "estimates/bootstrap." If you tick on "bootstrap standard errors," you will see an estimate of this statistical output, but more interesting are the bootstrap confidence interval and the bias-corrected percentile method two-tailed significance. Amos in this case told me that the 95% confidence interval was 0.111 to 0.195 with an associated *p*-value of .0017. This is the output that tells me that the size of the indirect effect is greater than one would expect by chance, that is, that the size of the indirect effect is statistically significant.

This is quite a useful tool in the Amos program that a lot of people don't know about. Use it and tell others about this feature.

AMOS GRAPHICS MODEL TO PERFORM BASIC CATEGORICAL MODERATION

The same preconditions apply to preparing your data for Amos as to preparing your data for an SPSS categorical moderation regression: (1) check that you have properly dummy-coded your categorical ModV (again, if you have more than two levels for this variable, then you will have more than one dummy variable); and (2) multiply your IV by the dummy variable(s). Once you have done this in SPSS, connect your dataset to Amos Graphics, and construct the following path model:

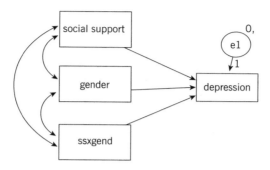

There are several things to note here, particularly if you are new to SEM: (1) you need to draw the double-headed arrows between the three predictors (these are called "covariances"); and (2) you need to insert a residual term for the DV (called "errdep" here because it is the error term for the DV). You will find, if you created the variables and set this model up correctly, that you will obtain results very similar to what you would get from multiple regression. I notice that a few of the estimates will be off in the hundredths or thousandths place due to rounding error, but basically all of the estimates will be identical. If you don't obtain the same results, then you have done something different between the two analyses.

AMOS GRAPHICS MODEL TO PERFORM BASIC CONTINUOUS MODERATION

The same model applies for continuous moderation, except, of course, that the ModV will be continuous (and possibly centered) rather than dummy coded. This is the way it will look:

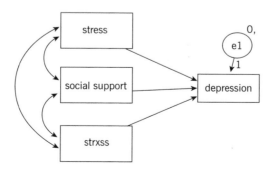

In this case, I have set up a model to examine Cohen and Wills's (1985) buffering hypothesis—namely, would social support moderate the stress-to-depression relationship? If you run this analysis, you should obtain a virtually identical result to the multiple regression analysis of this moderation hypothesis reported in Chapter 5.

Mplus SYNTAX TO PERFORM BASIC MEDIATION (WITH BOOTSTRAPPING)

Prepare your data as an .ascii file (and one must specify in the syntax the format in .ascii as well—in this case it is three fields of 8.2), and then use this syntax in Mplus to estimate the key statistical outputs:

```
TITLE: Mediation example
  DATA: FILE IS
  mediation.dat;
  FORMAT IS 3F8.2;
  VARIABLE: NAMES ARE
  PLE
  Grat
  SHS ;

  USEVARIABLES ARE
  PLE
  Grat
  SHS ;

  ANALYSIS:
  bootstrap = 1000;
  !ESTIMATOR = ML;

  MODEL:
  SHS on grat PLE;
  grat on PLE;

  Model indirect:
  SHS IND grat PLE
  OUTPUT: SAMPSTAT STDYX RESIDUAL tech4 modindices (all);
  PLOT: TYPE=PLOT2;
```

Mplus will first of all generate sample statistics that include zero-order correlations among all three variables:

SAMPLE STATISTICS

Means

	GRAT	SHS	PLE
1	36.538	4.972	1.987

Covariances

	GRAT	SHS	PLE
GRAT	28.84		
SHS	3.962	1.803	
PLE	1.539	0.426	0.878

Correlations

	GRAT	SHS	PLE
GRAT	1.000		
SHS	0.549	1.000	
PLE	0.306	0.338	1.000

The following outputs report the unstandardized and standardized coefficients and standard errors, as well as the R^2s of the two predicted variables. The underlined values are used to compute Sobel's z-score and CIs.

MODEL RESULTS

	Estimate	S.E.	Est./S.E.	Two-Tailed P-Value
SHS ON				
GRAT	0.123	0.013	9.662	0.000
PLE	0.269	0.067	4.045	0.000
GRAT ON				
PLE	1.752	0.282	6.215	0.000
Intercepts				
GRAT	33.057	0.705	46.908	0.000
SHS	-0.056	0.442	-0.127	0.899
Residual Variances				
GRAT	26.150	2.369	11.037	0.000
SHS	1.201	0.082	14.679	0.000

STANDARDIZED MODEL RESULTS

	StdYX Estimate
SHS ON	
GRAT	0.492
PLE	0.188
GRAT ON	
PLE	0.306
Intercepts	
GRAT	6.155
SHS	-0.042
Residual Variances	
GRAT	0.907
SHS	0.666

R-SQUARE

Observed Variable	Estimate
GRAT	0.093
SHS	0.334

And finally, the bootstrapped outcomes are presented next. The unstandardized estimates are reported first, and then the standardized estimates.

TOTAL, TOTAL INDIRECT, SPECIFIC INDIRECT, AND DIRECT EFFECTS

	Estimate	S.E.	Est./S.E.	Two-Tailed P-Value
Effects from PLE to SHS				
Sum of indirect	0.215	0.041	5.237	0.000
Specific indirect				
SHS				
GRAT				
PLE	0.215	0.041	5.237	0.000

STANDARDIZED TOTAL, TOTAL INDIRECT, SPECIFIC INDIRECT, AND
DIRECT EFFECTS

STDYX Standardization

	Estimate	S.E.	Est./S.E.	Two-Tailed P-Value
Effects from PLE to SHS				
Sum of indirect	0.150	0.027	5.566	0.000
Specific indirect				
SHS				
GRAT				
PLE	0.150	0.027	5.566	0.000

You may notice that the standardized indirect effect (0.150) is identical to that obtained by other methods.

Mplus SYNTAX TO PERFORM BASIC MODERATION

The syntax for basic moderation is the following. If you decide to center the IV and ModV, do so and create the product term (stress × social support) before uploading data into Mplus, but remember that it is not necessary to center the main effects before creating the product term.

```
TITLE: moderation example
 DATA: FILE IS
 moderation.dat;
 FORMAT IS 4F8.2;
 VARIABLE: NAMES ARE
 depress
 stress
 socsup
 strsxsoc;

 USEVARIABLES ARE
 depress
 stress
 socsup
 strsxsoc;
```

```
ANALYSIS:
ESTIMATOR = ML;

MODEL:
depress on stress socsup strsxsoc;

OUTPUT: SAMPSTAT STDYX RESIDUAL tech4 modindices (all);
PLOT: TYPE=PLOT2;
```

Sample (descriptive) statistics are generated like this:

```
SAMPLE STATISTICS
    Means
         DEPRESS      STRESS      SOCSUP     STRSXSOC

  1       0.321       -0.003      0.000      -0.002

    Covariances
         DEPRESS      STRESS      SOCSUP     STRSXSOC

DEPRESS    0.064
STRESS     0.035        0.142
SOCSUP    -0.055       -0.002      0.484
STRSXSOC  -0.009        0.013     -0.015      0.061

    Correlations
         DEPRESS      STRESS      SOCSUP     STRSXSOC

DEPRESS    1.000
STRESS     0.369        1.000
SOCSUP    -0.311       -0.007      1.000
STRSXSOC  -0.151        0.135     -0.089      1.000
```

The most important outputs are the unstandardized and standardized coefficients and standard errors:

```
MODEL RESULTS

                                              Two-Tailed
                 Estimate   S.E.   Est./S.E.   P-Value

DEPRESS   ON
   STRESS       0.268     0.048      5.531      0.000
   SOCSUP      -0.120     0.026     -4.596      0.000
   STRSXSOC    -0.240     0.074     -3.237      0.001
```

Intercepts
     DEPRESS   0.321   0.018   17.763   0.000

Residual Variances
     DEPRESS   0.046   0.005   8.396   0.000

STANDARDIZED MODEL RESULTS

STDYX Standardization

	Estimate	S.E.	Est./S.E.	Two-Tailed P-Value
DEPRESS ON				
STRESS	0.398	0.067	5.906	0.000
SOCSUP	-0.329	0.069	-4.790	0.000
STRSXSOC	-0.234	0.071	-3.293	0.001
Intercepts				
DEPRESS	1.266	0.104	12.210	0.000
Residual Variances				
DEPRESS	0.716	0.064	11.140	0.000

The key output is whether the product term evidences statistical significance, which it does here (p = .001). The output should be identical to that produced by SPSS and Amos analyses, and everything is provided here to graph the result except the standard deviations of the IV and ModV.

Appendix B

Resources for Researchers Who Use Mediation and Moderation

Quite a number of resources exist on the Internet for researchers who wish to conduct cutting-edge mediation and moderation analyses, and more are coming online every day. My goal in this chapter is to compile a list of resources for individuals who would like to use the most up-to-date analytical approach available. The need for this chapter, by the way, derives from the fact that the widely used statistical programs that most people know about (e.g., SPSS, SAS) don't perform mediation or moderation in a dedicated fashion. By this I mean that one cannot go into SPSS and pull down from the ANALYZE menu a menu box for "mediation," stipulate an IV, a MedV, and a DV, go into an OPTIONS menu to specify certain alternative ways to compute it, and then click OKAY to get the result. What one must do (as you know, if you read Chapters 3 and 4) is run several analyses and then piece the results together, often with the help of an outside program (e.g., Preacher's website). Several people have written SPSS and SAS macros and scripts to make these programs do what we want them to do, and they are a great step forward. And then there is my stand-alone program, called Mediation & Moderation (M&M for short), that will do basic mediation and moderation analyses. So there is help on the horizon; one just needs to be resourceful in finding and using these tools. I enumerate these resources in this Appendix, and they fall into three main groups: (1) informative websites, (2) downloadable programs/macros, and (3) books and articles. Scan through and pick and choose those items that will be most beneficial to you.

There is one last concern that I should probably mention before getting into the list. Be aware that this list is being compiled shortly before the book is going into print, and of course websites have a habit of disappearing and morphing into other sites, so some of these URLs may no longer be current when you are sitting and reading this page in the book. However, I have an updated list of resources on the companion website for this book (see **www.guilford.com/jose-materials**), so you can always check there to get the most recent links.

INFORMATIVE WEBSITES

David Kenny's Website

Dr. Kenny is Professor of Psychology in the Department of Psychology at the University of Connecticut. His home page URL is **http://davidakenny.net/kenny.htm**. Most people interested in mediation and moderation will want to check out four specific subpages listed on the home page:

1. The "Mediation" section: **http://davidakenny.net/cm/mediate.htm**.
2. The "Moderation" section: **http://davidakenny.net/cm/moderation.htm**.
3. The "Downloads" section, **http://davidakenny.net/downloads.htm**, for a useful manuscript.

   People interested in learning how to use the HLM program to conduct lower level multilevel modeling-based mediation will find a document written by Josephine Korchmaros and David Kenny that describes in great detail how to conduct this type of analysis.
4. A new item called "data-to-text": **http://davidakenny.net/dtt/datatotext.htm**.

   This Webpage is very exciting because it includes two relevant macros, one each for mediation and moderation. What Kenny has done here is write very complete SPSS macros that start with quantitative data, run through the proper analyses, and finally output text that describes what the analyses have found.

I recommend that users check back to this website frequently because Professor Kenny frequently updates the site and adds new and helpful information and macros.

David MacKinnon's Website

Dr. MacKinnon is the Director of the Research in Prevention Laboratory (RIPL) and is a Professor of Psychology at Arizona State University. From his RIPL website, click on "Mediation": **http://www.public.asu.edu/~davidpm/ripl/mediate.htm**.

A large amount of information is located on this page, including definitions and critical information about how to calculate indirect effects in mediation, lists of books and publications on the topic, and links to papers describing a number of programs designed to assist researchers perform mediation analyses. Dr. MacKinnon has intensively investigated the method of statistical mediation for several decades, and his written papers on the topic are considered to be authoritative. His book, *Introduction to Statistical Mediation Analysis* (2008) is the most comprehensive and complete treatment of mediation in print, and I highly recommend that students of mediation and moderation purchase a copy and take their knowledge about these techniques to a higher level.

One last comment: The RIPL group has made available a useful tool named PRODCLIN (find it at **http://www.public.asu.edu/~davidpm/ripl/Prodclin**), which calculates confidence intervals for mediation results. At this writing, the program is available in FORTRAN, SAS, and R. Hopefully a macro for SPSS will be available soon as well. This particular statistical output is offered as an alternate way to assess statistical significance to the usual "*p* less than .05" method that is ingrained in many statistical programs and macros. You can find the online calculator for MacKinnon's confidence interval program at: **http://www.amp.gatech.edu/RMediation**.

Kris Preacher's Website

Dr. Preacher is an Assistant Professor in the Quantitative Methods program at Vanderbilt University and an associate of the KU Center for Research Methods and Data Analysis (CRMDA). His home page is available at **http://www.vanderbilt.edu/psychological_sciences/bio/kristopher-preacher**.

Dr. Preacher has included a variety of different statistical resources, not just focused on mediation and moderation, and they are all very interesting and useful, but I'd like to highlight the most relevant items for researchers wishing to conduct state-of-the-art mediation and moderation.

1. The "Interactive calculators" section: **http://www.quantpsy.org/calc.htm**.
   a. The oldest and most well-known calculator would be the Sobel test calculator, which has been working online for more than 10 years now. One calculates *B*'s and *SE*s with two regressions and enters this information into this online calculator to obtain the Sobel *z*-score.
   b. Preacher has added a "Monte Carlo method for assessing mediation," which is similar to the bootstrapping method for computing the significance of an indirect effect in mediation. It is founded on the R statistical system, which is rapidly becoming a frequently used medium for these types of analyses.
   c. A related item is the "Monte Carlo method for assessing multilevel mediation," which is similar to the item immediately preceding, but for multilevel modeling mediation.
   d. The last item of note (in this context) is the interactive calculation tool to probe interactions. Whether the interaction is obtained in regression, latent curve analysis, or HLM, this tool will determine simple slopes and regions of significance (i.e., the Johnson–Neyman lines), which are immensely helpful in the interpretation of moderation results.

2. The "Mediation & moderation material" section (14 items on mediation and 2 for moderation): **http://www.quantpsy.org/medn.htm**.

   a. One of the more interesting links listed here is the link to a Facebook page, "Statistical mediation and moderation analysis": **https://www. facebook.com/mediation.and.moderation.analysis**. The site includes a fascinating list of discussion topics that many people will find useful, and I think that it uses the strength of Facebook, namely interactivity, very well; it is easier to post questions, enter into dialogues, and learn from other people's posts than in other contexts.

   b. Preacher has written a number of SPSS and SAS macros and scripts that perform mediation in a variety of different ways. Of particular note are the macros that perform bootstrapping, multiple mediation, and moderated mediation.

Andrew Hayes's Website

Dr. Hayes is an Associate Professor of Communication and an Adjunct Associate Professor of Psychology at The Ohio State University, and he is a long-time collaborator with Kris Preacher on the topic of mediation. This address takes you to his homepage: **www.afhayes.com**.

If you click on "SPSS, SAS, and Mplus macros and code," (**http://www.afhayes. com/spss-sas-and-mplus-macros-and-code.html**) you will find a number of macros relevant to mediation and moderation. These can be obtained through this website or through Kris Preacher's website, as they are coauthored outputs. I particularly draw attention to the macro that can compute mediation on nonlinear relationships among the variables. See this informative paper on this topic:

Hayes, A. F., & Preacher, K. J. (2010). Quantifying and testing indirect effects in simple mediation models when the constituent paths are nonlinear. *Multivariate Behavioral Research*, 45, 627–660.

Another macro named MODPROBE allows the user to probe significant interactions (moderations) to determine regions of significance and nonsignificance, which enhances the user's ability to interpret the meaning of the obtained pattern.

Alexander Shackman's Website

Dr. Shackman is located in the Laboratory for Affective Neuroscience, University of Wisconsin, and if you click on "Quantitative methods" on his home page, you will find a useful compendium of mediation–moderation information (as well as other quantitative resources): **http://psyphz.psych.wisc.edu/~shackman/mediation_ moderation_resources.htm#Resources_for_Mediation_and_Moderation_A**. The items on this list include helpful online information, a list of seminal published papers, and online calculators and downloadable macros. I would say that this list is up-to-date and fairly complete.

Paul Jose's Website

(I guess I'll write about myself in the first person. Third person is stuffy when you're talking about yourself.) I am an Associate Professor of Psychology in the School of Psychology at Victoria University of Wellington in New Zealand. I have posted information on how to perform mediation and moderation analyses on my home page (**http://www.victoria.ac.nz/psyc/staff/paul-jose.aspx**), and I have it linked under "The Help Centre." Interested people can review a number of pages that explain how to conduct both mediation and moderation with linear regression. Further, I have two online graphing/calculator functions. One is MedGraph (Jose, 2008a), which computes the Sobel z-test and depicts the mediation result in graphical form: **http://www.victoria.ac.nz/psyc/paul-jose-files/medgraph/medgraph.php**. It computes only single mediation and utilizes only continuous variables. The other online applet is ModGraph (Jose, 2008b), which both graphs the moderation result and calculates simple slopes: **http://www.victoria.ac.nz/psyc/paul-jose-files/modgraph/modgraph.php**. It has the option of either continuous or categorical moderation, but like MedGraph, it computes only single moderation. If you have double moderation, you would have to graph the result in two passes. You can either perform these calculations online or download an Excel macro in each case to perform the calculations on your own computer.

Psychwiki Website

Psychwiki.com is building a set of pages that inform people about statistical techniques such as mediation: **http://www.psychwiki.com/wiki/Mediation**. At this time it does not have a page for moderation, but the mediation page includes links to the key websites and macros listed here, and over time it will be an excellent place to keep track of recent developments.

CALCULATORS, APPLETS, AND MACROS

In addition to the macros described herein, there are a number of others that users may wish to know about.

Daniel Soper's Calculators

Daniel Soper presents a pair of mediation calculators under the heading of "Mediation models": **http://www.danielsoper.com/statcalc/default.aspx#c11**. One calculates the size of the indirect effect through multiplying the a and b paths, and the other calculates Sobel's z-score.

MMRPOWER Calculator

Aguinis, Boik, and Pierce (2001) have created an applet called MMRPOWER to compute power requirements for moderated multiple regression, and it is described in Aguinis's book (2004), *Regression Analysis for Categorical Moderators*.

Jeremy Dawson's Macros to Graph Interactions

Mr. Dawson (a Research Fellow at Aston Business School in the United Kingdom) has offered macros to graph both two-way and three-way interactions that will prove to be very helpful for individuals who want to graph their moderation results. It is located at **http://www.jeremydawson.co.uk/slopes.htm**.

You can use either standardized or unstandardized coefficients, and the Excel macros take the statistical information and graph the results very quickly and easily.

Jason Newsom's SPSS Macros

Dr. Newsom is an Associate Professor in the Institute on Aging at Portland State University and is a coeditor of a useful book titled *Longitudinal Data Analysis: A Practical Guide for Researchers in Aging, Health, and Social Sciences* (Newsom, Jones, & Hofer, 2011). He has written two SPSS macros that obtain simple slopes for moderation (with either a continuous or categorical moderator): **http://www.upa.pdx.edu/IOA/ newsom/macros.htm**.

Karl Wuensch's Summary

Dr. Wuensch has compiled an extensive online library of his own as well as others' resources on a wide range of statistical topics, but this page contains material specific to moderation and mediation: **http://core.ecu.edu/psyc/wuenschk/stathelp/ StatHelp.htm**.

BOOKS AND SEMINAL ARTICLES

For the novice in this area, I would recommend beginning with the following books and articles as a way to learn about the key issues in conducting these two statistical techniques. The key word here is *beginning*, because there are many other resources that the voracious learner will want to consume on his or her way to becoming a competent, skilled researcher (see all of the references at the end of the book).

Books

Aguinis, H. (2004). *Regression analysis for categorical moderators*. New York: Guilford Press.
Aiken, L. S., & West, S. G. (1991). *Multiple regression: Testing and interpreting interactions.* Newbury Park, CA: Sage.
MacKinnon, D. P. (2008). *Introduction to statistical mediation analysis*. Mahwah, NJ: Erlbaum.

Articles

Baron, R. M., & Kenny, D. A. (1986). The moderator–mediator variable distinction in social psychological research: Conceptual, strategic, and statistical considerations. *Journal of Personality and Social Psychology, 51*, 1173–1182.
Cole, D. A., & Maxwell, S. E. (2003). Testing mediational models with longitudinal data: Questions and tips in the use of structural equation modeling. *Journal of Abnormal Psychology, 112*, 558–577.
Hayes, A. F. (2009). Beyond Baron and Kenny: Statistical mediation analysis in the new millennium. *Communication Monographs, 76*, 408–420.
Holmbeck, G. N. (1997). Toward terminological, conceptual, and statistical clarity in the study of mediators and moderators: Examples from the child-clinical and pediatric psychology literatures. *Journal of Consulting and Clinical Psychology, 65*, 599–610.
Kenny, D. A. (2008). Reflections on mediation. *Organizational Research Methods, 11*, 353–358.
MacKinnon, D. P., Fairchild, A. J., & Fritz, M. S. (2007). Mediation analysis. *Annual Review of Psychology, 58*, 593–614.
MacKinnon, D. P., Lockwood, C. M., Hoffman, J. M., West, S. G., & Sheets, V. (2002). A comparison of methods to test mediation and other intervening variables. *Psychological Methods, 7*, 83–104.
Preacher, K. J., & Hayes, A. F. (2004). SPSS and SAS procedures for estimating indirect effects in simple mediation models. *Behavior Research Methods, Instruments, and Computers, 36*, 717–731.
Shrout, P. E., & Bolger, N. (2002). Mediation in experimental and nonexperimental studies: New procedures and recommendations. *Psychological Methods, 7*, 422–445.

I compiled this list of available resources some time ago, and I suspect that by the time you read the printed book, some addresses might have changed. I am additionally confident that some new resources will be available that I missed because this list is frozen in time. It goes without saying that you should Google frequently on certain key terms (e.g., "graphing moderation"), because new utilities are being made available all of the time.

References

Abelson, R. P. (1995). *Statistics as principled argument*. Hillsdale, NJ: Erlbaum.

Abrahams, N. M., & Alf, E., Jr. (1972). Pratfalls in moderator research. *Journal of Applied Psychology, 56*, 245–251.

Aguinis, H. (2004). *Regression analysis for categorical moderators*. New York: Guilford Press.

Aguinis, H., Boik, R. J., & Pierce, C. A. (2001). A generalized solution for approximating the power to detect effects of categorical moderator variables using multiple regression. *Organizational Research Methods, 4*, 291–323.

Aiken, L. S., & West, S. G. (1991). *Multiple regression: Testing and interpreting interactions*. Newbury Park, CA: Sage.

Algina, J., & Moulder, B. C. (2001). A note on estimating the Joreskog–Yang model for latent variable interaction using LISREL 8.3. *Structural Equation Modeling, 8*, 40–52.

Allison, P. D. (1977). Testing for interaction in multiple regression analysis. *American Journal of Sociology, 83*, 144–153.

Arbuckle, J. L. (2007). *Amos 4.0 User's Guide*. Chicago: SPSS.

Baron, R. M., & Kenny, D. A. (1986). The moderator–mediator variable distinction in social psychological research: Conceptual, strategic, and statistical considerations. *Journal of Personality and Social Psychology, 51*, 1173–1182.

Bauer, D. J., Preacher, K. J., & Gil, K. M. (2006). Conceptualizing and testing random indirect effects and moderated mediation in multilevel models: New procedures and recommendations. *Psychological Methods, 11*, 142–163.

Bentler, P. M. (2005). *EQS 6 Structural equations program manual*. Encino, CA: Multivariate Software.

Bernstein, P. L. (1996). *Against the gods: The remarkable story of risk*. New York: Wiley.

Bickel, R. (2007). *Multilevel analysis for applied research: It's just regression*. New York: Guilford Press.

Bijleveld, C. C. J. H., & van der Kamp, L. J. T. (1998). *Longitudinal data analysis: Designs, models and methods*. London: Sage.

Blalock, H. M. (1964). *Causal inferences in nonexperimental research*. Chapel Hill, NC: University of North Carolina.

Bollen, K. A., & Paxton, P. (1998). Interactions of latent variables in structural equation models. *Structural Equation Modeling, 5*, 266–293.

Bryant, F. B., & Veroff, J. (2006). *Savoring: A new model of positive experience.* Hillsdale, NJ: Erlbaum.

Bryk, A., & Raudenbush, S. W. (1992). *Hierarchical linear models for social and behavioral research: Applications and data analysis methods.* Newbury Park, CA: Sage.

Bryk, A. S., Raudenbush, S. W., & Congdon, R. (1996). *HLM 4 for Windows* [Computer software]. Chicago, IL: Scientific Software International.

Byrne, B. (2009). *Structural equation modeling with Amos: Basic concepts, applications, and programming.* New York: Taylor & Francis.

Chernick, M. R. (1999). *Bootstrap methods: A practitioner's guide.* New York: Wiley.

Chinn, C. A., & Brewer, W. F. (2001). Models of data: A theory of how people evaluate data. *Cognition and Instruction, 19*, 323–393.

Cohen, J. (1978). Partialed products *are* interactions; partialed powers *are* curve components. *Psychological Bulletin, 85*, 858–866.

Cohen, J. (1988). *Statistical power analysis for the behavioral sciences* (2nd ed.). Hillsdale, NJ: Erlbaum.

Cohen, J. (1992). A power primer. *Psychological Bulletin, 112*, 155–159.

Cohen, J., & Cohen, P. (1975). *Applied multiple regression/correlation analysis for the behavioral sciences.* Hillsdale, NJ: Erlbaum.

Cohen, J., & Cohen, P. (1983). *Applied multiple regression/correlation analysis for the behavioral sciences* (2nd ed.). Hillsdale, NJ: Erlbaum.

Cohen, J., Cohen, P., West, S. G., & Aiken, L. S. (2003). *Applied multiple regression/correlation analysis for the behavioral sciences* (3rd ed.). Mahwah, NJ: Erlbaum.

Cohen, S., & Wills, T. A. (1985). Stress, social support, and the buffering hypothesis. *Psychological Bulletin, 98*, 310–357.

Cole, D. A., & Maxwell, S. E. (2003). Testing mediational models with longitudinal data: Questions and tips in the use of structural equation modeling. *Journal of Abnormal Psychology, 112*, 558–577.

Collins Compact English Dictionary. (2000). Glasgow: Collins.

Conger, A. J. (1974). A revised definition for suppressor variables: A guide to their identification and interpretation. *Educational and Psychological Measurement, 34*, 35–46.

Cooley, E. J., & Keesey, J. C. (1981). Moderator variables in life stress and illness relationship. *Journal of Human Stress, 7*, 35–40.

Cronbach, L. J. (1987). Statistical tests for moderator variables: Flaws in analyses recently proposed. *Psychological Bulletin, 102*, 414–417.

Cronbach, L. J., & Furby, L. (1970). How should we measure "change" or should we? *Psychological Bulletin, 74*, 68–80.

Darlington, R. B. (1968). Multiple regression in psychological research and practice. *Psychological Bulletin, 69*, 161–182.

Dictionary.com. Definition for "exacerbate." Retrieved September 16, 2011, from *http://dictionary.reference.com/*.

Duncan, O. D. (1970). Partials, partitions, and paths. In E. F. Borgatta & G. W. Bohrnstedt (Eds.), *Sociological methodology* (pp. 38–47). San Francisco: Jossey-Bass.

Duncan, O. D. (1975). *Introduction to structural equation models.* New York: Academic Press.

Edwards, J. R., & Lambert, L. S. (2007). Methods for integrating moderation and mediation: A general analytical framework using moderated path analysis. *Psychological Methods, 12,* 1–22.

Emmons, R. A., & McCullough, M. E. (2003). Counting blessings versus burdens: An experimental investigation of gratitude and subjective well-being in daily life. *Journal of Personality and Social Psychology, 84*(2), 377–389.

Fairchild, A. J., & MacKinnon, D. P. (2009). A general model for testing mediation and moderation effects. *Prevention Science, 10,* 87–99.

Fisher, R. A. (1935). *The design of experiments.* Oxford: Oliver & Boyd.

Fisher, R. A. (1950). *Contributions to mathematical statistics.* New York: Wiley.

Frazier, P. A., Tix, A. P., & Barron, K. E. (2004). Testing moderator and mediator effects in counseling psychology research. *Journal of Counseling Psychology, 51,* 115–134.

Fritz, M. S., & MacKinnon, D. P. (2007). Required sample size to detect the mediated effect. *Psychological Science, 18,* 233–239.

Funk & Wagnalls standard college dictionary. (1978). Toronto, Ontario, Canada: Fitzhenry & Whiteside.

G*Power. Retrieved September 17, 2011 at *http://www.psycho.uni-duesseldorf.de/aap/projects/gpower/.*

Gallagher, M. W., Howard, W. J., & Stump, K. N. (2010). Longitudinal mediation within SEM: Using LISREL and MPlus to analyze mediation within longitudinal panel models. KUant Guides. Retrieved October 14, 2010, from *http://quant.ku.edu/pdf/15.%20Longitudinal%20Mediation.pdf.*

Galton, F. (1962). *Hereditary genius: An inquiry into its laws and consequences.* London: Macmillan/Fontana. (Original work published 1869)

Gaylord-Harden, N. K., Cunningham, J., Holmbeck, G. N., & Grant, K. E. (2010). Suppressor effects in coping research with African American adolescents from low-income communities. *Journal of Consulting and Clinical Psychology, 78,* 843–855.

Gelman, A., & Hill, J. (2007). *Data analysis using regression and multilevel/hierarchical models.* Cambridge, UK: Cambridge University Press.

Hang, Do Thi Le. (2007). *Stress, coping, and adjustment in New Zealand and Vietnamese students.* Unpublished master's thesis, Victoria University of Wellington, Wellington, New Zealand.

Hardy, M. (1993). *Regression with dummy variables.* Newbury Park, CA: Sage.

Hayes, A. F. (2009). Beyond Baron and Kenny: Statistical mediation analysis in the new millennium. *Communication Monographs, 76,* 408–420.

Hayes, A. F., & Matthes, J. (2009). Computational procedures for probing interactions in OLS and logistic regression: SPSS and SAS implementations. *Behavior Research Methods, 41,* 924–936.

Hayes, A. F., & Preacher, K. J. (2010). Quantifying and testing indirect effects in simple mediation models when the constituent paths are nonlinear. *Multivariate Behavioral Research, 45,* 627–660.

Heise, D. R. (1975). *Causal analysis.* New York: Wiley.

Henderson, C. (1998). The SPSS GLM procedure, or What happened to ANOVA? Retrieved November 2005, from *http://www.unt.edu/benchmarks/archives/1998/july98/GLM.htm.*

Hess, J., Hu, Y., & Blair, E. (2010). On testing moderation effects in experiments using logistic regression. Unpublished paper. Retrieved September 24, 2010, from *http://www.cba.uh.edu/jhess/documents/OnTestingModerationEffectsinExperimentsUsingLogisticRegressionAug172009.doc.*

Holmbeck, G. (1989). Masculinity, femininity, and multiple regression: Comment on Zeldow, Daugherty, and Clark's "Masculinity, femininity, and psychosocial adjustment in medical students: A 2-year follow-up." *Journal of Personality Assessment, 53,* 583–599.

Holmbeck, G. N. (1997). Toward terminological, conceptual, and statistical clarity in the study of mediators and moderators: Examples from the child-clinical and pediatric psychology literatures. *Journal of Consulting and Clinical Psychology, 65,* 599–610.

Holmbeck, G. N. (2002). Post-hoc probing of significant moderational and mediational effects in studies of pediatric populations. *Journal of Pediatric Psychology, 27,* 87–96.

Horst, P. (1941). The role of predictor variables which are independent of the criterion. *Social Science Research Bulletin, 48,* 431–436.

Howell, D. C. (2007). *Statistical methods for psychology* (6th ed.). Belmont, CA: Thomson Wadsworth.

Hoyle, R. (Ed.). (1995). *Structural equation modeling: Concepts, issues, and applications.* Thousand Oaks, CA: Sage.

Huang, B., Sivaganesan, S., Succop, P., & Goodman, E. (2004). Statistical assessment of mediational effects for logistic mediational models. *Statistics in Medicine, 23,* 2713–2728.

Hull, C. L. (1943). *Principles of behavior.* New York: Appleton-Century.

Hyman, H. H. (1955). *Survey design and analysis.* Glencoe, IL: Free Press.

Jaccard, J., & Wan, C. K. (1996). *LISREL approaches to interaction effects in multiple regression* (Sage University Paper Series: Quantitative applications in the social sciences, series no. 07-114). Thousand Oaks, CA: Sage.

James, L. R., & Brett, J. M. (1984). Mediators, moderators, and tests for mediation. *Journal of Applied Psychology, 69,* 307–321.

James, L. R., Mulaik, S. A., & Brett, J. M. (1982). *Causal analysis: Assumptions, models, and data.* Beverly Hills, CA: Sage.

Johnson, P. O., & Fay, L. C. (1950). The Johnson–Neyman technique, its theory and applications. *Psychometrika, 15(4),* 349–367.

Joreskog, K. G., & Sorbom, D. (1998). *LISREL 8.54.* Lincolnwood, IL: Scientific Software International.

Joreskog, K. G., & Yang, F. (1996). Nonlinear structural equation models: The Kenny–Judd model with interaction effects. In G. Marcoulides & R. Schumacker (Eds.), *Advanced structural equation modeling* (pp. 57–87). Mahwah, NJ: Erlbaum.

Jose, P. E. (2008a). *MedGraph-I: A programme to graphically depict mediation among three variables: The Internet version, version 3.0.* Wellington, New Zealand: Victoria University of Wellington. Retrieved from *http://www.victoria.ac.nz/psyc/paul-jose-files/medgraph/medgraph.php.*

Jose, P. E. (2008b). *ModGraph-I: A programme to compute cell means for the graphical display of moderational analyses: The Internet version, Version 2.0.* Wellington, New Zealand: Victoria University of Wellington. Retrieved from *http://www.victoria.ac.nz/psyc/paul-jose-files/modgraph/modgraph.php.*

Jose, P. E., & Brewer, W. F. (1984). Development of story liking: Character identi-fication, suspense, and outcome resolution. *Developmental Psychology, 20,* 911–924.

Jose, P. E., & Brown, I. (2008). When does the gender difference in rumination begin? Gender and age differences in the use of rumination by early adolescents. *Journal of Youth and Adolescence, 37*(2), 180–192.

Jose, P. E., Lim, B. T., & Bryant, F. B. (2012). Does savoring increase happiness? A daily diary study. *Journal of Positive Psychology, 7*(3), 176–187.

Jose, P. E., Ryan, N., & Pryor, J. (2012). Does social connectedness lead to a greater sense of well-being in adolescence? *Journal of Research on Adolescence, 22*(2), 235–251.

Jose, P. E., & Schurer, K. (2010). Cultural differences in coping among New Zealand adolescents. *Journal of Cross-Cultural Psychology, 41,* 3–18.

Jose, P. E., & Weir, K. (in press). Adolescent sense of control: A downward exten-sion of the Shapiro Control Inventory to pre- and early adolescents. *Journal of Genetic Psychology.*

Kam, C. D., & Franzese, R. J. (2007). *Modeling and interpreting interactive hypotheses in regression analysis.* Ann Arbor, MI: University of Michigan Press.

Kantardzic, M. (2003). *Data mining: Concepts, models, methods, and algorithms.* Totowa, NJ: Wiley-IEEE Press.

Kenny, D. A. (1979). *Correlation and causality.* New York: Wiley.

Kenny, D. A. (2007). Mediation. Retrieved August 29, 2007, from *http://davidakenny. net/cm/mediate.htm.*

Kenny, D. A. (2008). Reflections on mediation. *Organizational Research Methods, 11,* 353–358.

Kenny, D. A., & Judd, C. M. (1984). Estimating the nonlinear and interactive effects of latent variables. *Psychological Bulletin, 96,* 201–210.

Kenny, D. A., Korchmaros, J. D., & Bolger, N. (2003). Lower level mediation in mul-tilevel models. *Psychological Methods, 8,* 115–128.

Klein, A. G., & Moosbrugger, H. (2000). Maximum likelihood estimation of latent interaction effects with the LMS method. *Psychometrika, 65,* 457–474.

Kline, R. B. (2004). *Principles and practice of structural equation modeling* (2nd ed.). New York: Guilford Press.

Kraemer, H. C., & Thiemann, S. (1987). *How many subjects? Statistical power analysis in research.* Newbury Park, CA: Sage.

Kromrey, J. D., & Foster-Johnson, L. (1998). Mean centering in moderated multiple regression: Much ado about nothing. *Educational and Psychological Measure-ment, 58,* 42–67.

Krull, J. L., & MacKinnon, D. P. (1999). Multilevel mediation modeling in group-based intervention studies. *Evaluation Review, 23,* 418–444.

Krus, D. J., & Wilkinson, S. M. (1986). Demonstration of properties of a suppressor variable. *Behavior Research Methods, Instruments and Computers, 18,* 21–24.

Lerner, M. J. (1980). *The belief in a just world: A fundamental delusion.* New York: Plenum Press.

Lin, G. C., Wen, Z., Marsh, H. W., & Lin, H. S. (2010). Structural equation models of latent interactions: Clarification of orthogonalizing and double mean centering strategies. *Structural Equation Modeling, 17,* 374–391.

Little, T. D., Bovaird, J. A., & Widaman, K. F. (2006). On the merits of orthogonalizing powered and product terms: Implications for modeling interactions among latent variables. *Structural Equation Modeling, 13*(4), 497–519.

Little, T. D., Card, N. A., Bovaird, J. A., Preacher, K. J., & Crandall, C. S. (2007). Structural equation modeling of mediation and moderation with contextual factors. In T. D. Little, J. A. Bovaird, & N. A. Card (Eds.), *Modeling contextual effects in longitudinal studies* (pp. 207–230). Mahwah, NJ: Erlbaum.

Little, T. D., Schnabel, K. U., & Baumert, J. (2000). *Modeling longitudinal and multilevel data: Practical issues, applied approaches and specific examples.* Mahwah, NJ: Erlbaum.

Lyubomirsky, S., & Lepper, H. (1999). A measure of subjective happiness: Preliminary reliability and construct validation. *Social Indicators Research, 46,* 137–155.

MacCallum, R. C., & Mar, C. M. (1995). Distinguishing between moderator and quadratic effects in multiple regression. *Psychological Bulletin, 118,* 405–421.

MacCorquodale, K., & Meehl, P. (1948). On a distinction between hypothetical constructs and intervening variables. *Psychological Review, 55,* 95–107.

MacKinnon, D. P. (2008). *Introduction to statistical mediation analysis.* Mahwah, NJ: Erlbaum.

MacKinnon, D. P., & Dwyer, J. H. (1993). Estimating mediated effects in prevention studies. *Evaluation Review, 17,* 144–158.

MacKinnon, D. P., Fairchild, A. J., & Fritz, M. S. (2007). Mediation analysis. *Annual Review of Psychology, 58,* 593–614.

MacKinnon, D. P., Fritz, M. S., Williams, J., & Lockwood, C. M. (2007). Distribution of the product confidence limits for the indirect effect: Program PRODCLIN. *Behavior Research Methods, 39,* 384–389.

MacKinnon, D. P., Lockwood, C. M., Brown, C. H., & Hoffman, J. M. (2007). The intermediate endpoint effect in logistic and probit regression. *Clinical Trials, 4,* 499–513.

MacKinnon, D. P., Lockwood, C. M., Hoffman, J. M., West, S. G., & Sheets, V. (2002). A comparison of methods to test mediation and other intervening variables. *Psychological Methods, 7,* 83–104.

MacKinnon, D. P., Lockwood, C. M., & Williams, J. (2004). Confidence limits for the indirect effect: Distribution of the product and resampling methods. *Multivariate Behavioral Research, 39,* 99–128.

MacKinnon, D. P., Warsi, G., & Dwyer, J. H. (1995). A simulation study of mediated effect measures. *Multivariate Behavioral Research, 30,* 41–62.

Maxwell, S. E., & Cole, D. A. (2007). Bias in cross-sectional analyses of longitudinal mediation. *Psychological Methods, 12,* 23–44.

Maxwell, S. E., & Delaney, H. D. (1993). Bivariate median splits and spurious statistical significance. *Psychological Bulletin, 113,* 181–190.

McClelland, G. H., & Judd, C. M. (1993). Statistical difficulties of detecting interactions and moderator effects. *Psychological Bulletin, 114,* 376–390.

McCullough, M. E., Emmons, R. A., & Tsang, J. A. (2002). The grateful disposition: A conceptual and empirical topography. *Journal of Personality and Social Psychology, 82,* 112–127.

Milfont, T. L., & Duckitt, J. (2010). The Environmental Attitudes Inventory: A valid and reliable measure to assess the structure of environmental attitudes. *Journal of Environmental Psychology, 30,* 80–94.

Milfont, T. L., Duckitt, J., & Wagner, C. (2010). A cross-cultural test of the value–attitude–behaviour hierarchy. *Journal of Applied Social Psychology, 40*, 2791–2813.

Moosbrugger, H., Schermelleh-Engel, K., & Klein, A. (1997). Methodological problems of estimating latent interaction effects. *Methods of Psychological Research Online, 2*, 95–111.

Moulder, B. C., & Algina, J. (2002). Comparison of methods for estimating and testing latent variable interactions. *Structural Equation Modeling, 9*, 1–19.

Muller, D., Judd, C. M., & Yzerbyt, V. Y. (2005). When moderation is mediated and mediation is moderated. *Journal of Personality and Social Psychology, 89*, 852–863.

Muthen, B., & Asparouhov, T. (2003). Modeling interactions between latent and observed continuous variables using maximum-likelihood estimation in Mplus. *Mplus Web Notes: No. 6.*

Newsom, J., Jones, R. N., & Hofer, S. M. (2011). *Longitudinal data analysis: A practical guide for researchers in aging, health, and social sciences.* New York: Routledge Academic.

Nolen-Hoeksema, S. (1994). An interactive model for the emergence of gender differences in depression in adolescence. *Journal of Research on Adolescence, 4*(4), 519–534.

Norman, D. (1977). *Memory and attention: An introduction to human information processing.* New York: Wiley.

Paulhus, D. L., Robins, R. W., Trzesniewski, K. H., & Tracy, J. L. (2004). Two replicable suppressor situations in personality research. *Multivariate Behavioral Research, 39*, 303–328.

Pearl, J. (2000). *Causality: Models, reasoning, and inference.* Cambridge, UK: Cambridge University Press.

Pedhazur, E. J. (1997). *Multiple regression in behavioral research: Explanation and prediction* (3rd ed.). Fort Worth, TX: Harcourt Brace.

Ping, R. A. (1996). Latent variable interaction and quadratic effect estimation: A two-step technique using structural equation analysis. *Psychological Bulletin, 119*, 166–175.

Potthoff, R. F. (1964). On the Johnson–Neyman technique and some extensions thereof. *Psychometrika, 29*, 241–256.

Preacher, K. J., & Hayes, A. F. (2004). SPSS and SAS procedures for estimating indirect effects in simple mediation models. *Behavior Research Methods, Instruments, and Computers, 36*, 717–731.

Preacher, K. J., & Hayes, A. F. (2005). *SPSS and SAS macros for estimating and comparing indirect effects in multiple mediator models.* Retrieved December 6, 2006, from *http://www.comm.ohio-state.edu/ahayes/SPSS%20programs/indirect.htm.*

Preacher, K. J., & Hayes, A. F. (2008). Asymptotic and resampling strategies for assessing and comparing indirect effects in multiple mediator models. *Behavior Research Methods, 40*, 879–891.

Preacher, K. J., & Kelley, K. (2011). Effect size measures for mediation models: Quantitative strategies for communicating indirect effects. *Psychological Methods, 16*, 93–115.

Preacher, K. J., Rucker, D. D., & Hayes, A. F. (2007). Assessing moderated mediation hypotheses: Theory, method, and prescriptions. *Multivariate Behavioral Research, 42,* 185–227.

Preacher, K. J., Zyphur, M. J., & Zhang, Z. (2010). A general multilevel SEM framework for assessing multilevel mediation. *Psychological Methods, 15*(3), 209–233.

Raudenbush, S. W., & Bryk, A. S. (2002). *Hierarchical linear models: Applications and data analysis methods* (2nd ed.). Newbury Park, CA: Sage.

Raudenbush, S. W., Bryk, A. S., & Congdon, R. (2000). *HLM 5 for Windows* [Computer software]. Skokie, IL: Scientific Software International.

Raudenbush, S. W., Bryk, A. S., & Congdon, R. (2004). *HLM 6 for Windows* [Computer software]. Skokie, IL: Scientific Software International.

Raudenbush, S. W., & Sampson, R. (1999). Assessing direct and indirect associations in multilevel designs with latent variables. *Sociological Methods and Research, 28*(2), 123–153.

Rogosa, D. (1988). Myths about longitudinal research. In K. W. Schaie, R. T. Campbell, W. M. Meredith, & S. C. Rawlings (Eds.), *Methodological issues in aging research* (pp. 171–209). New York: Springer.

Rose, B., Holmbeck, G. N., Coakley, R. M., & Franks, L. (2004). Mediator and moderator effects in developmental and behavioral pediatric research. *Journal of Developmental and Behavioral Pediatrics, 25,* 58–67.

Rosenblueth, A., & Rioch, D. M. (1933). Temporal and spatial summation in autonomic systems. *American Journal of Physiology, 106,* 365–380.

Rozeboom, W. W. (1956). Mediation variables in scientific theory. *Psychological Review, 63,* 249–264.

Rudolph, K. D., & Troop-Gordon, W. (2010). Personal-accentuation and contextual-amplification models of pubertal timing: Predicting youth depression. *Development and Psychopathology, 22,* 433–451.

Salsburg, D. (2001). *The lady tasting tea: How statistics revolutionized science in the twentieth century.* New York: Freeman.

Schumacker, R. E., & Lomax, R. G. (2004). *A beginner's guide to structural equation modeling* (2nd ed.). Mahwah, NJ: Erlbaum.

Schwartz, S. H. (1994). Are there universal aspects in the structure and contents of human values? *Journal of Social Issues, 50,* 19–45.

Scialfa, C. T. (1987). A BASIC program to determine regions of significance using the Johnson–Neyman technique. *Behavior Research Methods, 19*(3), 349–352.

Selig, J. P., & Preacher, K. J. (2008, June). Monte Carlo method for assessing mediation: An interactive tool for creating confidence intervals for indirect effects [Computer software]. Available from *http://quantpsy.org/.*

Selig, J. P., & Preacher, K. J. (2009). Mediation models for longitudinal data in developmental research. *Research in Human Development, 6,* 144–164.

Shrout, P. E., & Bolger, N. (2002). Mediation in experimental and nonexperimental studies: New procedures and recommendations. *Psychological Methods, 7,* 422–445.

Simon, H. A. (1952). On the definition of the causal relation. *Journal of Philosophy, 49,* 517–528.

Singer, J. D., & Willett, J. B. (2003). *Applied longitudinal data analysis: Modeling change and event occurrence.* Oxford: Oxford University Press.

Skinner, B. F. (1938). *Behavior of organisms*. New York: Appleton-Century.

Sobel, M. E. (1982). Asymptotic intervals for indirect effects in structural equation models. In S. Leinhart (Ed.), *Sociological methodology 1982* (pp. 290–312). San Francisco: Jossey-Bass.

Sockloff, A. L. (1976). The analysis of nonlinearity via linear regression with polynomial and product variables: An examination. *Review of Educational Research, 46*, 267–291.

Southwood, K. E. (1978). Substantive theory and statistical interactions: Five models. *American Journal of Sociology, 83*, 154–203.

Spencer, S. J., Zanna, M. P., & Fong, G. T. (2005). Establishing a causal chain: Why experiments are often more effective than mediational analyses in examining psychological processes. *Journal of Personality and Social Psychology, 89*, 845–851.

Stolzenberg, R. M. (1980). The measurement and decomposition of causal effects in nonlinear and nonadditive models. *Sociological Methodology, 11*, 459–488.

Tabachnick, B. G., & Fidell, L. S. (2001). *Using multivariate statistics*. New York: Allyn & Bacon.

Tofighi, D., & MacKinnon, D. P. (2011). RMediation: An R package for mediation analysis confidence intervals. *Behavior Research Methods, 43*, 692–700.

Tolman, E. C. (1938). The determinants of behavior at a choice point. *Psychological Review, 45*, 1–41.

Triandis, H. C. (1995). *Individualism and collectivism*. Boulder, CO: Westview Press.

Warren, H. C. (1920). *Human psychology*. Boston: Houghton Mifflin.

Watkins, P. C., Woodward, K., Stone, T., & Kolts, R. L. (2003). Gratitude and happiness: Development of a measure of gratitude, and relationships with subjective well-being. *Social Behavior and Personality, 31*, 431–451.

Weir, K., & Jose, P. E. (2008). A comparison of the response styles theory and the hopelessness theory of depression in preadolescents. *Journal of Early Adolescence, 28*, 356–374.

West, S. G., & Aiken, L. S. (1997). Toward understanding individual effects in multiple component prevention programs: Design and analysis strategies. In K. Bryant, M. Windle, & S. West (Eds.), *The science of prevention: Methodological advances from alcohol and substance abuse research* (pp. 167–209). Washington, DC: American Psychological Association.

Wirtz, P. W. (2007). Advances in causal chain development and testing in alcohol research: Mediation, suppression, moderation, mediated moderation, and moderated mediation. *Alcoholism: Clinical and Experimental Research, 31*, 57–63.

Wright, S. (1921). Correlation and causation. *Journal of Agricultural Research, 20*, 557–585.

Yuan, Y., & MacKinnon, D. P. (2009). Bayesian mediation analysis. *Psychological Methods, 14*(4), 301–322.

Zedeck, S. (1971). Problems with the use of "moderator variables." *Psychological Bulletin, 76*, 295–310.

Author Index

Subject Index

An *f* following a page number indicates a figure; a *t* following a page number indicates a table.

About the Author

Paul E. Jose, PhD, is Associate Professor of Psychology and Director of the Roy McKenzie Centre for the Study of Families at Victoria University of Wellington in New Zealand. He received his doctorate in Developmental Psychology from Yale University, completed his postdoctoral work at the University of Illinois at Champaign–Urbana, and taught and conducted research at Loyola University Chicago for 15 years. Dr. Jose's research interests include gender differences in spoken discourse, moral development, cross-cultural comparisons of adolescent coping and family dynamics, children's preparation and motivation for academic achievement, adolescent anxiety and depression, and positive psychology. He has used mediation and moderation for over 20 years in his work.